Annual Editions:
Technologies, Social Media,
and Society, 20/e

Edited by Daniel Mittleman
DePaul University

http://create.mcgraw-hill.com

ISBN-10: 1259170985   ISBN-13: 9781259170980

Contents

Preface

A NOTE TO THE READER

In vetting articles for *Technologies, Social Media, and Society* from the sea of contenders, I have tried to continue in the tradition of the previous editors. The writers are journalists, computer scientists, lawyers, economists, policy analysts, and academics, the kinds of professions you would expect to find represented in a collection on the social implications of computing. They write for newspapers, business and general circulation magazines, academic journals, professional publications, and, more and more for websites. Their writing is mostly free from both the unintelligible jargon and the breathless enthusiasm that prevents people from forming clear ideas about computing and social media policy. This is by design, of course, and I hope that after reading the selections you agree.

Annual Editions: Technologies, Social Media, and Society is organized around important dimensions of society rather than of computing. This book's major themes are the economy, community, politics considered broadly, and the balance of the risk and reward of new technology. The introduction begins the conversation with an article by the late Neil Postman that provides us with an excellent five-point framework for modeling conversation and evaluation of ideas presented in almost every article that follows.

The units are organized to lead us through several of the critical issues of our day. You may notice that many of these issues (nature of community and friendships, causes of unemployment, intellectual property, freedom of speech, as examples) only tangentially seem to be technology or social media issues. This, too, is by design and serves as evidence for how intertwined technology policy has become with other social and economic policy decisions in the world today.

We are living during a very exciting time, comparable to the twenty-five or so years that followed the invention of Gutenberg's printing press. The principal modes for communication and collaboration in our society are changing faster than we know how to make public policy or evolve culture to deal with them. As such, business models, property rules, international treaty rules, and a myriad of other economic and social norms are experiencing both evolution and revolution, often with unanticipated or controversial outcomes. At the same time, these technological advances are empowering masses of people around the world who just a generation ago had little or no access to real opportunity. And technological advances are making available incredible new gains in medicine and productivity.

A word of caution. Each article has been selected because it is topical, interesting, and (insofar as the form permits) nicely written. To say that an article is interesting or well-written, however, does not mean that it is right. This is as true of both the facts presented in each article and the point of view of the author. I hope you will approach these articles as you might a good discussion among friends. You may not agree with all opinions, but you will come away nudged in one direction or another by reasoned arguments, holding a richer, more informed view of important issues.

This book includes several features I hope will be helpful to students and professionals. A topic guide lists each key issue and the articles that explore that issue. Included with each article are Learning Outcomes, Critical Thinking study/discussion questions, and Internet References.

The Internet References include links to articles and videos that guide a deeper dive into the topic at hand. The use of videos further supports multiple learning styles among the students using this reader.

Though some of the critical thinking questions can be answered from within the article, many more invite further investigation, in essence, allowing each reader to construct their own understanding of the article topic. I hope the articles I gathered for this volume, along with the materials provided with them, initiate further discussion and further interest in these controversial issues of our day. They are intended to get the discussion flowing, not to provide definitive answers.

I want *Annual Editions: Technologies, Social Media, and Society* to spark your interest for exploring some of the most important discussions of the time: those about the promises and risks engendered by new developments in information technology and social media.

A NOTE TO INSTRUCTORS

We invite you to provide feedback both to me (at danny@ cdm.depaul.edu) and to the editorial team at McGraw-Hill (at debra.henricks@mheducation.com). Suggestions and recommendations of new articles for inclusion in next year's edition of this reader are welcome. In addition, I encourage all adopting instructors to drop me a note as I would love to know who is using this reader and what I might do to make your teaching a more enjoyable and productive effort.

Editor

Daniel Mittleman is an Associate Professor in the College of Computing and Digital Media at DePaul University. He teaches coursework in virtual collaboration, user-focused web design, and social impact of technology. Dr. Mittleman's research is in collaboration engineering, focusing on the design of team processes, software, and physical environment to support virtual work. His work experience includes several years providing IT systems support at

Ticketmaster Corporation, as well as consulting projects with several Fortune 500 corporations and federal government agencies.

Academic Advisory Board

Members of the Academic Advisory Board are instrumental in the final selection of articles for each edition of ANNUAL EDITIONS. Their review of articles for content, level, and appropriateness provides critical direction to the editors and staff. We think that you will find their careful consideration well reflected in this volume.

Ghassan Alkadi
Southeastern Louisiana University

David Allen
Temple University

James Barnard
Embry-Riddle Aeronautical University, Daytona Beach

Peggy Batchelor
Furman University

Beverly Bohn
Park University

Maria I. Bryant
College of Southern Maryland

Cliff Cockerham
Whites Creek High School

Arthur I. Cyr
Carthage College

Peter A. Danielson
University of British Columbia

Michael J. Day
Northern Illinois University

Therese DonGiovanni O'Neil
Indiana University of Pennsylvania

Kenneth Fidel
DePaul University

Norman Garrett
Eastern Illinois University

David C. Gibbs
University of Wisconsin—Stevens Point

Keith Harman
Oklahoma Baptist University

Marc D. Hiller
University of New Hampshire

Malynnda A. Johnson
Carroll University

Patricia A. Joseph
Slippery Rock University

John Karayan
Woodbury University

Donna Kastner
California State University—Fullerton

Edward Kisailus
Canisius College

Eugene J. Kozminski
Aquinas College

Christine Kukla
North Central College

Rick Lejk
University of North Carolina—Charlotte

Xiangdong Li
New York City College of Technology

David Little
High Point University

Michael Martel
Ohio University

Ottis L. Murray
University of North Carolina—Pembroke

Gail Niklason
Weber State College

Morris Pondfield
Towson University

Scott Rader
University of St. Thomas

Ramona R. Santa Maria
Buffalo State College, SUNY

Thomas Schunk
SUNY Orange County Community College

Keith Stearns
University of Wisconsin—Eau Claire

Edwin Tjoe
St. John's University

Lawrence E. Turner
Southwestern Adventist University

Lih-Ching Chen Wang
Cleveland State University

Caroline Shaffer Westerhof
California National University and Kaplan University

Fred Westfall
Troy University

Rene Weston-Eborn
Weber State College

Nathan White
McKendree University

Correlation Guide

The *Annual Editions* series provides students with convenient, inexpensive access to current, carefully selected articles from the public press. **Annual Editions: Technologies, Social Media, and Society, 20/e** is an easy-to-use reader that presents articles on important topics such as the *economy, the workplace, social participation,* and many more. For more information on *Annual Editions* and other *McGraw-Hill Create*™ titles, visit www.mcgrawhillcreate.com.

This convenient guide matches the articles in **Annual Editions: Technologies, Social Media, and Society, 20/e** with **Business Driven Technology, 6/e** by Baltzan.

Business Driven Technology, 6/e by Baltzan	Annual Editions: Technologies, Social Media, and Society, 20/e
Chapter 1: Business Driven Technology	AmazonFresh is Jeff Bezos' Last Mile Quest for Total Retail Domination How Google Dominates Us How to Spot the Future The Lost Steve Jobs Tapes
Chapter 2: Identifying Competitive Advantages	Can Online Piracy Be Stopped by Laws? The Lost Steve Jobs Tapes A Small World After All?
Chapter 3: Strategic Initiatives for Implementing Competitive Advantages	AmazonFresh is Jeff Bezos' Last Mile Quest for Total Retail Domination The Secret Life of Data in the Year 2020 What Facebook Knows
Chapter 4: Measuring the Success of Strategic Initiatives	
Chapter 5: Organizational Structures That Support Strategic Initiatives	Can Online Piracy Be Stopped by Laws? Google's European Conundrum: When Does Privacy Mean Censorship? Network Insecurity: Are We Losing the Battle against Cyber Crime? The Tricky Business of Innovation: Can You Patent a Magic Trick?
Chapter 6: Valuing Organizational Information	How Google Dominates Us The Secret Life of Data in the Year 2020
Chapter 7: Storing Organizational Information—Databases	Network Insecurity: Are We Losing the Battle against Cyber Crime?
Chapter 8: Accessing Organizational Information—Data Warehouse	
Chapter 9: Enabling the Organization—Decision Making	
Chapter 10: Extending the Organization—Supply Chain Management	AmazonFresh is Jeff Bezos' Last Mile Quest for Total Retail Domination
Chapter 11: Building a Customer-centric Organization—Customer Relationship Management	AmazonFresh is Jeff Bezos' Last Mile Quest for Total Retail Domination Licence to Text Social Media: Why It Will Change the World
Chapter 12: Integrating the Organization from End-to-End—Enterprise Resource Planning	
Chapter 13: Creating Innovative Organizations	Five Things We Need to Know about Technological Change From Smart House to Networked Home How to Spot the Future I Used Google Glass: The Future, but with Monthly Updates
Chapter 14: Ebusiness	AmazonFresh is Jeff Bezos' Last Mile Quest for Total Retail Domination Social Media: Why It Will Change the World
Chapter 15: Creating Collaborative Partnerships	Licence to Text Social Media: Why It Will Change the World
Chapter 16: Integrating Wireless Technology in Business	
Chapter 17: Building Software to Support an Agile Organization	
Chapter 18: Managing Organizational Projects	
Chapter 19: Outsourcing in the 21st Century	How Technology Is Destroying Jobs 7 Reasons Why Sweatshops Still Persist
Chapter 20: Developing a 21st-Century Organization	Network Insecurity: Are We Losing the Battle against Cyber Crime? The Secret Life of Data in the Year 2020

This convenient guide matches the articles in **Annual Editions: Technologies, Social Media, and Society, 20/e** with **M: Information Systems, 3/e** by Baltzan.

M: Information Systems, 3/e by Baltzan	Annual Editions: Technologies, Social Media, and Society, 20/e
Chapter 1: Management Information Systems: Business Driven MIS	AmazonFresh is Jeff Bezos' Last Mile Quest for Total Retail Domination 7 Reasons Why Sweatshops Still Persist
Chapter 2: Decision + Processes: Value Driven Business	AmazonFresh is Jeff Bezos' Last Mile Quest for Total Retail Domination
Chapter 3: Ebusiness: Electronic Business Value	Licence to Text Social Media: Why It Will Change the World
Chapter 4: Ethics + Information Security: MIS Business Concerns	Network Insecurity: Are We Losing the Battle against Cyber Crime?
Chapter 5: Infrastructures: Sustainable Technologies	How Google Dominates Us Network Insecurity: Are We Losing the Battle against Cyber Crime?
Chapter 6: Data: Business Intelligence	The Secret Life of Data in the Year 2020 What Facebook Knows
Chapter 7: Networks: Mobile Business	From Smart House to Networked Home How to Spot the Future I Used Google Glass: The Future, but with Monthly Updates The Secret Life of Data in the Year 2020
Chapter 8: Enterprise Applications: Business Communications	AmazonFresh is Jeff Bezos' Last Mile Quest for Total Retail Domination Licence to Text
Chapter 9: Systems Development + Project Management: Corporate Responsibility	How Technology Is Destroying Jobs 7 Reasons Why Sweatshops Still Persist

This convenient guide matches the articles in **Annual Editions: Technologies, Social Media, and Society, 20/e** with **Management Information Systems for the Information Age, 9/e** by Haag/Cummings.

Management Information Systems for the Information Age, 9/e by Haag/Cummings	Annual Editions: Technologies, Social Media, and Society, 20/e
Chapter 1: The Information Age in Which You Live: Changing the Face of Business	Five Things We Need to Know about Technological Change New Document Sheds Light on Government's Ability to Search iPhones What Facebook Knows
Chapter 2: Major Business Initiatives: Gaining Competitive Advantage with IT	AmazonFresh is Jeff Bezos' Last Mile Quest for Total Retail Domination Licence to Text The Secret Life of Data in the Year 2020
Chapter 3: Databases and Data Warehouses: Supporting the Analytics-Driven Organization	
Chapter 4: Analytics, Decision Support, and Artificial Intelligence: Brainpower for Your Business	From Smart House to Networked Home Google's European Conundrum: When Does Privacy Mean Censorship? The Secret Life of Data in the Year 2020 What Facebook Knows
Chapter 5: Electronic Commerce: Strategies for the New Economy	AmazonFresh is Jeff Bezos' Last Mile Quest for Total Retail Domination How Google Dominates Us The Lost Steve Jobs Tapes Social Media: Why It Will Change the World
Chapter 6: Systems Development: Phases, Tools, and Techniques	
Chapter 7: Infrastructure, Cloud Computing, Metrics, and Business Continuity Planning: Building and Sustaining the Dynamic Enterprise	AmazonFresh is Jeff Bezos' Last Mile Quest for Total Retail Domination
Chapter 8: Protecting People and Information: Threats and Safeguards	Can Online Piracy Be Stopped by Laws? Network Insecurity: Are We Losing the Battle against Cyber Crime? The Tricky Business of Innovation: Can You Patent a Magic Trick?
Chapter 9: Emerging Trends and Technologies: Business, People, and Technology Tomorrow	Augmented Reality is Finally Getting Real How to Spot the Future From Smart House to Networked Home I Used Google Glass: The Future, but with Monthly Updates

Topic Guide

This topic guide suggests how the selections in this book relate to the subjects covered in your course. **All the articles that relate to each topic are listed below the bold-faced term.**

Artificial intelligence

Deception Is Futile When Big Brother's Lie Detector Turns Its Eyes on You
From Smart House to Networked Home
How Google Dominates Us
I Used Google Glass: The Future, but with Monthly Updates
The Secret Life of Data in the Year 2020
What Facebook Knows

Big data

AmazonFresh is Jeff Bezos' Last Mile Quest for Total Retail Domination
How Google Dominates Us
The Secret Life of Data in the Year 2020
What Facebook Knows

Business models

AmazonFresh is Jeff Bezos' Last Mile Quest for Total Retail Domination
Can Online Piracy Be Stopped by Laws?
Five Things We Need to Know about Technological Change
How Google Dominates Us
How to Spot the Future
Licence to Text
The Lost Steve Jobs Tapes
The Patent Problem
7 Reasons Why Sweatshops Still Persist
Social Media: Why It Will Change the World
What Facebook Knows

Censorship

Google's European Conundrum: When Does Privacy Mean Censorship?
Internet Freedom and Human Rights

Community and participation

R U Friends 4 Real?
Relationships, Community, and Identity in the New Virtual Society
A Small World After All?
What Facebook Knows

Cultural issues

Five Things We Need to Know about Technological Change
Google's European Conundrum: When Does Privacy Mean Censorship?
The Individual in a Networked World: Two Scenarios
I Used Google Glass: The Future, but with Monthly Updates
Licence to Text
R U Friends 4 Real?
Relationships, Community, and Identity in the New Virtual Society
A Small World After All?
Social Media: Why It Will Change the World
The Tricky Business of Innovation: Can You Patent a Magic Trick?
What Facebook Knows

Cybercrime

A Beginner's Guide to Building Botnets—with Little Assembly Required
Can Online Piracy Be Stopped by Laws?
Internet Freedom and Human Rights
Network Insecurity: Are We Losing the Battle against Cyber Crime?
The Truth about Video Games and Gun Violence

Economy

A Beginner's Guide to Building Botnets—with Little Assembly Required
How Technology Is Destroying Jobs
Network Insecurity: Are We Losing the Battle against Cyber Crime?

Emerging technology

Augmented Reality Is Finally Getting Real
Deception Is Futile When Big Brother's Lie Detector Turns Its Eyes on You
Five Things We Need to Know about Technological Change
From Smart House to Networked Home
How Google Dominates Us
How Technology Is Destroying Jobs
How to Spot the Future
I Used Google Glass: The Future, but with Monthly Updates
The Individual in a Networked World: Two Scenarios
The Secret Life of Data in the Year 2020

Ethics

A Beginner's Guide to Building Botnets—with Little Assembly Required
Bride of Stuxnet
Can Online Piracy Be Stopped by Laws?
Deception Is Futile When Big Brother's Lie Detector Turns Its Eyes on You
Five Things We Need to Know about Technological Change
Network Insecurity: Are We Losing the Battle against Cyber Crime?
New Document Sheds Light on Government's Ability to Search iPhones
The Patent Problem
7 Reasons Why Sweatshops Still Persist
The Tricky Business of Innovation: Can You Patent a Magic Trick?

Futurism

AmazonFresh is Jeff Bezos' Last Mile Quest for Total Retail Domination
Augmented Reality Is Finally Getting Real
From Smart House to Networked Home
How Google Dominates Us
How to Spot the Future
I Used Google Glass: The Future, but with Monthly Updates
The Individual in a Networked World: Two Scenarios
The Information: How the Internet Gets Inside Us
Licence to Text
The Secret Life of Data in the Year 2020
Social Media: Why It Will Change the World
What Facebook Knows

Hacking

A Beginner's Guide to Building Botnets—with Little Assembly Required
Bride of Stuxnet
Hacking the Lights Out
Network Insecurity: Are We Losing the Battle against Cyber Crime?

Innovation

AmazonFresh is Jeff Bezos' Last Mile Quest for Total Retail Domination
Augmented Reality Is Finally Getting Real
Deception Is Futile When Big Brother's Lie Detector Turns Its Eyes on You

Unit 1

UNIT

Prepared by: Daniel Mittleman, *DePaul University*

Introduction

Consider the automobile: a wonderful invention a little over a century ago that enabled us to travel faster and farther than we previously could by horse. The invention of the automobile, though, meant the end of horse-drawn carriages. That trade off, perhaps, was positive; it certainly changed man's relationship to the horse. The automobile created or advanced whole new fields of work from highway construction to petroleum engineering. It created jobs for gas station attendants, parking valets, mechanics, and car salesmen. It also eliminated many jobs for blacksmiths, stable boys, and street sweeps.

More than that, however, the automobile opened up the practicality of suburban living, shopping malls, and super highways. It enabled much of what we now think of as Americana such as carpooling, Route 66, drive in movies, and drive thru ATMs. But it also fed America's need for oil, which has contributed to hostilities in the Middle East, oil spills in Alaska and the Gulf of Mexico, and controversy about overland oil pipelines.

All of this happened because someone in the late 19th century attached a gasoline engine to a buggy chassis and connected it to turn the wheels.

What follows this opening essay is a book of readings: a collection of recent newspaper, magazine, and journal articles as well as extended blog posts from notable authors. It is possible to step through the collected articles and read each as a disconnected essay, much as you might read a typical monthly magazine that has a loose theme, if any theme at all, connecting the articles.

You might decide you like some of the articles: they amuse you, they stimulate you to think, or they contain information you can put to practical use. And you might decide you dislike other articles that bore you, or don't seem at all relevant to your life interests, or both. In truth, you could read the articles presented in this book in just that fashion. But to do so would miss the point of the whole exercise of the course you are currently taking.

What this book—and presumably your course—is about is the evaluation of recent technological advances on our economics, our politics, our culture, and on us. You may find readings in the book addressing the nature of friendships on Facebook; the question of erasing incorrect or embarrassing—but correct—information about you that has made its way online; how you can become a hacker (or hire a hacker to do your dirty work for you); why Google and Amazon and Facebook are so dominant; why Hollywood is working overtime to criminalize unauthorized downloading of media; how buying amazing inexpensive cellphones or clothing can get someone killed halfway around the world; or how Google Glass might impact your life next year.

These readings address a myriad of intertwining issues about personal privacy, personal security, national security, job security, and the future of commerce. Getting one's head around the ideas from these articles—and the implications that stem from the ideas—is not a simple matter.

So, what differentiates this book—this reader—from a magazine, and what differentiates you reading this material inside a course rather than on your own, is the use of a framework or model to help make sense of the complexities.

We present several frameworks over the course of this book, but no other is as useful as the one originally presented by Neil Postman in 1998.[1] In short, Postman presents five ideas.

1. All technological change is a trade-off. That is, every new technology introduces advantages and disadvantages.
2. Advantages and disadvantages of new technologies are never distributed evenly among the world's populace. There are always winners and losers.
3. Embedded within each new technology is one—maybe more—underlying new idea. Often this idea is not immediately apparent; sometimes it is fairly abstract. But the idea will be there and its impact may turn out to dwarf the technology itself.
4. Technological change is not additive, it is ecological. That is, a new technology cannot simply be added to our world; its adoption changes our world.
5. Adopted technologies become mythic. The existence of new technologies, once they diffuse to regular use, are taken for granted as though they have always been there and they cannot possibly be removed.

These ideas can be applied as a framework, a modeled approach, to evaluate almost every article in this reader—and I encourage you to do so. Spend some time reading Postman's five ideas and then, as you read articles in subsequent units, ask yourself how Postman would react to the article?

- What are the trade-offs this new technology presents?
- Who are the winners and losers as this technology becomes diffused into regular use?
- What grand idea(s) underlies this new technology and how does this idea impact our economic, social, cultural, or political institutions?
- How is diffusion of this technology changing structures, patterns, or norms in our world?

Perhaps some articles do not focus on the technology itself, but on the ideas, patterns, or outcomes already occurring. Even so, applying Postman's framework is an excellent approach to making sense of the reading.

In the case of the automobile, Postman's ideas provide a strong structure for analysis. The automobile clearly had its advantages: faster travel led to more mobility and greater opportunity for many. On the other hand, it has contributed to air pollution and a breakdown of urban neighborhoods.

Clearly the winners and losers from the diffusion of the automobile into common use go far beyond the parking lot attendant and stable boy. Auto workers unionized through bloody and violent fights in the 1930s. Detroit was built on money from the automobile and, today, Detroit and Michigan are close to bankruptcy as most of that business has moved elsewhere. Oil cartels have made some in the Middle East obscenely wealthy, but have led to subjugation and death of countless others. Roadside businesses flourished from the 1930s to 1950s as the U.S. Highway system was built; then those same businesses failed in the 1960s and 1970s and the U.S. Interstate Highway system replaced it.

Postman suggests that embedded in every new technology is one or more powerful abstract ideas. Henry Ford and other automobile pioneers might have imagined American suburbia, but they could not foresee it as it has evolved. Nor could they have foreseen the varied implications of a split urban/suburban American population. While they knew their autos required gasoline, they could not have predicted the global political ramifications that the demand for a consistent, low-priced oil and gas supply would portend.

Clearly the automobile changed our world. But it did so not by adding a new tool to it, rather by enabling enormous shifts in societal structures. In doing so, it became mythic, celebrated in song, in movie, and in idiom like "as American as apple pie and Chevrolet."

While few information technologies have yet had the opportunity to embed themselves in culture as deeply as the automobile, you just may find parallels to draw.

Note

1. Neil Postman, "Five Things We Need to Know about Technological Change," *Address to New Tech '98 Conference,* March 27, 1998.

Article Prepared by: Daniel Mittleman, *DePaul University*

Five Things We Need to Know about Technological Change

Neil Postman

Learning Outcomes

After reading this article, you will be able to:

- Understand what is meant by "technology." Understand what is meant by technological change.

- Argue for and against the idea that "all technological change is a trade-off."

- Argue for and against the idea that "technological change is not additive; it is ecological."

Good morning your Eminences and Excellencies, ladies, and gentlemen.

The theme of this conference, "The New Technologies and the Human Person: Communicating the Faith in the New Millennium," suggests, of course, that you are concerned about what might happen to faith in the new millennium, as well you should be. In addition to our computers, which are close to having a nervous breakdown in anticipation of the year 2000, there is a great deal of frantic talk about the 21st century and how it will pose for us unique problems of which we know very little but for which, nonetheless, we are supposed to carefully prepare. Everyone seems to worry about this—business people, politicians, educators, as well as theologians.

> **The human dilemma is as it has always been, and it is a delusion to believe that the technological changes of our era have rendered irrelevant the wisdom of the ages and the sages.**

At the risk of sounding patronizing, may I try to put everyone's mind at ease? I doubt that the 21st century will pose for us problems that are more stunning, disorienting or complex than those we faced in this century, or the 19th, 18th, 17th, or for that matter, many of the centuries before that. But for those who are excessively nervous about the new millennium, I can provide, right at the start, some good advice about how to confront it. The advice comes from people whom we can trust, and whose thoughtfulness, it's safe to say, exceeds that of President Clinton, Newt Gingrich, or even Bill Gates. Here is what Henry David Thoreau told us: "All our inventions are but improved means to an unimproved end." Here is what Goethe told us: "One should, each day, try to hear a little song, read a good poem, see a fine picture, and, if possible, speak a few reasonable words." Socrates told us: "The unexamined life is not worth living." Rabbi Hillel told us: "What is hateful to thee, do not do to another." And here is the prophet Micah: "What does the Lord require of thee but to do justly, to love mercy and to walk humbly with thy God." And I could say, if we had the time, (although you know it well enough) what Jesus, Isaiah, Mohammad, Spinoza, and Shakespeare told us. It is all the same: There is no escaping from ourselves. The human dilemma is as it has always been, and it is a delusion to believe that the technological changes of our era have rendered irrelevant the wisdom of the ages and the sages.

. . . all technological change is a trade-off. . . . a Faustian bargain.

Nonetheless, having said this, I know perfectly well that because we do live in a technological age, we have some special problems that Jesus, Hillel, Socrates, and Micah did not and could not speak of. I do not have the wisdom to say what we ought to do about such problems, and so my contribution must confine itself to some things we need to know in order to address the problems. I call my talk *Five Things We Need to Know About Technological Change.* I base these ideas on my thirty years of studying the history of technological change but I do not think these are academic or esoteric ideas. They are the sort of things everyone who is concerned with cultural stability and balance should know and I offer them to you in the hope that you will find them useful in thinking about the effects of technology on religious faith.

First Idea

The first idea is that all technological change is a trade-off. I like to call it a Faustian bargain. Technology giveth and technology taketh away. This means that for every advantage a new technology offers, there is always a corresponding disadvantage. The disadvantage may exceed in importance the advantage, or the advantage may well be worth the cost. Now, this may seem to be a rather obvious idea, but you would be surprised at how many people believe that new technologies are unmixed blessings. You need only think of the enthusiasms with which most people approach their understanding of computers. Ask anyone who knows something about computers to talk about them, and you will find that they will, unabashedly and relentlessly, extol the wonders of computers. You will also find that in most cases they will completely neglect to mention any of the liabilities of computers. This is a dangerous imbalance, since the greater the wonders of a technology, the greater will be its negative consequences.

Think of the automobile, which for all of its obvious advantages, has poisoned our air, choked our cities, and degraded the beauty of our natural landscape. Or you might reflect on the paradox of medical technology which brings wondrous cures but is, at the same time, a demonstrable cause of certain diseases and disabilities, and has played a significant role in reducing the diagnostic skills of physicians. It is also well to recall that for all of the intellectual and social benefits provided by the printing press, its costs were equally monumental. The printing press gave the Western world prose, but it made poetry into an exotic and elitist form of communication. It gave us inductive science, but it reduced religious sensibility to a form of fanciful superstition. Printing gave us the modern conception of nationwide, but in so doing turned patriotism into a sordid if not lethal emotion. We might even say that the printing of the Bible in vernacular languages introduced the impression that God was an Englishman or a German or a Frenchman—that is to say, printing reduced God to the dimensions of a local potentate.

Perhaps the best way I can express this idea is to say that the question, "What will a new technology do?" is no more important than the question, "What will a new technology undo?" Indeed, the latter question is more important, precisely because it is asked so infrequently. One might say, then, that a sophisticated perspective on technological change includes one's being skeptical of Utopian and Messianic visions drawn by those who have no sense of history or of the precarious balances on which culture depends. In fact, if it were up to me, I would forbid anyone from talking about the new information technologies unless the person can demonstrate that he or she knows something about the social and psychic effects of the alphabet, the mechanical clock, the printing press, and telegraphy. In other words, knows something about the costs of great technologies.

Idea Number One, then, is that culture always pays a price for technology.

Second Idea

This leads to the second idea, which is that the advantages and disadvantages of new technologies are never distributed evenly among the population. This means that every new technology benefits some and harms others. There are even some who are not affected at all. Consider again the case of the printing press in the 16th century, of which Martin Luther said it was "God's highest and extremest act of grace, whereby the business of the gospel is driven forward." By placing the word of God on every Christian's kitchen table, the mass-produced book undermined the authority of the church hierarchy, and hastened the breakup of the Holy Roman See. The Protestants of that time cheered this development. The Catholics were enraged and distraught. Since I am a Jew, had I lived at that time, I probably wouldn't have given a damn one way or another, since it would make no difference whether a pogrom was inspired by Martin Luther or Pope Leo X. Some gain, some lose, a few remain as they were.

Let us take as another example, television, although here I should add at once that in the case of television there are very few indeed who are not affected in one way or another. In America, where television has taken hold more deeply than anywhere else, there are many people who find it a blessing, not least those who have achieved high-paying, gratifying careers in television as executives, technicians, directors, newscasters and entertainers. On the other hand, and in the long run, television may bring an end to the careers of school teachers since school was an invention of the printing press and must stand or fall on the issue of how much importance the printed word will have in the future. There is no chance, of course, that television will go away but school teachers who are enthusiastic about its presence always call to my mind an image of some turn-of-the-century blacksmith who not only is singing the praises of the automobile but who also believes that his business will be enhanced by it. We know now that his business was not enhanced by it; it was rendered obsolete by it, as perhaps an intelligent blacksmith would have known.

The questions, then, that are never far from the mind of a person who is knowledgeable about technological change are these: Who specifically benefits from the development of a new technology? Which groups, what type of person, what kind of industry will be favored? And, of course, which groups of people will thereby be harmed?

. . . there are always winners and losers in technological change.

These questions should certainly be on our minds when we think about computer technology. There is no doubt that the computer has been and will continue to be advantageous to large-scale organizations like the military or airline companies or banks or tax collecting institutions. And it is equally clear that the computer is now indispensable to high-level researchers in physics and other natural sciences. But to what extent has computer technology been an advantage to the masses of people? To steel workers, vegetable store owners, automobile mechanics, musicians, bakers, bricklayers, dentists, yes, theologians, and most of the rest into whose lives the computer now intrudes? These people have had their private matters made more accessible to powerful institutions. They are more easily tracked and controlled; they are subjected to more examinations, and are increasingly mystified by the decisions made about them. They are more than ever reduced to mere numerical objects. They are being buried by junk mail. They are easy targets for advertising agencies and political institutions.

In a word, these people are losers in the great computer revolution. The winners, which include among others computer companies, multi-national corporations and the nation state, will, of course, encourage the losers to be enthusiastic about computer technology. That is the way of winners, and so in the beginning they told the losers that with personal computers the average person can balance a checkbook more neatly, keep better track of recipes, and make more logical shopping lists. Then they told them that computers will make it possible to vote at home, shop at home, get all the entertainment they wish at home, and thus make community life unnecessary. And now, of course, the winners speak constantly of the Age of Information, always implying that the more information we have, the better we will be in solving significant problems—not only personal ones but large-scale social problems, as well. But how true is this? If there are children starving in the world—and there are—it is not because of insufficient information. We have known for a long time how to produce enough food to feed every child on the planet. How is it that we let so many of them starve? If there is violence on our streets, it is not because we have insufficient information. If women are abused, if divorce and pornography and mental illness are increasing, none of it has anything to do with insufficient information. I dare say it is because something else is missing, and I don't think I have to tell this audience what it is. Who knows? This age of information may turn out to be a curse if we are blinded by it so that we cannot see truly where our problems lie. That is why it is always necessary for us to ask of those who speak enthusiastically of computer technology, why do you do this? What interests do you represent? To whom are you hoping to give power? From whom will you be withholding power?

I do not mean to attribute unsavory, let alone sinister motives to anyone. I say only that since technology favors some people and harms others, these are questions that must always be asked. And so, that there are always winners and losers in technological change is the second idea.

Third Idea

Here is the third. Embedded in every technology there is a powerful idea, sometimes two or three powerful ideas. These ideas are often hidden from our view because they are of a somewhat abstract nature. But this should not be taken to mean that they do not have practical consequences.

The third idea is the sum and substance of what Marshall McLuhan meant when he coined the famous sentence, "The medium is the message."

Perhaps you are familiar with the old adage that says: To a man with a hammer, everything looks like a nail. We may extend that truism: To a person with a pencil, everything looks like a sentence. To a person with a TV camera, everything looks like an image. To a person with a computer, everything looks like data. I do not think we need to take these aphorisms literally. But what they call to our attention is that every technology has a prejudice. Like language itself, it predisposes us to favor and value certain perspectives and accomplishments. In a culture without writing, human memory is of the greatest importance, as are the proverbs, sayings and songs which contain the accumulated oral wisdom of centuries. That is why Solomon was thought to be the wisest of men. In Kings I we are told he knew 3,000 proverbs. But in a culture with writing, such feats of memory are considered a waste of time, and proverbs are merely irrelevant fancies. The writing person favors logical organization and systematic analysis, not proverbs. The telegraphic person values speed, not introspection. The television person values immediacy, not history. And computer people, what shall we say of them? Perhaps we can say that the computer person values information, not knowledge, certainly not wisdom. Indeed, in the computer age, the concept of wisdom may vanish altogether.

The consequences of technological change are always vast, often unpredictable and largely irreversible.

The third idea, then, is that every technology has a philosophy which is given expression in how the technology makes people use their minds, in what it makes us do with our bodies, in how it codifies the world, in which of our senses it amplifies, in which of our emotional and intellectual tendencies it disregards. This idea is the sum and substance of what the great Catholic prophet, Marshall McLuhan meant when he coined the famous sentence, "The medium is the message."

Fourth Idea

Here is the fourth idea: Technological change is not additive; it is ecological. I can explain this best by an analogy. What happens if we place a drop of red dye into a beaker of clear water? Do we have clear water plus a spot of red dye? Obviously not. We have a new coloration to every molecule of water. That is what I mean by ecological change. A new medium does not add something; it changes everything. In the year 1500, after the printing press was invented, you did not have old Europe plus the printing press. You had a different Europe. After television, America was not America plus television. Television gave a new coloration to every political campaign, to every home, to every school, to every church, to every industry, and so on.

That is why we must be cautious about technological innovation. The consequences of technological change are always vast, often unpredictable and largely irreversible. That is also why we must be suspicious of capitalists. Capitalists are by definition not only personal risk takers but, more to the point, cultural risk takers. The most creative and daring of them hope to exploit new technologies to the fullest, and do not much care what traditions are overthrown in the process or whether or not a culture is prepared to function without such traditions. Capitalists are, in a word, radicals. In America, our most significant radicals have always been capitalists—men like Bell, Edison, Ford, Carnegie, Sarnoff, Goldwyn. These men obliterated the 19th century, and created the 20th, which is why it is a mystery to me that capitalists are thought to be conservative. Perhaps it is because they are inclined to wear dark suits and grey ties.

I trust you understand that in saying all this, I am making no argument for socialism. I say only that capitalists need to be carefully watched and disciplined. To be sure, they talk of family, marriage, piety, and honor but if allowed to exploit new technology to its fullest economic potential, they may undo the institutions that make such ideas possible. And here I might just give two examples of this point, taken from the American encounter with technology. The first concerns education. Who, we may ask, has had the greatest impact on American education in this century? If you are thinking of John Dewey or any other education philosopher, I must say you are quite wrong. The greatest impact has been made by quiet men in grey suits in a suburb of New York City called Princeton, New Jersey. There, they developed and promoted the technology known as the standardized test, such as IQ tests, the SATs and the GREs. Their tests redefined what we mean by learning, and have resulted in our reorganizing the curriculum to accommodate the tests.

A second example concerns our politics. It is clear by now that the people who have had the most radical effect on American politics in our time are not political ideologues or student protesters with long hair and copies of Karl Marx under their arms. The radicals who have changed the nature of politics in America are entrepreneurs in dark suits and grey ties who manage the large television industry in America. They did not mean to turn political discourse into a form of entertainment. They did not mean to make it impossible for an overweight person to run for high political office. They did not mean to reduce political campaigning to a 30-second TV commercial. All they were trying to do is to make television into a vast and unsleeping money machine. That they destroyed substantive political discourse in the process does not concern them.

Fifth Idea

I come now to the fifth and final idea, which is that media tend to become mythic. I use this word in the sense in which it was used by the French literary critic, Roland Barthes. He used the word "myth" to refer to a common tendency to think of our technological creations as if they were God-given, as if they were a part of the natural order of things. I have on occasion asked my students if they know when the alphabet was invented. The question astonishes them. It is as if I asked them when clouds and trees were invented. The alphabet, they believe, was not something that was invented. It just is. It is this way with many products of human culture but with none more consistently than technology. Cars, planes, TV, movies, newspapers—they have achieved mythic status because they are perceived as gifts of nature, not as artifacts produced in a specific political and historical context.

When a technology become mythic, it is always dangerous because it is then accepted as it is, and is therefore not easily susceptible to modification or control. If you should propose to the average American that television broadcasting should not begin until 5 P.M. and should cease at 11 P.M., or propose that there should be no television commercials, he will think the idea ridiculous. But not because he disagrees with your cultural agenda. He will think it ridiculous because he assumes you are proposing that something in nature be changed; as if you are suggesting that the sun should rise at 10 A.M. instead of at 6.

The best way to view technology is as a strange intruder.

Whenever I think about the capacity of technology to become mythic, I call to mind the remark made by Pope John Paul II. He said, "Science can purify religion from error and superstition. Religion can purify science from idolatry and false absolutes."

What I am saying is that our enthusiasm for technology can turn into a form of idolatry and our belief in its beneficence can be a false absolute. The best way to view technology is as a strange intruder, to remember that technology is not part of God's plan but a product of human creativity and hubris, and that its capacity for good or evil rests entirely on human awareness of what it does for us and to us.

Conclusion

And so, these are my five ideas about technological change. First, that we always pay a price for technology; the greater the technology, the greater the price. Second, that there are always winners and losers, and that the winners always try to persuade the losers that they are really winners. Third, that there is embedded in every great technology an epistemological, political or social prejudice. Sometimes that bias is greatly to our advantage. Sometimes it is not. The printing press annihilated the oral tradition; telegraphy annihilated space; television has humiliated the word; the computer, perhaps, will degrade community life. And so on. Fourth, technological change is not additive; it is ecological, which means, it changes everything and is, therefore too important to be left entirely in the hands of Bill Gates. And fifth, technology tends to become mythic; that is, perceived as part of the natural order of things, and therefore tends to control more of our lives than is good for us.

If we had more time, I could supply some additional important things about technological change but I will stand by these for the moment, and will close with this thought. In the past, we experienced technological change in the manner of sleepwalkers. Our unspoken slogan has been "technology über alles," and we have been willing to shape our lives to fit the requirements of technology, not the requirements of culture. This is a form of stupidity, especially in an age of vast technological change. We need to proceed with our eyes wide open so that we may use technology rather than be used by it.

Critical Thinking

1. All U.S. schoolchildren learn that the first message Samuel F. B. Morse transmitted over his newly invented telegraph were the words, "What hath God wrought." What they probably do not learn is that Morse was quoting from the poem of Balaam in the Book of Numbers, chapter 23. Read the text of this poem.
2. The overview to this unit presents two ways to understand technical and scientific discoveries. In which camp is Morse? Richard Lewontin, a Harvard geneticist, says ("The Politics of Science," *The New York Review of Books,* May 9, 2002) that "The state of American science and its relation to the American state are the product of war." What does he mean?

Create Central

www.mhhe.com/createcentral

Internet References

Ian Goldin: Navigating Our Global Future [TED Talk]
www.ted.com/talks/ian_goldin_navigating_our_global_future.html

Technology Trends That Are Reshaping Our World [Interview with Tom Standage]
http://knowledge.ckgsb.edu.cn/2013/09/10/technology/tom-standage-technology-trends

Article

Prepared by: Daniel Mittleman, *DePaul University*

The Information: How the Internet Gets Inside Us

Adam Gopnik

Learning Outcomes

After reading this article, you will be able to:

- Articulate different visions for the future of networked technology.

- Understand how different views can be formed from the same set of existing data.

- Understand how views of the future are anchored by what is known and valued in the present.

When the first Harry Potter book appeared, in 1997, it was just a year before the universal search engine Google was launched. And so Hermione Granger, that charming grind, still goes to the Hogwarts library and spends hours and hours working her way through the stacks, finding out what a basilisk is or how to make a love potion. The idea that a wizard in training might have, instead, a magic pad where she could inscribe a name and in half a second have an avalanche of news stories, scholarly articles, books, and images (including images she shouldn't be looking at) was a Quidditch broom too far. Now, having been stuck with the library shtick, she has to go on working the stacks in the Harry Potter movies, while the kids who have since come of age nudge their parents. "Why is she doing that?" they whisper. "Why doesn't she just Google it?"

That the reality of machines can outpace the imagination of magic, and in so short a time, does tend to lend weight to the claim that the technological shifts in communication we're living with are unprecedented. It isn't just that we've lived one technological revolution among many; it's that our technological revolution is the big social revolution that we live with. The past twenty years have seen a revolution less in morals, which have remained mostly static, than in means: you could already say "fuck" on HBO back in the eighties; the change has been our ability to tweet or IM or text it. The set subject of our novelists is information; the set obsession of our dons is what it does to our intelligence.

The scale of the transformation is such that an ever-expanding literature has emerged to censure or celebrate it. A series of books explaining why books no longer matter is a paradox that Chesterton would have found implausible, yet there they are, and they come in the typical flavors: the eulogistic, the alarmed, the sober, and the gleeful. When the electric toaster was invented, there were, no doubt, books that said that the toaster would open up horizons for breakfast undreamed of in the days of burning bread over an open flame; books that told you that the toaster would bring an end to the days of creative breakfast, since our children, growing up with uniformly sliced bread, made to fit a single opening, would never know what a loaf of their own was like; and books that told you that sometimes the toaster would make breakfast better and sometimes it would make breakfast worse, and that the cost for finding this out would be the price of the book you'd just bought.

All three kinds appear among the new books about the Internet: call them the Never-Betters, the Better-Nevers, and the Ever-Wasers. The Never-Betters believe that we're on the brink of a new utopia, where information will be free and democratic, news will be made from the bottom up, love will reign, and cookies will bake themselves. The Better-Nevers think that we would have been better off if the whole thing had never happened, that the world that is coming to an end is superior to the one that is taking its place, and that, at a minimum, books and magazines create private space for minds in ways that twenty-second bursts of information don't. The Ever-Wasers insist that at any moment in modernity something like this is going on, and that a new way of organizing data and connecting users is always thrilling to some and chilling to others—that something like this is going on is exactly what makes it a modern moment. One's hopes rest with the Never-Betters; one's head with the Ever-Wasers; and one's heart? Well, twenty or so books in, one's heart tends to move toward the Better-Nevers, and then bounce back toward someplace that looks more like home.

Among the Never-Betters, the N.Y.U. professor Clay Shirky—the author of "Cognitive Surplus" and many articles and blog posts proclaiming the coming of the digital millennium—is the breeziest and seemingly most self-confident.

"Seemingly," because there is an element of overdone provocation in his stuff (So people aren't reading Tolstoy? Well, Tolstoy *sucks*) that suggests something a little nervous going on underneath. Shirky believes that we are on the crest of an ever-surging wave of democratized information: the Gutenberg printing press produced the Reformation, which produced the Scientific Revolution, which produced the Enlightenment, which produced the Internet, each move more liberating than the one before. Though it may take a little time, the new connective technology, by joining people together in new communities and in new ways, is bound to make for more freedom. It's the *Wired* version of Whig history: ever better, onward and upward, progress unstopped. In John Brockman's anthology "Is the Internet Changing the Way You Think?," the evolutionary psychologist John Tooby shares the excitement—"We see all around us transformations in the making that will rival or exceed the printing revolution"—and makes the same extended parallel to Gutenberg: "Printing ignited the previously wasted intellectual potential of huge segments of the population. . . . Freedom of thought and speech—where they exist—were unforeseen offspring of the printing press."

Shirky's and Tooby's version of Never-Betterism has its excitements, but the history it uses seems to have been taken from the back of a cereal box. The idea, for instance, that the printing press rapidly gave birth to a new order of information, democratic and bottom-up, is a cruel cartoon of the truth. If the printing press *did* propel the Reformation, one of the biggest ideas it propelled was Luther's newly invented absolutist anti-Semitism. And what followed the Reformation wasn't the Enlightenment, a new era of openness and freely disseminated knowledge. What followed the Reformation was, actually, the Counter-Reformation, which used the same means—i.e., printed books—to spread ideas about what jerks the reformers were, and unleashed a hundred years of religious warfare. In the seventeen-fifties, more than two centuries later, Voltaire was still writing in a book about the horrors of those other books that urged burning men alive in auto-da-fé. Buried in Tooby's little parenthetical—"where they exist"—are millions of human bodies. If ideas of democracy and freedom emerged at the end of the printing-press era, it wasn't by some technological logic but because of parallel inventions, like the ideas of limited government and religious tolerance, very hard won from history.

Of course, if you stretch out the time scale enough, and are sufficiently casual about causes, you can give the printing press credit for anything you like. But all the media of modern consciousness—from the printing press to radio and the movies—were used just as readily by authoritarian reactionaries, and then by modern totalitarians, to reduce liberty and enforce conformity as they ever were by libertarians to expand it. As Andrew Pettegree shows in his fine new study, "The Book in the Renaissance," the mainstay of the printing revolution in seventeenth-century Europe was not dissident pamphlets but royal edicts, printed by the thousand: almost all the new media of that day were working, in essence, for kinglouis.gov.

Even later, full-fledged totalitarian societies didn't burn books. They burned *some* books, while keeping the printing presses running off such quantities that by the mid-fifties Stalin was said to have more books in print than Agatha Christie. (Recall that in "1984" Winston's girlfriend works for the Big Brother publishing house.) If you're going to give the printed book, or any other machine-made thing, credit for all the good things that have happened, you have to hold it accountable for the bad stuff, too. The Internet *may* make for more freedom a hundred years from now, but there's no historical law that says it has to.

Many of the more knowing Never-Betters turn for cheer not to messy history and mixed-up politics but to psychology—to the actual expansion of our minds. The argument, advanced in Andy Clark's "Supersizing the Mind" and in Robert K. Logan's "The Sixth Language," begins with the claim that cognition is not a little processing program that takes place inside your head, Robby the Robot style. It is a constant flow of information, memory, plans, and physical movements, in which as much thinking goes on out there as in here. If television produced the global village, the Internet produces the global psyche: everyone keyed in like a neuron, so that to the eyes of a watching Martian we are really part of a single planetary brain. Contraptions don't change consciousness; contraptions are part of consciousness. We may not act better than we used to, but we sure think differently than we did.

Cognitive entanglement, after all, is the rule of life. My memories and my wife's intermingle. When I can't recall a name or a date, I don't look it up; I just ask her. Our machines, in this way, become our substitute spouses and plug-in companions. Jerry Seinfeld said that the public library was everyone's pathetic friend, giving up its books at a casual request and asking you only to please return them in a month or so. Google is really the world's Thurber wife: smiling patiently and smugly as she explains what the difference is between eulogy and elegy and what the best route is to that little diner outside Hackensack. The new age is one in which we have a know-it-all spouse at our fingertips.

But, if cognitive entanglement exists, so does cognitive exasperation. Husbands and wives deny each other's memories as much as they depend on them. That's fine until it really counts (say, in divorce court). In a practical, immediate way, one sees the limits of the so-called "extended mind" clearly in the mob-made Wikipedia, the perfect product of that new vast, super-sized cognition: when there's easy agreement, it's fine, and when there's widespread disagreement on values or facts, as with, say, the origins of capitalism, it's fine, too; you get both sides. The trouble comes when one side is right and the other side is wrong and doesn't know it. The Shakespeare authorship page and the Shroud of Turin page are scenes of constant conflict and are packed with unreliable information. Creationists crowd cyberspace every bit as effectively as evolutionists, and extend their minds just as fully. Our trouble is not the over-all absence of smartness but the intractable power of pure stupidity, and no machine, or mind, seems extended enough to cure that.

The books by the Better-Nevers are more moving than those by the Never-Betters for the same reason that Thomas Gray was at his best in that graveyard: loss is always the great poetic subject. Nicholas Carr, in "The Shallows," William Powers, in

"Hamlet's BlackBerry," and Sherry Turkle, in "Alone Together," all bear intimate witness to a sense that the newfound land, the ever-present BlackBerry-and-instant-message world, is one whose price, paid in frayed nerves and lost reading hours and broken attention, is hardly worth the gains it gives us. "The medium does matter," Carr has written. "As a technology, a book focuses our attention, isolates us from the myriad distractions that fill our everyday lives. A networked computer does precisely the opposite. It is designed to scatter our attention. . . . Knowing that the depth of our thought is tied directly to the intensity of our attentiveness, it's hard not to conclude that as we adapt to the intellectual environment of the Net our thinking becomes shallower."

These three Better-Nevers have slightly different stories to tell. Carr is most concerned about the way the Internet breaks down our capacity for reflective thought. His testimony about how this happened in his own life is plangent and familiar, but he addles it a bit by insisting that the real damage is being done at the neurological level, that our children are having their brains altered by too much instant messaging and the like. This sounds impressive but turns out to be redundant. Of course the changes are in their brains; where else would they be? It's the equivalent of saying that playing football doesn't just affect a kid's fitness; it changes the muscle tone that creates his ability to throw and catch footballs.

Powers's reflections are more family-centered and practical. He recounts, very touchingly, stories of family life broken up by the eternal consultation of smartphones and computer monitors:

> Somebody excuses themselves for a bathroom visit or a glass of water and doesn't return. Five minutes later, another of us exits on a similarly mundane excuse along the lines of "I have to check something.". . . Where have all the humans gone? To their screens of course. Where they always go these days. The digital crowd has a way of elbowing its way into everything, to the point where a family can't sit in a room together for half an hour without somebody, or everybody, peeling off. . . . As I watched the Vanishing Family Trick unfold, and played my own part in it, I sometimes felt as if love itself, or the acts of heart and mind that constitute love, were being leached out of the house by our screens.

He then surveys seven Wise Men—Plato, Thoreau, Seneca, the usual gang—who have something to tell us about solitude and the virtues of inner space, all of it sound enough, though he tends to overlook the significant point that these worthies were not entirely in favor of the kinds of liberties that we now take for granted and that made the new dispensation possible. (He knows that Seneca instructed the Emperor Nero, but sticks in a footnote to insist that the bad, fiddling-while-Rome-burned Nero asserted himself only after he fired the philosopher and started to act like an Internet addict.)

Similarly, Nicholas Carr cites Martin Heidegger for having seen, in the mid-fifties, that new technologies would break the meditational space on which Western wisdoms depend. Since Heidegger had not long before walked straight out of his own meditational space into the arms of the Nazis, it's hard to have much nostalgia for this version of the past. One feels the same doubts when Sherry Turkle, in "Alone Together," her touching plaint about the destruction of the old intimacy-reading culture by the new remote-connection-Internet culture, cites studies that show a dramatic decline in empathy among college students, who apparently are "far less likely to say that it is valuable to put oneself in the place of others or to try and understand their feelings." What is to be done? Other Better-Nevers point to research that's supposed to show that people who read novels develop exceptional empathy. But if reading a lot of novels gave you exceptional empathy university English departments should be filled with the most compassionate and generous-minded of souls, and, so far, they are not.

One of the things that John Brockman's collection on the Internet and the mind illustrates is that when people struggle to describe the state that the Internet puts them in they arrive at a remarkably familiar picture of disassociation and fragmentation. Life was once whole, continuous, stable; now it is fragmented, multi-part, shimmering around us, unstable and impossible to fix. The world becomes Keats's "waking dream," as the writer Kevin Kelly puts it.

The odd thing is that this complaint, though deeply felt by our contemporary Better-Nevers, is identical to Baudelaire's perception about modern Paris in 1855, or Walter Benjamin's about Berlin in 1930, or Marshall McLuhan's in the face of three-channel television (and Canadian television, at that) in 1965. When department stores had Christmas windows with clockwork puppets, the world was going to pieces; when the city streets were filled with horse-drawn carriages running by bright-colored posters, you could no longer tell the real from the simulated; when people were listening to shellac 78s and looking at color newspaper supplements, the world had become a kaleidoscope of disassociated imagery; and when the broadcast air was filled with droning black-and-white images of men in suits reading news, all of life had become indistinguishable from your fantasies of it. It was Marx, not Steve Jobs, who said that the character of modern life is that everything falls apart.

We must, at some level, *need* this to be true, since we think it's true about so many different kinds of things. We experience this sense of fracture so deeply that we ascribe it to machines that, viewed with retrospective detachment, don't seem remotely capable of producing it. If all you have is a hammer, the saying goes, everything looks like a nail; and, if you think the world is broken, every machine looks like the hammer that broke it.

It is an intuition of this kind that moves the final school, the Ever-Wasers, when they consider the new digital age. A sense of vertiginous overload is the central experience of modernity, they say; at every moment, machines make new circuits for connection and circulation, as obvious-seeming as the postage stamps that let nineteenth-century scientists collaborate by mail, or as newfangled as the Wi-Fi connection that lets a sixteen-year-old in New York consult a tutor in Bangalore. Our new confusion is just the same old confusion.

Among Ever-Wasers, the Harvard historian Ann Blair may be the most ambitious. In her book "Too Much to Know:

Managing Scholarly Information Before the Modern Age," she makes the case that what we're going through is like what others went through a very long while ago. Against the cartoon history of Shirky or Tooby, Blair argues that the sense of "information overload" was not the consequence of Gutenberg but already in place before printing began. She wants us to resist "trying to reduce the complex causal nexus behind the transition from Renaissance to Enlightenment to the impact of a technology or any particular set of ideas." Anyway, the crucial revolution was not of print but of paper: "During the later Middle Ages a staggering growth in the production of manuscripts, facilitated by the use of paper, accompanied a great expansion of readers outside the monastic and scholastic contexts." For that matter, our minds were altered less by books than by index slips. Activities that seem quite twenty-first century, she shows, began when people cut and pasted from one manuscript to another; made aggregated news in compendiums; passed around précis. "Early modern finding devices" were forced into existence: lists of authorities, lists of headings.

Everyone complained about what the new information technologies were doing to our minds. Everyone said that the flood of books produced a restless, fractured attention. Everyone complained that pamphlets and poems were breaking kids' ability to concentrate, that big good handmade books were ignored, swept aside by printed works that, as Erasmus said, "are foolish, ignorant, malignant, libelous, mad." The reader consulting a card catalogue in a library was living a revolution as momentous, and as disorienting, as our own. The book index was the search engine of its era, and needed to be explained at length to puzzled researchers—as, for that matter, did the Hermione-like idea of "looking things up." That uniquely evil and necessary thing the comprehensive review of many different books on a related subject, with the necessary oversimplification of their ideas that it demanded, was already around in 1500, and already being accused of missing all the points. In the period when many of the big, classic books that we no longer have time to read were being written, the general complaint was that there wasn't enough time to read big, classic books.

Blair's and Pettegree's work on the relation between minds and machines, and the combination of delight and despair we find in their collisions, leads you to a broader thought: at any given moment, our most complicated machine will be taken as a model of human intelligence, and whatever media kids favor will be identified as the cause of our stupidity. When there were automatic looms, the mind was like an automatic loom; and, since young people in the loom period liked novels, it was the cheap novel that was degrading our minds. When there were telephone exchanges, the mind was like a telephone exchange, and, in the same period, since the nickelodeon reigned, moving pictures were making us dumb. When mainframe computers arrived and television was what kids liked, the mind was like a mainframe and television was the engine of our idiocy. Some machine is always showing us Mind; some entertainment derived from the machine is always showing us Non-Mind.

Armed with such parallels, the Ever-Wasers smile condescendingly at the Better-Nevers and say, "Of course, some new machine is always ruining everything. We've all been here before." But the Better-Nevers can say, in return, "What if the Internet is actually doing it?" The hypochondriac frets about this bump or that suspicious freckle and we laugh—but sooner or later one small bump, one jagged-edge freckle, will be the thing for certain. Worlds really do decline. "Oh, they always say that about the barbarians, but every generation has its barbarians, and every generation assimilates them," one Roman reassured another when the Vandals were at the gates, and next thing you knew there wasn't a hot bath or a good book for another thousand years.

And, if it was ever thus, how did it ever get to be thus in the first place? The digital world is new, and the real gains and losses of the Internet era are to be found not in altered neurons or empathy tests but in the small changes in mood, life, manners, feelings it creates—in the texture of the age. There is, for instance, a simple, spooky sense in which the Internet is just a loud and unlimited library in which we now live—as if one went to sleep every night in the college stacks, surrounded by pamphlets and polemics and possibilities. There is the sociology section, the science section, old sheet music and menus, and you can go to the periodicals room anytime and read old issues of the *New Statesman*. (And you can whisper loudly to a friend in the next carrel to get the hockey scores.) To see that that is so is at least to drain some of the melodrama from the subject. It is odd and new to be living in the library; but there isn't anything odd and new about the library.

Yet surely having something wrapped right around your mind is different from having your mind wrapped tightly around something. What we live in is not the age of the extended mind but the age of the inverted self. The things that have usually lived in the darker recesses or mad corners of our mind—sexual obsessions and conspiracy theories, paranoid fixations and fetishes—are now out there: you click once and you can read about the Kennedy autopsy or the Nazi salute or hog-tied Swedish flight attendants. But things that were once external and subject to the social rules of caution and embarrassment—above all, our interactions with other people—are now easily internalized, made to feel like mere workings of the id left on its own. (I've felt this myself, writing anonymously on hockey forums: it is easy to say vile things about Gary Bettman, the commissioner of the N.H.L., with a feeling of glee rather than with a sober sense that what you're saying should be tempered by a little truth and reflection.) Thus the limitless malice of Internet commenting: it's not newly unleashed anger but what we all think in the first order, and have always in the past socially restrained if only thanks to the look on the listener's face—the monstrous music that runs through our minds is now played out loud.

A social network is crucially different from a social circle, since the function of a social circle is to curb our appetites and of a network to extend them. Everything once inside is outside, a click away; much that used to be outside is inside, experienced in solitude. And so the peacefulness, the serenity that we feel away from the Internet, and which all the Better-Nevers rightly testify to, has less to do with being no longer harried by others than with being less oppressed by the force of your own inner life. Shut off your computer, and your self stops raging quite as much or quite as loud.

It is the wraparound presence, not the specific evils, of the machine that oppresses us. Simply reducing the machine's presence will go a long way toward alleviating the disorder. Which points, in turn, to a dog-not-barking-in-the-nighttime detail that may be significant. In the Better-Never books, television isn't scanted or ignored; it's celebrated. When William Powers, in "Hamlet's BlackBerry," describes the deal his family makes to have an Unplugged Sunday, he tells us that the No Screens agreement doesn't include television: "For us, television had always been a mostly communal experience, a way of coming together rather than pulling apart." ("Can you please turn off your damn computer and come watch television with the rest of the family," the dad now cries to the teen-ager.)

Yet everything that is said about the Internet's destruction of "interiority" was said for decades about television, and just as loudly. Jerry Mander's "Four Arguments for the Elimination of Television," in the nineteen-seventies, turned on television's addictive nature and its destruction of viewers' inner lives; a little later, George Trow proposed that television produced the absence of context, the disintegration of the frame—the very things, in short, that the Internet is doing now. And Bill McKibben ended his book on television by comparing watching TV to watching ducks on a pond (advantage: ducks), in the same spirit in which Nicholas Carr leaves his computer screen to read "Walden."

Now television is the harmless little fireplace over in the corner, where the family gathers to watch "Entourage." TV isn't just docile; it's positively benevolent. This makes you think that what made television so evil back when it was evil was not its essence but its omnipresence. Once it is not everything, it can be merely something. The real demon in the machine is the tirelessness of the user. A meatless Monday has advantages over enforced vegetarianism, because it helps release the pressure on the food system without making undue demands on the eaters. In the same way, an unplugged Sunday is a better idea than turning off the Internet completely, since it demonstrates that we can get along just fine without the screens, if only for a day.

Hermione, stuck in the nineties, never did get her iPad, and will have to manage in the stacks. But perhaps the instrument of the new connected age was already in place in fantasy. For the Internet screen has always been like the palantír in Tolkien's "Lord of the Rings"—the "seeing stone" that lets the wizards see the entire world. Its gift is great; the wizard can see it all. Its risk is real: evil things will register more vividly than the great mass of dull good. The peril isn't that users lose their knowledge of the world. It's that they can lose all sense of proportion.

You can come to think that the armies of Mordor are not just vast and scary, which they are, but limitless and undefeatable, which they aren't.

Thoughts are bigger than the things that deliver them. Our contraptions may shape our consciousness, but it is our consciousness that makes our credos, and we mostly live by those. Toast, as every breakfaster knows, isn't really about the quality of the bread or how it's sliced or even the toaster. For man cannot live by toast alone. It's all about the butter.

Critical Thinking

1. Gopnik wraps this article in a reference to Harry Potter. What point is he making with this reference, and how does this point tie to the central thesis of the article? Can you think of another fictional reference from before 1997 and how those characters might have differed had the author known of the Internet?

2. The three kinds of books referenced in the article represent three kinds of thinking about the Internet. Why do you think authors who write about the Internet come to such different conclusions regarding its impact on our civilization? Is it differences in the information each author has, differences in their underlying assumptions about the nature of man and technology, differences in their view of societal values and goals, or something else?

3. Among the Web Resources for this article are text interviews with authors from each of the three kinds of books. Do you notice any differences in how the authors communicate their attitudes and views about the Internet?

Create Central

www.mhhe.com/createcentral

Internet References

Interview: Tom Standage
www.abc.net.au/news/2012-08-24/interview-tom-standage/4221934

On Bubbles, Facebook, and Playing for Keeps: 10 Questions with Clay Shirky
www.wired.com/business/2012/06/on-bubbles-facebook-and-playing-for-keeps-ten-questions-with-clay-shirky

Q&A: Author Nicholas Carr on the Terrifying Future of Computing
www.wired.com/techbiz/people/magazine/16-01/st_qa

Technopessimism Is Bunk
www.pbs.org/newshour/businessdesk/2013/07/technopessimism-is-bunk.html

Transcript for Ann Blair Interview on Information Overload
http://ttbook.org/book/transcript/transcript-ann-blair-information-overload

Article

Prepared by: Daniel Mittleman, *DePaul University*

The Secret Life of Data in the Year 2020

A futurist for Intel shows how geotags, sensor outputs, and big data are changing the future. He argues that we need a better understanding of our relationship with the data we produce in order to build the future we want.

BRIAN DAVID JOHNSON

Learning Outcomes

After reading this article, you will be able to:

- Understand the concept of "big data."
- Understand both the risks and rewards of big data.

My job as Intel's futurist is to look 10 to 15 years out and model how people will act and interact with devices in the future. I explore a vision for all computational devices. Basically if it has a chip in it, it's within my view. The driving force behind this work is incredibly pragmatic. The process of designing, developing, manufacturing, and deploying our platforms takes around 10 years. It's of vital business importance today for Intel to understand the landscape a decade from now. That's why in 2010 we started work on 2020.

When you look to 2020 and beyond, you can't escape big data. Big data—extremely large sets of data related to consumer behavior, social network posts, geotagging, sensor outputs, and more—is a big problem. Intel is at the forefront of the big data revolution and all the challenges therein. Our processors are how data gets from one place to another. If anyone should have insight into how to make data do things we want it to do, make it work for the future, it should be Intel.

That's where I come in. I model what it will feel like to be a human 10 years from now. I build models that explore what it will feel like to experience big data as an average person. An integral part of this work is collaborating with Genevieve Bell. She's an Intel fellow, a cultural anthropologist by training, and one of the best minds working in this area. Together, we've been exploring 2020 through the lens of what we call "the Secret Life of Data."

For most people in 2020, it will feel like data has a life of its own. With the massive amount of sensors we have littering our lives and landscapes, we'll have information spewing from everywhere. Our cars, our buildings, and even our bodies will expel an exhaust of data, information, and 1s and 0s at an incredible volume.

Why will most people think that their data has a life of its own? Well, because it's true. We will have algorithms talking to algorithms, machines talking to machines, machines talking to algorithms, sensors and cameras gathering data, and computational power crunching through that data, then handing it off to more algorithms and machines. It will be a rich and secret life separate from us and for me incredibly fascinating.

But as we begin to build the Secret Life of Data, we must always remember that data is meaningless all by itself. The 1s and 0s are useless and meaningless on their own. Data is only useful and indeed powerful when it comes into contact with people.

This brings up some interesting questions and fascinating problems to be solved from an engineering standpoint. When we are architecting these algorithms, when we are designing these systems, how do we make sure they have an understanding of what it means to be human? The people writing these algorithms must have an understanding of what people will do with that data. How will it fit into their lives? How will it affect their daily routine? How will it make their lives better?

The Mysterious Resident of Glencoe and Wren Roads

At Intel, solving the problem of how data will interact with other data in the future is not an esoteric pursuit. When I talk about making people's lives better and having a deep understanding of how data will make their lives better, I'm not speaking in the abstract. I work with the people who are writing those algorithms and the people building the systems. Take Rita, for instance, who just had a baby last year. Rita did an experiment recently that will show you exactly what I mean when I say that algorithms need to understand people.

To test out this approach, Rita developed a prototype and programmed a personal tracking system. She allowed her smartphone to track and record all of her movements throughout her day. She wanted to test how the software understood who she was and what she did with her day.

After allowing her device and the software to track her every movement for a month, she checked out the report. The initial findings of the sensors and algorithms had learned some very specific information about her. The system told her that she "lived" in three primary places. The first location was spot on. It showed that she lived in her own home. It even showed the location on a map. Okay, that was right.

Second, it reported that she lived on the Jones Farm Campus of Intel. Okay, that was correct, as well. Rita spends most of her time at work when she's not at home. But the third data point really enraged Rita.

The third data point showed that Rita lived at the intersection of Glencoe and Wren roads. This really made her mad. I didn't completely understand. I asked why. She showed me on the map.

"There's nothing at Glencoe and Wren," she said. It's a stop sign in the middle of nowhere. All it had to do is look at any mapping program and it would show nothing there. How could I live there if there is no building there? It's ridiculous. We need to program these things to understand what it really means to be human. Just because I stopped in this place twice a day on my way to and from work doesn't mean I live there. It's so simple to fix. We just have to understand how people really live and not base it on just data points. People are the most important data points."

That really is my challenge: How do we come up with the requirements and problems to build into the 2020 platform? The Secret Life of Data research and development work I've been doing with Genevieve Bell tells us that one approach is to start looking at data as if it were a person.

The Algorithm: More Human Than a Human?

In the era of big data, how do we make sense of all this massive amount of information? We need new ways of conceptualizing and thinking about data that is not the traditional binary view that we have taken for the last 50 years.

If we begin to think of data as having a life of its own, and we are programming systems to enable them to have this life, then ultimately we are designing this data and the algorithms that process it to be human. One approach is to think about data as having responsibilities.

When I say responsibilities, I'm not just talking about the responsibility to keep the data safe and secure, but also a responsibility to deliver the data in the right context—to tell the story right. It's akin to making sure that a person understands your family history, the subtle nuances of your father and grandmother and great-grandmother. It is the responsibility of history, and it cannot be taken lightly.

The research and development that Bell and I have been doing explores what is the only way to make sense of all this complex information—by viewing data, massive data sets, and the algorithms that really utilize big data as being human. Data doesn't spring full formed from nowhere. Data is created,

generated, and recorded. And the unifying principle behind all of this data is that it was all created by humans. We create the data, so essentially our data is an extension of ourselves, an extension of our humanity.

Ultimately in these systems, our data will need to start interacting with other data and devices. There will be so much data and so many devices that our data will need to take on a life of its own just to be efficient and not drive us crazy. But how do these systems understand and examine who we and our data are in the complex reality of big data that is basically too big for us to understand? This is where science fiction, androids, and Philip K. Dick and William Gibson come in.

Science Fiction and the Literary Origins of Android Data

In 1969, Philip K. Dick wrote the novel *Do Androids Dream of Electric Sheep?* The book is a meditation on what it means to be human and how the lines between that humanity and machines can become hazy—if not completely impossible to determine. The book eventually was developed into the science-fiction movie masterpiece *Blade Runner* by director Ridley Scott.

Just a few years after writing *Androids*, Dick further developed his ideas about humanity and the constructs that we build. He gave a speech called "The Android and the Human" at the University of British Columbia in February 1972, where he explored his new way of thinking: "I have, in some of my stories and novels, written about androids or robots or simulacra—the name doesn't matter; what is meant is artificial constructs masquerading as humans. . . . Now, to me, that theme seems obsolete. The constructs do not mimic humans; they are, in many deep ways, actually human already."

Thirty-six years later, another science-fiction legend, William Gibson, gave a speech at the Vancouver Institute called "Googling the Cyborg." Gibson is best known for popularizing the cyberpunk movement in books like *Neuromancer* (Ace, 1984) and *Pattern Recognition* (Putnam, 2003). In his speech, Gibson contemplated what it means to be a cyborg. He had a good time poking fun at popular culture's images of the man–machine hybrid with its carnal jacks, and he challenged his audience to think of the cyborg in a different way.

Gibson said he believes that the human and machine union has already happened, and it is called the Internet. He sees the Internet as "the largest man-made object on the planet" and says that the "real-deal cyborg will be deeper and more subtle and exist increasingly at the particle level."

Gibson's coupling of our humanity and the humanity of our data gives us another image of our constructs. We produce data and we write algorithms, and when we do this at the increasing scale (which will be coming in the next decade), we will need to begin to imagine who we are and who our data and our algorithms might be in a very different light.

The Android Is Your Data

Using these science-fiction visions, we can begin to develop a way to conceptualize the data. From the view of this narrative, our data—the data we created—becomes a kind of simulacrum of ourselves. Like Philip K. Dick's androids and William Gibson's cyborgs, data becomes a way to embody who we are, but at the same time it remains external. It allows us to examine who we are and also what we want to do with these systems. As we begin to architect these systems, often the reality is too hard to handle: It's too complex for us to make any meaningful design decisions. We need these representations, these androids, to be our proxies.

By thinking about data, large data sets, and the algorithms that make use of this information as human—or, in Dick's language, androids—we are giving these complex systems a kind of narrative and characteristics that help programmers, system architects, and even regular folks to understand data's "bigness."

To understand what we want from the algorithms, these systems become less complex because we can understand them not only as an extension of ourselves but also a collection of human entities. If we understand them as human, then we know how to talk to them. We know how to ask for things. We know what to expect. We can hold them responsible, and we can even have an understanding for how far we can trust them.

But this humanness doesn't really look like the humanness of Dick or even Gibson. This humanness is not trying to trick us into thinking that it is human like us, and it doesn't exist on the particle level. Today, our understanding of humanity and intelligence is being challenged. Every year we get new products with increasing intelligence. These range from the amazing to the downright funny, but the reality of these systems looks more like a Furby toy having a conversation with the iPhone's Siri service than two superhuman androids having a chat.

This concept of humanity is more about our relationships to other people, other pieces of data, and the complex web of relationships that make up our very culture. Humanity shouldn't really be defined by Alan Turing's test (designed to fool a person into thinking an AI was a human over teletype) or even Dick's Voight-Kampff empathy test. How we define humanity is by our relationship to others—the connections we have to other people and their data.

And one day, humanity may be defined by how our personal data interacts with and is connected to other people's data. We have to come to grips with the idea that this interconnected humanness that moves from data to data, algorithm to algorithm, might happen without us knowing anything about it. It very well could happen in the Secret Life of Data.

Do Algorithms Dream of Electric Sheep?

I think that there is something lovely about the idea that our data could have a life of its own. For too long, computers, computational power, and even software have been thought of as cold mathematical pursuits. In reality, the digital world is simply an extension of our world. Data and computational power are, at their core, human. With Genevieve Bell, these new models have given us a way to architect a future that is both more efficient and more human. And I think that's awesome.

To answer the question "Do algorithms dream of electric sheep?" becomes complicated. First we can say "Yes," because we programmed them to do so. Next we could say "No," because the complex neurological structures of the human dream state will not be modeled in algorithms or software anytime soon. But finally, we might need to say "Maybe," and we will just have to wait and ask them.

These questions of how we interact with data, and how data interacts with itself, may seem removed from our daily experience right now. That's only because we've already come to expect our relationship with information to be a seamless exchange of signals that brings us closer to what we want. When we swipe a fare card to enter a subway, we expect the metal turnstile to turn for us. When we check in on Facebook, we expect our status update to change instantly. When we enter our credit-card numbers into a Web site like Amazon, we expect that the product we purchased is on its way, that our account has already been debited, and that a record of the transaction has already been stored in a database to provide us with more recommendations at a later date. We only truly notice how much we interact with data when something goes wrong, when the metal subway turnstile doesn't spin.

But this current state of affairs can't last. Data is becoming too big. We need to start paying attention to the data we create and what we want it to do for us.

What I find incredibly exciting about this vision for the future is that it is real. Big data is coming, and in many instances it's already here. So it's not a matter of *if* this will happen; it's not even a question of *when*. For me, the real question is *how*. How do we want this to happen? What do we want it to do for us? How will it make the lives of every person on the planet better?

In 2010, Intel chief technology officer Justin Rattner said, "Science and technology have progressed to the point where what we build is only constrained by the limits of our own imaginations." Imagining what the secret life of data could be is the real challenge; once we've done that, then all we have to do is go and build it.

That's just engineering. The difficult part is changing the story we tell ourselves about the future we're going to live in. If we can do that, then we can change the future.

Critical Thinking

1. The introduction to the article says the author argues "we need a better understanding of our relationship with the data. . . ." What do you think "our relationship with data" means? And why is this relationship important?

2. What is big data? What are some examples of big data in your life today? (What products do you regularly use that rely on big data?) What are the trade-offs to you that this data exists in your life?

3. The author says, "Ultimately . . . our data will need to start interacting with other data and devices." What positive and

what negative might result if our data is able to interact with other data and other computer systems? How do we design systems and set policies to maximize the postive outcomes and minimize the negative outcomes?

Create Central

www.mhhe.com/createcentral

Internet References

Mapping the Future with Big Data

www.wfs.org/futurist/2013-issues-futurist/july-august-2013-vol-47-no-4/mapping-future-big-data

Researchers Steer Off Course to Show Potential Power of 'GPS Spoofing'

www.pbs.org/newshour/bb/science/july-dec13/gps_08-02.html

BRIAN DAVID JOHNSON is a futurist at Intel Corporation, where he is developing an actionable vision for computing in 2020. He speaks and writes extensively about future technologies in articles and scientific papers as well as science-fiction short stories and novels (*Science Fiction Prototyping: Designing the Future with Science Fiction, Screen Future: The Future of Entertainment Computing and the Devices We Love, Fake Plastic Love,* and *Nebulous Mechanisms: The Dr. Simon Egerton Stories*).

Unit 2

UNIT

Prepared by: Daniel Mittleman, *DePaul University*

Social Media and Participation

Almost every American college student knows that the First Amendment to the U.S. Constitution guarantees the right to practice any religion and to exercise free speech. What many may not know are the additional rights specified by the First Amendment: the right to peaceably assemble and the right to petition the government. The founders of the American government recognized that to establish and maintain a free and open society, not only must the ability to speak be protected, but the ability to gather in groups, form associations, and network must also be protected. Without those protections, citizens would not be able to form the critical mass necessary to feel safe standing up and petitioning the government.

For two hundred plus years, writers and commentators have recognized the relationship between association and democracy. Americans, through all its history, have actively joined clubs, guilds, leagues, lodges, societies, associations, chambers of commerce, and militia. Today, we have the technical means to communicate almost instantly and effortlessly across great distances. And with that, the bounds of traditional association are being abandoned.

Robert Putnam, in "Bowling Alone," argued that the civil associations, long the glue of vibrant American communities, were breaking down. Americans were not joining the PTA, the Boy Scouts, the local garden club, or bowling leagues in their former numbers. Putnam discovered that, although more people bowl than ever, participation in leagues was down by 40 percent since 1980.[1]

But it isn't that people are not associating any more, it is the environment of association that changes each generation, enabled by the newest technologies. Watching kids play from neighborhood stoops has given way to afterschool programs and nanny cams. Shopping in locally owned main street stores gave way to the commercial chains and protected space of shopping malls, which in turn are now giving way to Amazon and eBay. Playing little league has given way to massive multiplayer online role playing games (MMPORGs). After school malt shop gatherings (think: Happy Days) have given way to texting, Facebook, music sharing, and more gaming.

A French social observer, Émile Durkheim (1858–1917), argued that a vital society must have members who feel a sense of community. Community is easily evident in pre-industrial societies where kinship ties, shared religious beliefs, and customs reinforce group identity and shared values. Not so today in the United States, where a mobile population commutes long distances and retreats each evening to the sanctity and seclusion of individual homes. Contemporary visitors to the United States are struck by the cornucopia of cultural options available to Americans. They find a dizzying array of religions, beliefs, philosophical and political perspectives, modes of social interaction, entertainment venues and, now, digital gadgets.

One can argue that the new communications technologies permit associations that were never before possible. And that we Americans continue to network and assemble, but we do so following the lead of our youth via Facebook, Twitter, and other emerging online platforms.

Today, our cultural norms are coming to be defined by the preferences and behaviors of the millennial generation, with a yet unnamed—even more electronically connected, now teenage—generation (The iGeneration, perhaps?) nearing adulthood. I read a lot of social media statistics while preparing to write this essay. Here is my favorite: Eighty-three percent of American millennials sleep with their cell phones every night.[2] I can only imagine what the percentage must be for the generation that follows.

Today's teenagers are electronically connected. Ninety-four percent use Facebook, eighty-eight percent text; eighty percent text every day. Almost half of them stream TV over the Internet, a concept mostly foreign to baby boomers.[3]

So Americans still associate, with more and more of our social lives spent online. The questions we might ponder while reading the articles in this Unit are: How do modern computer and communication tools change the ways we associate? And how do these changes impact our sense of community and our shared identity?

Notes

1. See http://bowlingalone.com
2. See http://www.pewsocialtrends.org/files/2010/10/millennials-confident-connected-open-to-change.pdf
3. ibid.

Article

Prepared by: Daniel Mittleman, *DePaul University*

Relationships, Community, and Identity in the New Virtual Society

As we spend more of our social lives online, the definitions of relationships and families are shifting. A business futurist offers an overview of these trends and what they imply for organizations in the coming years.

ARNOLD BROWN

Learning Outcomes

After reading this article, you will be able to:

- Argue both for and against the notion of the Internet as a vehicle for social and political change

- Argue for and against the proposition that humans were more studious and attentive before the Internet.

In India, where for centuries marriages have been arranged by families, online dating services such as BharatMatrimony.com are profoundly changing embedded traditions.

MyGamma, a Singapore-based mobile phone social networking site, has millions of users throughout Asia and Africa, giving social networking capability to people across continents—no personal computer necessary.

In China, individuals have been participating in *wang hun* (online role-play marriages). These gaming sites are causing actual married couples to get divorced on the grounds that this constitutes adultery—even though no face-to-face meetings ever took place.

And Web sites such as GeneTree.com and Ancestry.com, which offer inexpensive cheek-swab DNA tests, link up people throughout the world who have similar DNA, thus combining genealogy, medical technology, and social networking.

Clearly the Internet has radically reshaped our social lives over the span of just a couple of decades, luring us into a virtual metaworld where traditional interactions—living, loving, belonging, and separating, as well as finding customers and keeping them—require new protocols.

Relationships Take on a Digital Dimension

The future of falling in love may be online. Dating sites, once considered a gimmicky way to meet and connect with new

people, have grown immensely in popularity, thanks in part to the convergence of information technologies and digital entertainment. Facilitating and managing relationships online is projected to become close to a billion-dollar industry in the United States in 2011.

In the new Virtual Society, we will see an increasing transition from basic matchmaking sites to sites that enable people to actually go out on online "dates" without ever leaving their desks. While face-to-face dating will never entirely disappear, the process—and even relationships themselves—will happen more and more in virtual space.

Especially for young people, relationships made in virtual space can be just as powerful and meaningful as those formed in the real world. Additionally, as more people gain access to broadband technologies, an increasing number are seeking social connectivity this way. There are already at least 500 million mobile broadband users globally. The speed and flexibility with which people communicate and socialize online will likely only continue to increase.

Technology doesn't just bring people together, though. As Douglas Rushkoff points out in *Program or Be Programmed* (OR Books, 2010), cyberspace creates a temporal and spatial separation from which it becomes seemingly easier to accomplish unpleasant interpersonal tasks. Hence, the *techno brush-off:* breaking up with a significant other via e-mail or text message.

This will increasingly be a dominant fixture of the global youth culture. Young people everywhere link up through IM, Twitter, blogs, smart-phones, and social networking sites that are proliferating at an accelerating rate. This is a critical point for businesses to understand. The emerging generation is part of what is, in essence, a vast new cross-border empire. It is marked by an instant awareness of what's new, what's hot, what's desirable—and what's not. This is the group that pollster John Zogby, in his book *The Way We'll Be* (Random House, 2008), calls the First Globals. His research shows that their expectations of products and services will be vastly different and that they will force businesses to redefine their offerings.

Young people will not, as their elders did, simply adapt to the technology. The new youth cyberculture will continue to find ways to adapt the technology to their needs and desires. For example, Ning, created in 2005 by Netscape co-founder Marc Andreessen, enables people to create their own individual social network—not join a preexisting world but actually build their own. A Web site called paper.li creates a personalized newspaper for you every day based on whom you follow on Twitter and whether or not they said anything particularly important in the last 24 hours (as measured by retweets). Your friend's brilliant blog post about last night's St. Patrick's Day party could appear directly next to Tim O'Reilly or Bruce Sterling's most recent missive on China's Internet policy. It's hard to imagine a local newspaper providing that sort of personalized content.

But online relationships are not exclusively reserved for young people. As the elderly become more comfortable with the Internet, they will increasingly turn to alternative spaces, such as virtual worlds, to find company or meet people with similar interests. By 2008, more than 20 million social networkers in the United States were over the age of 50, according to a study by Deloitte. There have been a slew of media reports playing up the fact that many seniors are joining Facebook and Twitter, as well as becoming an increasingly significant part of the growing commercial activity in virtual worlds.

Commercializing Communities

More and more people regard the virtual world as a place where they can establish and maintain safer, less demanding relationships on their own time. Ease, flexibility, and relative anonymity will continue to be three key components of dating online. Monetization will happen quickly, as virtual restaurants, movie theaters, concerts, and even wedding chapels are established.

In addition to using virtual worlds as test markets for real-life products and services, as is done now, businesses will offer a much wider variety of virtual products and services. Having these options would give a substantive feel to online relationships. The more real and satisfying these relationships can be made to seem, the more they will attract and hold people, and the more money they will generate.

Commercialized virtual venues such as upscale bars and coffeehouses could even be looked to as testing grounds to develop the social skills necessary to form meaningful human relationships. Businesses could use game applications like Mall World or Café World on Facebook as platforms to advertise various specials that occur in virtual space, ranging from coupons for those aforementioned simulations of bars and coffeehouses to discounts for two to "live" streaming concert events. Advertising boards could promote online activities and events such as speed dating in a virtual nightclub setting. All this will dramatically change the nature of relationships.

As social researchers have pointed out, the Internet is programming us as well, starting at an early age. For example, there are combination social networking and gaming sites for children such as Disney's Club Penguin. Children are developing social skills within these virtual worlds. What this will

mean in terms of how they will start, maintain, and end "real" friendships and relationships in the future is anyone's guess.

But the Internet can also strengthen family ties because it provides a continuously connected presence. In Norway, for example, one study showed that college students were in touch with their parents on average 10 times a week. Young people use mobile devices to Skype, text, upload photos and videos to Facebook, and more, with increasing frequency. Cyberspace enables families and friends to converse, in effect, as if they were in the same room. This is part of the reason that the Millennial generation reported feeling closer to their parents than did their older siblings during adolescence, according to the Pew Internet and American Life Survey.

So what does all this tell us? For one thing, the temporal and spatial "here-and-now" limitations that formerly characterized social interactions such as dating and family get-togethers have broken down. The composition of, and behavior in, relationships and households in the future will therefore change seriously. These trends are powerfully affecting how companies and organizations will design, sell, and market a wide range of products and services to consumers, with a growing emphasis on individualization and personalization. For instance, if relationships and families are more virtual, we should see an increase in the construction of new kinds of single-person housing units or dual sleeping quarters.

Family formation will need to be flexible and adaptive. The nuclear family was a response to the Industrial Age, in large measure replacing the extended family that characterized the Agricultural Era. It spurred vast economic shifts and led to new multibillion-dollar industries, from autos to washing machines to personal telephones. We are already seeing indications that the family is morphing into other forms as the Virtual Age approaches. Employers and governments will see their social, human resources, financial services, and benefits programs challenged, as the new economy takes great advantage of these multiple, newly unfolding personal relationships. For instance, should a "virtual spouse" be able to claim the Social Security benefits of a partner? The easy answer is, of course not. But what if it's the virtual spouse who is charged with monitoring the health of an aged parent remotely? What if he or she does the household bill-paying, or even contributes half of the household income? In other words, what if the virtual spouse performs many if not all of the tasks associated with a traditional spouse? And should the same polygamy laws applied to regular marriages also apply to virtual marriages? Should such marriages be subject to the same taxation laws?

With the advent of an electronic era, many social scientists and other "experts" decried what they saw as a loss of social capital—the so-called "Bowling Alone" theory—because people were supposedly decreasing their participation in such things as bowling leagues. The big mistake that the fearful always make is to equate change with destruction. The social turmoil of the 1970s was heralded by such observers as "the destruction of the family." But the family did not die; it just changed—and it is still changing.

Similarly, social capital is not going away; it is too intrinsic to human nature, although aspects of it may well be changing, and

The Reality of Virtual Feelings

Advances in brain research and multisensory perception could play an important role in the development of virtual relationships. Neural devices already allow people to control electronic equipment such as wheelchairs, televisions, and video games via brain–computer interfaces.

One day soon, avatars may also be controllable this way. Virtual reality may become so advanced that it could trick the brain into thinking the invented images it is responding to are real—and human emotions would follow accordingly. Avatars will cause people to feel love, hate, jealousy, etc. And as haptic technologies improve, our abilities to respond physically to our virtual partners will also improve.

Sexual pleasure may be routinely available without any inter-human stimulation at all.

If it becomes possible to connect virtual reality programs directly to the brain, thoughts and emotions may also be digitized, rendered binary and reduced to 0s and 1s. Feelings of satisfaction and pleasure (two key components in any relationship) could be created between avatars without any "real" stimulus at all. But would they be real or mimetic?

Once humans begin to perceive virtual social interactions as actually having occurred, it will greatly impact individuals, relationships, communities, and society as a whole.

—Arnold Brown

helped by the fact that they have what he calls "a safe autonomous pattern," in that their parents are only a speed dial away.

Sociologists describe two kinds of social ties: strong ties of family members and those with shared values, beliefs, and identities; and weak ties to acquaintances and other people with shallower connections. According to some researchers, the Internet and, in particular, mobile devices are enabling the strong community ties to be reinforced, often at the expense of the weak ties. At a time when technology is being lauded for encouraging diversity and facilitating cross-cultural communication, there is, consequently, a strong and growing countertrend: digital tribalism. Aside from strengthening ties to family and close friends, people are using the technology to find others with whom they share important affinities, ranging from genomes to beliefs to lifestyle choices. This digital form of tribalism is an unexpectedly strong trend, as observed by social critics such as Christine Rosen.

Information—including product and service information—spreads electronically with speed and power. Effectively getting a positive message on a tribal network could well be tomorrow's best marketing strategy. Although the tribal identity can be deep and solid, brand connections may not necessarily be so. Maintaining the connection will require constant monitoring of the electronic tribal village and quickness to reposition or reinforce when required.

Bridal showers, for instance, can be attended by distant guests through Skype, and e-registries allow gift givers to view what others have bought. There is much room for innovation here, in terms of bringing people together who would not otherwise be in the same place for business meetings, financial planning, meal sharing, celebrations, and more. Associations might capitalize on online events for far-flung and numerous businesses, professionals, and friends and families of members. Employers might do the same for their employees' personal networks, perhaps offering discounts, education, job postings, and new products to all "friends of friends."

Expat workers and members of the armed forces might be more easily enabled to stay in touch with their families if their employers organized better around online communications and communities. This would ease the burden on relocated personnel, improve morale, attract more people, increase productivity, and spin the sale of products and service to these populations. This could also be true for alumni networks and other diaspora groups.

it is important that you view these changes objectively if you want to understand what they are and what they mean to you.

Social ties are being created, strengthened, and—yes—weakened in an almost unbelievable variety of ways. This has to entail, as well, the remaking and establishing of both a deeper and a shallower social capital. Someone with more than 3,000 Facebook friends probably has more than 2,000 shallow friendships, but there's a tremendous amount of variety in that number; some of these friendships are viable clients, others may be service providers, others may be long-term friend prospects, or secret crushes, or members of a social circle to which the person with 3,000 friendships wants access; some of them will be annoying people encountered only once at a party, be grudgingly given the status of "friend" to avoid seeming rude. All of these friendships have their own unique value. But Facebook sees little difference among them outside of how they are designated in privacy settings (some people can see more private posts than others). Outside institutions don't recognize any distinction among these virtual friendships, if they recognize such friendships at all.

Sociologist Richard Ling has labeled the new communication phenomenon *micro-coordination*—as people are constantly planning, coordinating, and changing plans because their cyberconnections are always on. University of Southern California sociologist Manuel Castells says that adolescents today build and rebuild social networks via constant messaging. This is

The Identity Industry

Social scientists make the distinction between a found identity and a made identity. The found identity is one created by your circumstances—who your parents were, your ethnic background, your religion, your sex, where you went to school, your profession, and all the other external factors that people use to categorize and describe you. The made identity, on the other hand, is the one you create for yourself. It is how you wish to see yourself and how you want others to see you.

In the past, people who wanted to escape what they saw as the trap of their found identity did such things as change their name or appearance. They moved somewhere else. Now, and increasingly in the future, technology will let you make and remake your identity at will—virtually. This extraordinary, even revolutionary, development will profoundly affect fundamental societal values such as trust and reliability.

In addition to engaging directly online with other individuals, you can also interact with them through avatars, the images that represent you (or an idealized version of yourself) in virtual worlds. Each virtual world requires a separate avatar, so in effect you can be as many different people as there are virtual worlds. In the future, you will be able to create avatars that will literally take on lives of their own. They will, once created, be able to "think" on their own, without further input from you. They may be able to perform intensive research tasks for you, start and even manage online companies, maintain your social relationships by reading your Facebook updates and blog posts and analyzing them for significant news so you don't have to.

Increasingly, over time, distinctions between real and virtual identity will become less sharply defined, particularly for people who spend substantial amounts of time in the virtual world—or some enhanced combination of the real and the virtual. A company called Total Immersion combines 3-D and augmented reality technology on the Internet, inserting people and physical objects into live video feeds. According to the company's Web site, "this digital processing mixes real and virtual worlds together, in real time."

All this could lead to growing confusion about identity. We will go from "Who am I?" to "Who, when, and where am I?" What in the twentieth century was seen as a problem that needed treatment—multiple personalities—will increasingly be seen in the twenty-first century as a coping mechanism, greatly affecting the evolving economy, as multiple personas split their expenditures in multiple ways. Companies that provide such services will be a great growth industry as we move further into the "Who are you, really?" era.

Critical Thinking

1. Brown says that "clearly the Internet has radically reshaped our social lives over the span of just a couple of decades. . . ." Who is "our"? Ask your parents (or people of their generation) how the Internet has changed their social lives.
2. Brown distinguishes between found and made identitites. What are they?
3. Do you distinguish between your real and virtual identity? How is your online presentation different from your "real" identity? Do your friends come across differently online than they do in person?

Create Central

www.mhhe.com/createcentral

Internet References

A Thin Line
www.athinline.org

Crowdsourced Sleuthing Offers Extra Eyes and Ears, Some Wrong Turns
www.pbs.org/newshour/bb/science/jan-june13/technology_04-19.html

Christopher "Moot" Poole": The Case for Anonymity Online [TED Talk]
www.ted.com/talks/christopher_m00t_poole_the_case_for_anonymity_online.html

Kevin Allocca: Why Videos Go Viral
www.ted.com/talks/kevin_allocca_why_videos_go_viral.html

Pew Internet & American Life Project
www.pewinternet.org

ARNOLD BROWN is the chairman of Weiner, Edrich, Brown, Inc., and the coauthor (with Edie Weiner) of *FutureThink: How to Think Clearly in a Time of Change* (Pearson Prentice Hall, 2006). E-mail arnold@weineredrichbrown.com. Web site www.weineredrichbrown.com.

Originally published in the March/April 2011 issue of *The Futurist*. Copyright © 2011 by World Future Society, Bethesda, MD. Used with permission. www.wfs.org

Article   Prepared by: Daniel Mittleman, *DePaul University*

R U Friends 4 Real?

Psychologists are learning more about how teen friendships are changed by social networking and text messaging.

AMY NOVOTNEY

Learning Outcome

After reading this article, you will be able to:

• Articulate how social networking friends are both similar and different from face-to-face friends.

As the parents of most teenagers know, today's two-hour telephone calls with friends are often now conducted via marathon text messaging or Facebook sessions. And that cultural shift has psychologists asking lots of questions: What happens to adolescent friendships when so much interpersonal communication is via text? Or when fights between best friends explode via Facebook for all to see? And can "OMG—ROTFL" ("Oh my God! I'm rolling on the floor laughing!") via text really convey the same amusement as hearing the giggles of a best friend?

So far, the answers to those questions are mixed. Margarita Azmitia, PhD, a psychology professor at the University of California, Santa Cruz, who studies adolescent friendships, is among those who contend that these technologies have only changed some of the ways teens interact. Today's youth still count the friends they see and talk to every day among their closest, she says.

"The [qualities] teens value in friendships, like loyalty and trust, remain the same," Azmitia says. "Technology has just changed some of the ways kids can be friends with each other."

Other psychologists, however, say today's ways of communicating can change the message, and wonder what effect that has on adolescent friendships, and even teens' social development. For example, instead of learning how to handle the give and take of conversation—one of our most basic human attributes and a connection we all crave—teens instead are crafting and often constantly editing witty text responses, says Massachusetts Institute of Technology social psychologist Sherry Turkle, PhD.

"We're losing our sense of the human voice and what it means—the inflections, hesitations and the proof that someone isn't just giving you stock answers," says Turkle, whose book "Alone Together" (2011) is based on 15 years of research and observation of children and adult interactions with technology. "That's a radical thing to do to our relationships."

Outcasts Reaching Out

One of social networking's greatest benefits is its ability to bring meaningful friendships to people who might otherwise be shunned as outcasts. As research has shown, being friendless in high school can have lifelong consequences on a person's cognitive, social and moral development. In one study, published in *School Psychology Review,* educational psychologist Beth Doll, PhD, of the University of Nebraska–Lincoln, found that friendless adolescents are more likely to be unemployed, aggressive or have poor mental health as adults.

But thanks to text messaging and the Internet, socially anxious teens who might have been left out now have a voice. In a 2010 study with 626 children and teens, researchers at the Queensland University of Technology in Australia found that lonely adolescents reported using the Internet to make new friends, and that they communicated online significantly more frequently about personal and intimate topics than those who did not report loneliness. These teens also indicated that they communicated online more frequently because they did not feel as shy, were able to talk more comfortably and dared to say more (*Cyberpsychology, Behavior, and Social Networking,* 2010).

Further, in a 2010 study in *Computers in Human Behavior,* Malinda Desjarlais, PhD, a psychology professor at the University of Northern British Columbia, found that socially anxious teen boys who played computer games with friends reported better friendships than their socially anxious peers who used the computer by themselves. Online games, Desjarlais says, typically allow players to speak to each other via the computer—and the opportunity to communicate without making eye contact may put socially anxious boys at ease.

The Internet's capacity for social connection doesn't only benefit shy and lonely teens. In a study of 63 Cornell University undergraduates, researchers found that people reported higher self-esteem after spending time on their Facebook profile than after time spent looking into a mirror (*Cyberpsychology, Behavior and Social Networking,* 2011).

"Unlike a mirror, which reminds us of who we really are and may have a negative effect on self-esteem if that image does not match with our ideal, Facebook can show a positive version of ourselves," says Cornell communications professor Jeffrey Hancock, PhD, one of the study's co-authors. "We're not saying that it's a deceptive version of self, but it's a positive one."

New research also suggests that youth who use blogs, websites and email to discuss politics and current events become more socially engaged over time. Students who spent more time seeking out information and participating in political and civic discussions in online communities, for example, reported higher levels of volunteerism, including raising money for charity, working on a local political campaign and increased voting participation, even after controlling for their level of political interest and involvement. The three-year as-yet-unpublished study of 2,500 teens was led by Joseph Kahne, PhD, an education professor at Mills College.

Lyn Mikel Brown, EdD, has seen first-hand the positive effects of the Internet on teen relationships and civic engagement in her job as director of Hardy Girls Healthy Women, a nonprofit girls' advocacy organization based in Waterville, Maine. In one national media literacy program titled Powered by Girls and sponsored by Hardy Girls, teenage girls throughout the United States connect online via the social networking site Ning to discuss pop culture's positive and negative media representations of girls and women and create their own e-zine to raise awareness of these issues.

"It's easy to say that the Internet is bad and filled with porn, and that's the stuff that makes the news," says Brown, professor of education at Colby College. "What doesn't make the news is the degree to which girls are blogging and building coalitions around social and political projects. No, they may not be intimate, long-term relationships, but they impact girls' sense of self in really positive ways because they connect with people who really get them."

A Crisis of Connection?

But while the Internet may give teens a forum, it may also rob them of the richness of real-life friendships. Time spent online, after all, is time not spent *with* friends and could lessen the social support teens feel.

For example, a 2010 study with 99 undergraduates led by Holly Schiffrin, PhD, a psychology professor at the University of Mary Washington, found that those who spent more time on the Internet reported decreased well-being. Most of the students also reported that the Internet was less useful than face-to-face communication for building relationships and increasing emotional closeness with others (*Cyberpsychology, Behavior, and Social Networking*, 2010).

"I definitely think that technology can be used to build and maintain in-person relations, but it's not a satisfactory substitute for in-person relationships," Schiffrin says.

The Internet—and particularly online social networking websites—may also exacerbate the problems identified in a 2011 study in *Personality and Psychology Bulletin.* It found that people think their peers are happier than they really are, and this distortion of reality makes people lonely and dissatisfied with life. In the study, Dartmouth College business professor Alexander Jordan, PhD (a student in Stanford's graduate psychology department at the time) asked 80 college freshmen about how often they thought other students had negative experiences, such as getting dumped, receiving a bad grade or feeling overloaded with work.

Students were also asked to estimate how often their peers had positive experiences, such as going out with friends or acing tests.

Overall, the researchers found that students underestimated their peers' negative feelings (by 17 percent) and overestimated their positive emotions (by 6 percent).

"Online social networks are a great example of the type of public venue where people play up the positive and hide the negative, which can lead to the sense that one is alone in one's own struggles," Jordan says.

These findings also suggest that even though we all know we hide our own sad or lonely feelings from others, we don't realize how often others are doing the same.

"This anxiety around always 'performing' for others via social networking sites may lead to teenagers whose identities are shaped not by self-exploration and time alone to process their thoughts, but by how they are perceived by the online collective," Turkle says.

What remains to be seen is how well adolescent friendships managed via Facebook and text message affect teen development, and ultimately, how today's teens will develop relationships in adulthood, says New York University developmental psychologist Niobe Way, PhD, who has been studying friendships among teenagers for more than two decades. In a 2009 study in *Child Development,* Way and colleagues found that, among both American and Chinese middle-school students, the emotional support they got from close friends boosted their self-esteem and grade point averages more than support from their parents. Way, author of "Deep Secrets: Boys' Friendships and the Crisis of Connection" (2011), has also found that teenage boys who feel supported by and intimate with their friends are more likely to be academically engaged and do their homework than teens who report low support. Yet as social networking drives teens to decrease their face-to-face time with friends, how much intimacy do they really share?

"We know from the developmental literature that empathy and intimacy are fostered by looking at people's faces and reading people's emotions and spending time together physically," Way says, but it remains to be seen whether that can really be accomplished online. "We also know from the sociological literature that Americans are becoming less empathic and more emotionally disconnected from each other. We are facing a crisis of connection that most assuredly is not effectively addressed by less face-to-face contact."

Online friends can also make it less likely for young adults to create new adult friendships—a move that Way says may even put psychological and physical health in jeopardy.

"It's evident in the research that building real connections can help us thrive in life," Way says. "Friendships are a core part of that, and we just don't take them seriously enough."

Critical Thinking

1. How might the quality of conversation differ between phone, text, and social networking channels? In what ways is phone better? In what ways is each channel better and worse? What kinds of conversations would you choose to have on one channel over another?

2. How do Facebook friendships differ from traditional friendships? Are Facebook only friendships meaningful friendships? Why do you think so or not think so?

3. Do teens who use texting fail to learn the give-and-take of social communication, as Sherry Turkle suggests, or do they learn it differently? If the latter, differently in what ways?

Create Central

www.mhhe.com/createcentral

Internet References

Disruptions: More Connected, Yet More Alone
http://bits.blogs.nytimes.com/2013/09/01/disruptions-more-connected-yet-more-alone/?_r=1&

Immersion: A Do-It-Yourself Privacy Invasion/Metadata Visualization
http://cnnmoneytech.tumblr.com/post/54348171393/immersion-a-do-it-yourself-privacy-invasion-metadata

Sherry Turkle: Connected, But Alone? [TED Talk]
www.ted.com/talks/sherry_turkle_alone_together.html

Stefana Broadbent: How the Internet Enables Intimacy [TED Talk]
www.ted.com/talks/stefana_broadbent_how_the_internet_enables_intimacy.html

What's Not to Like? Using the Facebook 'Like' to Connect, Commune, Endorse
www.pbs.org/newshour/bb/media/jan-june13/dailydownload_02-11.html

AMY NOVOTNEY is a writer in Chicago.

Article   Prepared by: Daniel Mittleman, *DePaul University*

Licence to Text

Fewer young people are learning to drive. The biggest reason is the Internet—it's replacing the need for a car.

KATE LUNAU

Learning Outcomes

After reading this article, you will be able to:

- Extrapolate from data and anecdotes to what extent the reported trend of less auto ownership and use is real.

- Understand that changing patterns of Internet use may have systemic impacts on non-Internet behaviors of people, and on whole industries dependent on those behaviors.

This summer, Sarah Mohammed is going on a road trip. She and three of her friends plan to drive from Montreal, where they live, to the Okanagan Valley. "We're going to work on some orchards and vineyards in the Interior of B.C.," says Mohammed, 23. The trip is to mark her recent graduation from the University of King's College, in Halifax. "I just finished school and I want to do something different," she says. But on the long drive west, Mohammed won't be taking any shifts behind the wheel—she doesn't have a driver's licence. "Oh, I won't actually be driving. I'm just being a leech," she jokes.

Mohammed didn't go out of her way to avoid learning how to drive. "It's just something that kind of happened, because of the places I lived," she says. As a high school student in Toronto, "I just didn't bother." At university in Halifax, "everything was very accessible by bike or bus, and it wasn't really necessary." Now, in Montreal, she walks, bikes or takes the subway. Mohammed worries that, once she gets to the rural B.C. Interior, she'll be dependent on her friends for lifts. Of the four heading west, only two can drive. "I'll pretty much be at their mercy," she says.

Mohammed isn't alone. She's one of a growing number of younger people who shrug their shoulders at the idea of getting a driver's licence, leaving car companies fretting and older generations perplexed. Getting a licence used to be a rite of passage—one that brought younger people together, gave them access to jobs, opportunities and the glories of the open road. It meant adulthood, and freedom. "That moment when the keys got passed from dad or mom to you, and you could drive by

yourself, was a liberation," says Steve Penfold, who teaches a course on the history of the automobile at the University of Toronto. "It said, 'I'm trustworthy enough to drive a car. I'm bordering on adulthood.' " People remember their first car "like they remember nothing else," he says, and often they gave the car a name.

That feeling of freedom and coming of age was glorified in classic American movies and TV shows like *Grease, The Dukes of Hazzard* and *American Graffiti*. "Our idea of adolescence was invented in the 1940s and '50s, and cars were an important part of that," says Max Valiquette, managing director of strategy at Toronto-based ad agency Bensimon Byrne and a frequent commentator on youth culture. "Like making out in the back seat of a car, or going to a drive-through." Penfold has studied 1960s fast-food parking lots as "a meeting place for youth," where they'd hang out and flirt with the carhop, "and you couldn't get there without a car." On a Friday night, teenagers often did little else for fun but drive up and down the street. The ones with a driver's licence were heroes; others squabbled over who could ride shotgun up front.

Not anymore. "From World War II until just a few years ago, the number of miles driven annually on America's roads steadily increased," begins a recent report from Frontier Group, a think tank, and U.S. Public Interest Research Group (PIRG) Education Fund. "Then, at the turn of the century, something changed." From 2001 to 2009, the number of "vehicle miles" travelled by Americans aged 16 to 34 dropped 23 per cent. "It does come as a surprise," says Phineas Baxandall of U.S. PIRG, co-author of the report. "It's been such an article of faith that we're driving more and more, with more road congestion, more highway buildup, in a vicious cycle." But that's not the case—and the decline is happening in other countries, too.

In another new study, researchers from the University of Michigan Transportation Research Institute (UMTRI) found a drop in younger licensed drivers in more than half of 15 countries they surveyed, including Canada. Among 25- to 34-year-olds here, 92 per cent had a licence in 1999; 10 years later, 87 per cent did. In Canada, this decline occurred in every age group from 16 to 54.

In the U.S., Great Britain, Germany, Japan, Sweden, Norway and South Korea, the percentage of younger people with a licence also fell. One-third of all licensed drivers in the U.S. were under 30 in 1983; today, it's less than a quarter. This can't be pinned entirely on the recession. The drop in licensed drivers "predates the economic downturn," Baxandall says. Young people who have jobs and are doing well financially are also driving less.

Instead, they're opting for alternatives. Bike culture is flourishing, with bike-sharing networks popping up everywhere from Montreal to Washington and Honolulu. In 2009, Americans aged 16 to 34 took 24 per cent more bike trips than in 2001—even though that age group shrank in size by two per cent. They also walked 16 per cent more often, and increased the number of miles travelled on public transit by 40 per cent, according to the report Baxandall co-wrote. A 2011 survey from Zipcar, the car-sharing service, notes that 55 per cent of millennials (18 to 34) are making an effort to drive less, partly because of concern over the environment, and partly because of the cost of owning a car.

But the biggest reason for the move away from driving is the Internet—in some ways, it has replaced the need for a car, since how we connect has completely changed. According to the Zipcar survey, 68 per cent of 18- to 34-year-olds said they sometimes use social media to connect with friends and family instead of going out to see them. The Michigan study found that having a higher proportion of Internet users is associated with lower licensing rates among young people. If given the choice between having Internet access or a car, 46 per cent of all 18- to 24-year-old U.S. drivers say they'd take the Internet, according to technology researcher Gartner Inc. "Virtual contact through the Internet is replacing the need for physical contact," says Michael Sivak, head of UMTRI's Human Factors Group and the Michigan study's co-author. "They just don't need to be with others as often as they did in the past, because they can connect other ways than physically." Car manufacturers are all too aware of the shift. "For many baby boomers and Gen Xers, the car was a really important status symbol," says Sheryl Connelly, manager of Ford global consumer trends and futuring. "Today, it's a cellphone, and a lot of kids are getting one before they turn 16."

Everyone can now shop, watch movies, play games, listen to music and catch up with friends online. When kids do leave the house, many would rather take the bus and stay connected. Texting is the dominant daily mode of communication for teens, according to the Pew Research Center—but in every Canadian province, there's a ban on using hand-held cellphones while driving. "When you talk to people about why they don't drive, they'll say that when they're driving, they're not connected," Baxandall says.

For young people of any generation, "freedom is the most important thing," Valiquette says. "Cars used to represent that." Now, after insurance payments and parking permits and missed time on texting and Twitter—not to mention the process of getting a driver's licence, which, with the graduated system, can take years—cars represent the opposite. "They're a burden."

Growing up in Winnipeg, Erin Klassen had no interest in getting her driver's licence. When she turned 14, her family moved to North Bay, Ont.; there wasn't much of a public transit system there, Klassen says, "but a lot of my friends were a couple of years older, and they could pick me up in their car. It was never an issue. I'd throw them some money for gas, or buy them a coffee when we went out." In the final year of her bachelor's degree at the University of Toronto, she and a roommate drove to the East Coast. "She borrowed her father's car and I couldn't drive," Klassen says. "I was in charge of keeping her awake, and the music."

Klassen, 28, now works from home in west-end Toronto; she's the editor of an online magazine. She still doesn't drive, and neither does her live-in boyfriend. In her neighbourhood, "we have markets, clothing boutiques, coffee shops, restaurants," she says. "I can walk to get the things I need." Her boyfriend will probably get his licence eventually, but "I honestly can't see myself getting mine."

Of course, getting around without a car is much more easily accomplished in a city. Households in urban areas are 2.5 times more likely not to own one than those in rural areas, but younger people—those at the forefront of the trend away from driving—tend to prefer living in cities. According to a 2011 National Association of Realtors survey cited in Baxandall's report, 62 per cent of 18- to 29-year-olds said they'd prefer living in a "smart growth" community (with a mix of homes, restaurants, libraries and decent public transportation) instead of contributing to sprawl.

For some people, the idea of driving can be nerve-racking. Emma O'Neill grew up in the small town of Arnprior, Ont., where getting a licence was "a great thing, because it meant you could go to the city—Ottawa," about an hour away. But she was nervous, and says she only got her learner's permit at her parents' insistence. "My dad took me out in his truck for the first time, this huge massive thing. It was fun, but I was really scared." O'Neill later moved to Toronto for school and let her permit expire. In Toronto, "I don't really have any friends who drive cars," says O'Neill, 23. When she goes back to Arnprior to visit, she walks or bikes around town, or gets a lift from her parents.

One powerful incentive for getting a licence is still parenthood. Stephanie Kale grew up in Windsor, Ont., and lives in Ottawa; she didn't need to learn how to drive until she had a child almost three years ago. Then she got her licence and bought a car one week later. "My daughter was my motivation," says Kale, 32, who left her downtown apartment for a less expensive place further from the city core. Now she's in a better financial situation, and she's tempted to move back downtown and use her car less.

People who can't drive sometimes end up feeling like a mooch. If Mohammed's friends want to drink, she can't be the designated driver. On their road trip, "it's just crappy because it will always have to be one of them," she says, referring to her two friends who have their licences. They'll be bringing an arsenal of technology to B.C.—including a MacBook Pro laptop—but the driver can't use it on long boring stretches of highway, while Mohammed can check her phone and text any time. Even in Montreal, her inability to drive can leave her feeling dependent. When she spoke to *Maclean's,* she was about to have her wisdom teeth removed; a friend would be dropping her off at the appointment and picking her up afterwards. "I can't be that person for someone else," she says.

Despite these inconveniences, some people, like Dan Dubuc in Vancouver, B.C., say they'd rather not drive because of the environment. "I'm holding out until I can buy a reliable vehicle that isn't powered by fossil fuel," says Dubuc, 24, a student at Langara College. Maybe so, but it's hard to believe that if a driver's licence had the cachet it once did, so many would be holding out too. And such criticisms of the car are fairly recent. In the 1960s, "there was a godlike sense of the car being important," Penfold says. "You might have had one guy on the margins who didn't think the car was a positive force for society," but these days, more people share Dubuc's attitude, making cars seem less cool than ever.

With youth unemployment in Canada roughly double the national average, the cost of owning a car could discourage many young people from driving. But cars are getting more affordable. It took on average 18.8 weeks' worth of income (before tax) to pay off a new car in 2011, according to auto analyst Dennis DesRosiers. Ten years before, it would have taken three weeks longer. "Vehicle ownership in Canada is going up, not down," says DesRosiers, who adds that up to 90 per cent of the demand for new vehicles comes from existing car owners.

Car companies are trying to catch the interest of aloof younger buyers by creating vehicles that are an extension of their smartphones. Chevrolet MyLink, an "infotainment system," lets a driver connect her smartphone with the car to access personal music libraries, video and photo albums on a colour touchscreen (the latter two only work when the car is going less than five kilometres per hour). The Ford Sync system can stream music from the driver's phone through the vehicle's sound system, and reads incoming text messages aloud, among many other features.

Companies also use heavy product placement to make sure their products stay visible to younger drivers. "One of our most famous was the Camaro in *Transformers,*" says Rob Assimakopoulos, general director of marketing and communications of GM Canada. Ford, which has set its sights on social media marketing to reach millennials, launched its Fiesta in North America by recruiting bloggers to drive the car and create buzz. An ad for the Chevy Sonic, which played during the Super Bowl, featured the band OK Go using the car as a musical instrument—a very different way of perceiving vehicle performance.

Some manufacturers have accepted the fact that, for a growing number of people, cars are no longer an expression of personal identity. Peugeot, in turn, has launched a European program called Mu: members can visit a dealer to rent out whichever "mobility solution" best suits their needs that day, whether it's a scooter, van or bike. Maybe this is the car dealership of the future. Maybe we'll see more "self-driving cars," like one Google has developed, suggests Rudi Volti, professor emeritus of sociology at Pitzer College in Claremont, Calif.,

and an expert in car culture. He wonders if "a more European situation" will emerge, where people have cars but tend to use them for making day trips, and not for commuting to work. "I think there's always going to be a place for the private automobile," he says. "It's not just the freedom; it's the ability to be with whomever you want, or nobody at all."

But ironically, today it's actually easier for young people to be with whomever they want *without* a car. "You can have a conversation with 15 people online," Valiquette says. "That didn't exist 40 years ago." The licensed driver, once the source of envy among his friends, is stuck talking to the passengers in his car. Those passengers, with their smartphones in hand, are the ones to envy: they can chat virtually with anybody.

Mohammed hopes to get her driver's licence one day. "Someone mentioned to me that having your licence, it's a coming-of-age thing. On the grand list of stuff you've got to do in life," she says, "that's one that needs to be checked off the list." Eventually.

Critical Thinking

1. One part of the author's thesis is that millennials have less need to drive because the Internet has partially replaced the need to get together face to face. Given that the total miles travelled by 16–34-year-olds dropped marginally (23%) last decade, do you accept this thesis as reasonable? Why or why not?
2. This article is from a Canadian magazine and references mostly Canadian data and anecdotes. Do you think the trend reported applies equally to Americans? Why or why not?
3. If you were an auto industry executive and read the data in this article, how would you respond to it in terms of changing product design, changing your approach to marketing, or would you ignore this trend as a passing fad—if it exists at all?

Create Central

www.mhhe.com/createcentral

Internet References

Generation of Tech-Savvy Toddlers Go for Tablets over Teddy Bears
www.pbs.org/newshour/bb/science/jan-june13/techbabies_03-28.html

The Great Debate: Do Millennials Really Want Cars, or Not
http://business.time.com/2013/08/09/
the-great-debate-do-millennials-really-want-cars-or-not/?iid=obnetwork

Is Technology Wiring Teens to Have Better Brains?
www.pbs.org/newshour/bb/science/jan-june11/digitalbrain_01-05.html

Juan Enriquez: Will Our Kids Be a Different Species? [TED Talk]
www.ted.com/talks/juan_enriquez_will_our_kids_be_a_different_species.html

Social Media and Social Change: How Young People are Tapping into Technology
http://blogs.worldbank.org/youthink/social-media-and-social-change-how-young-people-are-tapping-technology

Article

Prepared by: Daniel Mittleman, *DePaul University*

The Truth about Video Games and Gun Violence

Aaron Alexis reportedly loved first-person shooters. Does that explain his mass killing at the Washington Navy Yard?

Erik Kain

Learning Outcomes

After reading this article, you will be able to:

- Summarize the research on the connection between video game playing and violence.

- Aritculate why it is difficult to research the relationship between video game playing and violence.

- Understand and articulate both the costs and benefits of game playing among a large subset of our population.

It was one of the most brutal video games imaginable—players used cars to murder people in broad daylight. Parents were outraged, and behavioral experts warned of real-world carnage. "In this game a player takes the first step to creating violence," a psychologist from the National Safety Council told the *New York Times*. "And I shudder to think what will come next if this is encouraged. It'll be pretty gory."

To earn points, Death Race encouraged players to mow down pedestrians. Given that it was 1976, those pedestrians were little pixel-gremlins[1] in a 2-D black-and-white universe that bore almost no recognizable likeness to real people.

Indeed, the debate about whether violent video games lead to violent acts by those who play them goes way back. The public reaction to Death Race can be seen as an early predecessor to the controversial Grand Theft Auto[2] three decades later and the many other graphically violent and hyper-real games of today, including the slew of new titles debuting at the E3 gaming[3]summit[3] this week in Los Angeles.

In the wake of the Newtown massacre and numerous other recent mass shootings,[4] familiar condemnations of and questions about these games have reemerged. Here are some answers.

Who's claiming video games cause violence in the real world?

Though conservatives tend to raise it more frequently, this bogeyman plays across the political spectrum, with regular calls for more research, more regulations, and more censorship. The tragedy in Newtown set off a fresh wave:

Donald Trump tweeted:[5] "Video game violence & glorification must be stopped—it's creating monsters!" Ralph Nader likened violent video games to "electronic child molesters."[6] (His outlandish rhetoric was meant to suggest that parents need to be involved in the media their kids consume.) MSNBC's Joe Scarborough asserted that the government has a right to regulate[7] video games, despite a Supreme Court ruling to the contrary.[8]

Unsurprisingly, the most over-the-top talk came from the National Rifle Association:

"Guns don't kill people. Video games, the media, and Obama's budget kill people," NRA Executive Vice President Wayne LaPierre said at a press conference[9] one week after the mass shooting at Sandy Hook Elementary. He continued without irony: "There exists in this country, sadly, a callous, corrupt and corrupting shadow industry that sells and stows violence against its own people through vicious, violent video games with names like Bulletstorm, Grand Theft Auto, Mortal Kombat, and Splatterhouse."

Has the rhetoric led to any government action?

Yes. Amid a flurry of broader legislative activity on gun violence,[10] since Newtown there have been proposals specifically focused on video games. Among them:

State Rep. Diane Franklin, a Republican in Missouri, sponsored a state bill[11] that would impose a 1 percent tax on violent games, the revenues of which would go toward "the treatment of mental-health conditions associated with exposure to violent video games." (The bill has since been withdrawn.) Vice President Joe Biden[12] has also promoted this idea.

Rep. Jim Matheson (D-Utah) proposed a federal bill[13] that would give the Entertainment Software Rating Board's ratings system the weight of the law, making it illegal to sell Mature-rated games to minors, something Gov. Chris Christie (R-N.J.) has also proposed for his home state.[14]

A bill introduced in the Senate by Sen. Jay Rockefeller (D-W.Va.) proposed studying the impact of violent video games on children.[15]

So who actually plays these games and how popular are they?

While many of the top selling games in history have been various Mario and Pokemon titles, games from the the first-person-shooter genre, which appeal in particular to teen boys and young men, are also huge sellers.

The new king of the hill is Activision's Call of Duty: Black Ops II, which surpassed Wii Play as the No. 1 grossing game[16] in 2012. Call of Duty is now one of the most successful franchises in video game history, topping charts year after year and boasting around 40 million active monthly users playing one of the franchise's games over the internet. (Which doesn't even include people playing the game offline.) There is already much anticipation for the release later this year of Call of Duty: Ghosts.

The Battlefield games from Electronic Arts also sell millions of units with each release. Irrational Games' BioShock Infinite, released in March, has sold nearly 4 million units and is one of the most violent games to date. (Read *MoJo*'s interview[17] with Irrational's cofounder and creative director, Ken Levine.)

What research has been done on the link between video games and violence, and what does it really tell us?

Studies on how violent video games affect behavior date to the mid 1980s, with conflicting results. Since then there have been at least two dozen studies[18] conducted on the subject.

"Video Games, Television, and Aggression in Teenagers," published by the University of Georgia in 1984, found that playing arcade games was linked to increases in physical aggression. But a study published a year later by the Albert Einstein College of Medicine, "Personality, Psychopathology, and Developmental Issues in Male Adolescent Video Game Use," found that arcade games have a "calming effect" and that boys use them to blow off steam. Both studies relied on surveys and interviews asking boys and young men about their media consumption.

Studies grew more sophisticated over the years, but their findings continued to point in different directions. A 2011 study found that people who had played competitive games, regardless of whether they were violent or not, exhibited increased aggression. In 2012, a different study found that cooperative playing in the graphically violent Halo II made the test subjects more cooperative even outside of video game playing.

Metastudies—comparing the results and the methodologies of prior research on the subject—have also been problematic.

One published in 2010 by the American Psychological Association, analyzing data from multiple studies and more than 130,000 subjects, concluded that "violent video games increase aggressive thoughts, angry feelings, and aggressive behaviors and decrease empathic feelings and pro-social behaviors." But results from another metastudy showed that most studies of violent video games over the years suffered from publication biases that tilted the results toward foregone correlative conclusions.

Why is it so hard to get good research on this subject?

"I think that the discussion of media forms—particularly games—as some kind of serious social problem is often an attempt to kind of corral and solve what is a much broader social issue," says Carly Kocurek, a professor of Digital Humanities at the Illinois Institute of Technology. "Games aren't developed in a vacuum, and they reflect the cultural milieu that produces them. So of course we have violent games."

There is also the fundamental problem of measuring violent outcomes ethically and effectively.

"I think anybody who tells you that there's any kind of consistency to the aggression research is lying to you," Christopher J. Ferguson, associate professor of psychology and criminal justice at Texas A&M International University, told *Kotaku*.[19] "There's no consistency in the aggression literature, and my impression is that at this point it is not strong enough to draw any kind of causal, or even really correlational links between video game violence and aggression, no matter how weakly we may define aggression."

Moreover, determining why somebody carries out a violent act like a school shooting can be very complex; underlying mental-health issues are almost always present. More than half of mass shooters[20] over the last 30 years had mental-health problems.

But America's consumption of violent video games must help explain our inordinate rate of gun violence, right?

Actually, no. A look at global video game spending per capita in relation to gun death statistics reveals that gun deaths in the United States far outpace those in other countries—including countries with higher per capita video game spending.

A 10-country comparison[21] from the *Washington Post* shows the United States as the clear outlier in this regard. Countries with the highest per capita spending on video games, such as the Netherlands and South Korea, are among the safest countries in the world when it comes to guns. In other words, America plays about the same number of violent video games per capita as the rest of the industrialized world, despite that we far outpace every other nation in terms of gun deaths.

Or, consider it this way: With violent video game sales almost always at the top of the charts,[22] why do so few gamers turn into homicidal shooters? In fact, the number of violent youth offenders in the United States fell by more than half between 1994 and 2010—while video game sales more than doubled since 1996. A working paper from economists on violence and video game sales published in 2011 found that higher rates of violent video game sales in fact correlated with a decrease in crimes, especially violent crimes.

I'm still not convinced. A bunch of mass shooters were gamers, right?

Some mass shooters over the last couple of decades have had a history with violent video games. The Newtown shooter, Adam Lanza, was reportedly "obsessed" with video games. Norway shooter Anders Behring Breivik was said to have played World of Warcraft for 16 hours a day until he gave up the game in favor of Call of Duty: Modern Warfare, which he claimed he used to train with a rifle.[23] Aurora theater shooter James Holmes was reportedly a fan of violent video games[24] and movies such as *The Dark Knight.* (Holmes reportedly went so far as to mimic the Joker by dying his hair prior to carrying out his attack.)

Jerald Block, a researcher and psychiatrist in Portland, Oregon, stirred controversy when he concluded that Columbine shooters Eric Harris and Dylan Klebold carried out their rampage after their parents took away their video games. According to the *Denver Post,*[25] Block said that the two had relied on the virtual world of computer games to express their rage, and that cutting them off in 1998 had sent them into crisis.

But that's clearly an oversimplification. The age and gender[26] of many mass shooters, including Columbine's, places them right in the target demographic for first-person-shooter (and most other) video games. And people between ages 18 and 25 also tend to report the highest rates of mental-health issues.[27] Harris and Klebold's complex mental-health problems have been well documented.[28]

To hold up a few sensational examples as causal evidence between violent games and violent acts ignores the millions of other young men and women who play violent video games and never go on a shooting spree in real life. Furthermore, it's very difficult to determine empirically whether violent kids are simply drawn to violent forms of entertainment, or if the entertainment somehow makes them violent. Without solid scientific data to go on, it's easier to draw conclusions that confirm our own biases.

How is the industry reacting to the latest outcry over violent games?

Moral panic over the effects of violent video games on young people has had an impact on the industry over the years, says Kocurek, noting that "public and government pressure has driven the industry's efforts to self regulate."

In fact, it is among the best when it comes to abiding by its own voluntary ratings system, with self-regulated retail sales of Mature-rated games to minors lower than in any other entertainment field.[14]

But is that enough? Even conservative judges think there should be stronger laws regulating these games, right?

There have been two major Supreme Court cases involving video games and attempts by the state to regulate access to video games. *Aladdin's Castle, Inc. v. City of Mesquite* in 1983 and *Brown v. Entertainment Merchants Association* in 2011.

"Both cases addressed attempts to regulate youth access to games, and in both cases, the court held that youth access can't be curtailed," Kocurek says.

In *Brown v. EMA,* the Supreme Court found that the research simply wasn't compelling enough to spark government action,

and that video games, like books and film, were protected by the First Amendment.

"Parents who care about the matter can readily evaluate the games their children bring home," Justice Antonin Scalia wrote when the Supreme Court deemed California's video game censorship bill unconstitutional in *Brown v. EMA.* "Filling the remaining modest gap in concerned-parents' control can hardly be a compelling state interest."

So how can we explain the violent acts of some kids who play these games?

For her part, Kocurek wonders if the focus on video games is mostly a distraction from more important issues. "When we talk about violent games," she says, "we are too often talking about something else and looking for a scapegoat."

In other words, violent video games are an easy thing to blame for a more complex problem. Public policy debates, she says, need to focus on serious research into the myriad factors that may contribute to gun violence. This may include video games—but a serious debate needs to look at the dearth of mental-health care[29] in America, our abundance of easily accessible weapons, our highly flawed background-check system, and other factors.

There is at least one practical approach to violent video games, however, that most people would agree on: Parents should think deliberately about purchasing these games for their kids. Better still, they should be involved in the games their kids play as much as possible so that they can know first-hand whether the actions and images they're allowing their children to consume are appropriate or not.

References

1. www.retrogamer.net/show_image.php?imageID=2833
2. www.theguardian.com/technology/grand-theft-auto
3. www.techradar.com/us/news/gaming/e3-2013-10-things-we-expect-from-the-show-1139138
4. www.motherjones.com/special-reports/2012/12/guns-in-america-mass-shootings
5. https://twitter.com/realDonaldTrump/status/280812064539283457
6. www.politico.com/story/2013/01/nader-inauguration-political-bullsh-t-86479.html?hp=r6
7. www.youtube.com/watch?v=CG1roDmFQAg
8. http://thinkprogress.org/alyssa/2011/06/27/254812/supreme-court-rules-against-video-game-censorship-7-2/
9. http://usnews.nbcnews.com/_news/2013/01/15/16524425-new-practice-range-app-says-its-from-nra-which-blamed-video-games-for-violence?lite
10. www.motherjones.com/mojo/2013/03/crazy-gun-laws-newtown
11. www.polygon.com/2013/1/16/3882840/mo-house-bill-violent-video-game-tax
12. www.geek.com/games/joe-biden-floats-idea-of-a-violent-video-game-tax-1555101/
13. http://venturebeat.com/2013/01/17/deja-vu-new-bill-would-give-esrb-ratings-the-force-of-law/

14. www.motherjones.com/mojo/2013/04/chris-christie-violent-video-games-guns

15. www.huffingtonpost.com/2012/12/19/video-games-sandy-hook_n_2330741.html

16. www.gamespot.com/news/npd-black-ops-ii-is-us-top-selling-game-of-2012-6402271

17. www.motherjones.com/media/2013/05/irrational-games-bioshock-infinite-creator-ken-levine-interview

18. http://kotaku.com/5976781/25-video-game-violence-studies-summarized

19. http://kotaku.com/5976733/do-video-games-make-you-violent-an-in+depth-look-at-everything-we-know-today

20. www.motherjones.com/politics/2012/11/jared-loughner-mass-shootings-mental-illness

21. www.washingtonpost.com/blogs/worldviews/wp/2012/12/17/ten-country-comparison-suggests-theres-little-or-no-link-between-video-games-and-gun-murders/

22. www.guardian.co.uk/world/interactive/2013/apr/30/violence-guns-best-selling-video-games

23. http://news.yahoo.com/norway-killer-sharpened-aim-playing-video-game-213107800.html

24. http://latimesblogs.latimes.com/lanow/2012/07/colorado-shooter-enjoyed-video-games-movies-school-friend-says.html

25. www.denverpost.com/headlines/ci_6300370

26. www.motherjones.com/politics/2012/07/mass-shootings-map

27. www.nimh.nih.gov/statistics/SMI_AASR.shtml

28. www.davecullen.com/columbine/faq.htm

29. www.motherjones.com/politics/2013/04/mental-health-crisis-mac-mcclelland-cousin-murder

Critical Thinking

1. Do we know whether video games cause violence in the real world? What do we actually know about the relationship between video games and violence, and what questions remain unanswered?

2. If someone who commits a violent act is also a video game player, is this evidence that video game playing causes violence? Explain your position.

3. Take a look at the web resources at the end of this article. Do politicians and newscasters accurately portray what we know about the relationship between video game playing and violence? What factors do you think influence those who speak out on this subject?

Create Central

www.mhhe.com/createcentral

Internet References

How Virtual Reality Games Can Impact Society, Encourage Prosperity
www.pbs.org/newshour/bb/business/july-dec13/games_07-11.html

Jane McGonigal: Gaming Can Make a Better World
www.ted.com/talks/jane_mcgonigal_gaming_can_make_a_better_world.html

Lawmakers Neglect Facts on Video Games and Gun Violence
www.psychologytoday.com/blog/talking-about-trauma/201306/lawmakers-neglect-facts-video-games-and-gun-violence

Media Figures Say Guns Don't Kill People, Video Games Do
http://mediamatters.org/blog/2013/09/17/media-figures-say-guns-dont-kill-people-video-g/195921

Navy Yard Shooting & Gun Violence Causes
www.colbertnation.com/the-colbert-report-videos/429165/september-18-2013/navy-yard-shooting—gun-violence-causes

Unit 3

UNIT

Prepared by: Daniel Mittleman, *DePaul University*

Privacy in a Digital World

Privacy is the yin to security's yang. They are two sides of the same dilemma we face in America today. We want our government to keep us secure. And to do so, they require the ability to conduct surveillance. But we also value our privacy and the constitutional protections designed to preserve that privacy. And some of us do not trust the government. Policies that make for more effective security often seem to erode our privacy. And policies that preserve our privacy hinder our government's ability to protect. In this unit we explore the status of privacy today on the Internet.

In a recent *New Yorker* article, Nicholas Thompson noted that "privacy snafus are to social networks as violence is to football. The whole point of social networks is to share stuff about people that's interesting, just as the whole point of football is to upend the guy with the ball. Every so often, someone gets paralyzed, which prompts us to add padding to the helmets or set new rules about tackling. Then we move on."[1] But we change the rules and add more security—both in football and in our computer networks and the injuries not only keep occurring, but they become larger and more dangerous than before.

Edward Tenner published a book chronicling what he calls "revenge effects" seventeen years ago. Revenge effects occur, he writes, "because new structures, devices, and organisms react with real people in real situations in ways we could not foresee."[2] Thus, when stronger football helmets were developed in the 1960s and 1970s, players began charging with their heads forward and spines straight, resulting in more broken necks and damaged spinal columns. Similarly, soldiers in Iraq have suffered more frequent brain injuries than those who served in Vietnam, largely the result of body armor and rapid evacuation of the wounded. We equip our soldiers with body armor to withstand small weapons fire and insurgents respond with head-trauma inducing rocket-propelled grenades and IEDs.[3] The moral of Tenner's story is to look beyond technological fixes for our predicaments to the social and economic systems in which they are embedded. "Technology giveth and technology taketh away."

Privacy concerns exist not just in the realm of our collective relationships with government. Large corporations have as much—perhaps more—information about us. Google's vast database of our web browsing and related history contains far more detailed personal interests and behaviors than any government could know.[4] And Facebook, is aiming to capture every one of everyone's relationships with objects, organizations, and each other.[5] What are the implications of having such personal and complete information about almost all of us sitting in corporate databases?

As the Patriot Act enacted during the Bush years has shown, a normal response of government during times of threatened public safety is to threaten civil liberties. In theory, a free press, a concerned citizenry, and the normal checks and balances built into our system should prevent the worst abuses. If only the federal government were all we had to worry about. In a world of networked computers, e-commerce, and social networking, we blithely hand over valuable data to providers of services we usually think of as free. To take a simple example, imagine that you're a Gmail subscriber. You may well think you have deleted private messages. But they are stored on a server, who knows where for who knows how long, with access by who knows whom. We Americans (but not Europeans and Canadians whose governments were farsighted enough to pass privacy legislation in the 1980s and 1990s) are in a privacy fix. It turns out that the fifty most visited websites install, on average, sixty-four "pieces of tracking technology" onto our computers. Who is the worst offender? Dictionary.com installs 234 files. The best-behaved is Wikipedia, which installs no tracking technology at all.

Notes

1. Nicholas Thompson, How to get Privacy Right, *New Yorker Magazine*, March 5, 2012
2. Edward Tenner, *Why Things Bite Back*, Vintage, 1996, p. 4.
3. Emily Singer, *Technology Review*, Brain Trauma in Iraq, 2008.
4. James Gleick, "How Google Dominates Us,'" *The New York Review of Books*, August 13, 2011.
5. Tom Simonite, "What Facebook Knows," *Technology Review*, July/August 2012.

Article

Prepared by: Daniel Mittleman, *DePaul University*

The Individual in a Networked World: Two Scenarios

Collaborative agent bots? A walled world under constant surveillance? Two information technology experts parse the future of human–network interaction.

LEE RAINIE AND BARRY WELLMAN

Learning Outcomes

After reading this article, you will be able to:

- Understand that the technologies we innovate do not guarantee either a utopian or dystopian future; we have options in how we choose to create policy and institutions around those technologies.

- Articulate characteristics of both utopian and dystopian futures.

- Define and describe the "Triple Revolution."

One of the most useful and formal futurism exercises in recent years was the work in 2006–2007 of the Metaverse Roadmap project. It was driven by John Smart, Jamais Cascio, and Jerry Paffendorf, and originally conceived of as a brief for the future of the World Wide Web as it became three-dimensional.

Once the leaders of the effort began to hear from several dozen thinkers, their own views branched in other directions. They had started their inquiries with the notion of a "Metaverse" that was first conceived by the influential science-fiction writer Neal Stephenson in his 1982 classic, *Snow Crash*. To Stephenson, the Metaverse was an immersive, virtual space with 3-D technologies.

Yet, the Metaverse Roadmap thinkers went beyond seeing the Metaverse as a virtual domain. They saw it as the "convergence of (1) virtually enhanced physical reality and (2) physically persistent virtual space. It is a fusion of both, while allowing users to experience it as either." In other words, it is the connection of the physical and virtual worlds. Although we do not foresee people living mostly in virtual space, the technological directions suggested by the Metaverse Roadmap provide guides for how networked individualism may proceed.

This is a future that has already come to pass in many respects. There is already a mad rush in Silicon Valley to create products to embed social interplay in most kinds of information and media encounters, and it will likely accelerate going forward. Moreover, in coming years a wider Metaverse will emerge as relatively ordinary objects—as well as computers and phones—will become ubiquitously networked with each other, and networked individuals will be able to augment their information through direct contact with databases and objects that have become smarter and more communicative.

Increased computing power may make people's involvements in virtual worlds more immersive and compelling, although experiences to date suggest that people are more apt to use computer networks that integrate with real life rather than becoming totally immersed in virtual worlds—with virtual game players the exception.

Ubiquitous computing, sometimes called "the Internet of things" (or "everyware"), describes human–computer interaction that goes beyond personal computing to an environment of objects processing information and networking with each other and humans. Objects would share information: appliances, utility grids, clothing and jewelry, cars, books, household and workplace furnishings, as well as buildings and landscapes. They would learn additional information and preferred methods of use by gathering data about people who are in their environment. For example, cars could tell each other not to be in the same lane at the same time, and bicycles could tell car doors not to open suddenly when the bikes pass by.

With all these trends rolling along into the future, there is still reason to be uncertain about how the environment of networked individuals will evolve. We offer two different scenarios that seem credible.

Scenario 1: Collaborative Agents in Augmented Reality

Waking up in a networked future, his digital agent's soft voice slowly grows into Harry Sanchez's hearing range. It's been monitoring his sleep rhythms and cross-referencing them with data from his ongoing brain scans to see when it's most appropriate to wake him. After stretching and rubbing the sleep from his eyes, Harry suddenly and happily recalls yesterday's purchase.

He found a collaborative coupon on the Web the other day for a deal on a new pair of augmented reality (AR) contact lenses and the haptic feedback implant that everyone's been raving about. The implantation was a simple and quick outpatient procedure that reminded him more of getting his ears pierced than of surgery. It was performed remotely by a doctor whose robot mimicked his every move. It was not as though Harry could really tell, however, since his AR glasses had "skinned" (covered) the robot with the doctor's virtual image. In this way, the doctor efficiently treats dozens of patients a day, projecting in from his home.

Now that he is awake, Harry eagerly slips in his new AR contact lenses for the first time. They instantly network with his microcomputer, smartphone, and the Internet. His personalized augmented overlay appears in his field of vision: the time and date, the weather and air quality, a few applications he left open from the previous night minimized into his peripheral vision, a faintly blinking icon notifying him of some messages he missed overnight, an icon notifying him of information updates on news stories aggregated for him by his agent, and an InterFace lifelog update showing what his friends did last night that is cross-referenced with the media they consumed and the tagged conversations they had. He sees a call for participating in a political smart mob in the virtual world, but he tells his agent to disregard it.

His agent also warns him about his health.

Harry hasn't been sleeping well, as his late-night virtual meetings with colleagues in China have taken a toll on his system. Yet, he's happy to not have to fly there ever since they've been able to collaborate long-distance by using the Cavecat productivity system with active walls and tables holding spreadsheets, texts, drawings, and videos.

As Harry settles in at the kitchen table, the surface notices that he's put down his morning cup of coffee. Finally, the news displays as manipulable augmented reality overlays of Harry's social network, with pictures of each network member blinking when she or he posts messages, videos, or lifelog entries.

The new haptic implant gives him a sensory understanding of the news: He can feel the continuing battle in Kabul, experiencing its sounds and vibrations as if he were at the scene. And it now feels as if the computer icons of his various applications have weight and texture. Having not found any urgent messages, Harry's agent organizes his correspondence by topic and relevance. Noticing a conversation he had that he does not want many network members to see, Harry has his agent make the information private across his entire InterFace network. His agent also sends out a quick update to his entire network, letting them know his plans for the day.

Harry is distracted by a knocking sound. His agent informs him that his best friend, Neal, is projecting in for their regular weekend virtual breakfast.

Though Harry and Neal only live 50 kilometers apart, this is a nice way for them to check in on one another and spend some time together. Harry hasn't shaved, and so he puts on his shiny-face skin before he opens the virtual door. He uses his new haptic chip to get the sensation of shaking his friend's hand. It's a little strange at first, since there's nothing actually present to shake, but his nervous system responds as though he had reached out and touched someone.

Harry and Neal chat about how everyone who was at the pub's avatar party last night has shared recordings of the evening with friends. Their agents have already automatically tagged these recordings with relevant information about people and location. Avatar parties have become popular these days. Everyone dresses like their favorite game character; some even come looking like one another. It can be a lot of fun role playing like this, and the collected and tagged videos are highly amusing as people's voices, looks, and even smells can be altered in the virtual world.

After visualizing and flipping through these tags for mentions of his name, Harry updates the conversation file with some witty things he thought of after the fact, and his agent forwards the updates to the relevant people. He also tells his agent to delete information about last night's embarrassing ice-cube escapade at the avatar party, and to ask his friends to delete their versions.

Harry's agent softly chimes in just as he's saying goodbye to Neal, reminding him that he has to meet his sister Merril today. The agents settle on a place downtown. Harry projects himself into the restaurant's virtual space. The restaurant keeps a good online presence, with a nice menu, list of ingredients, health report, and real-time webcam view. It's local and the tables there get automatically reserved.

As Harry gets ready for the day, his agent presents him with a few clothing options. He decides to wear the new trousers suggested by his girlfriend, but calls up another app to make sure his sister would also approve. Harry's girlfriend had tagged the info to the trousers while doing some virtual window shopping and had a pair in his size set aside after asking his belt how big it was.

Not wanting to be late, Harry has his agent arrange a car for him through a collaborative consumption app that recognizes his high trust score. He rarely uses a car, as his fridge automatically schedules grocery deliveries. Slipping his microcomputer into his pocket, Harry goes to the car, has his agent set the restaurant's coordinates, and leans back to check his messages as the car pulls out.

Scenario 2: A Walled and Surveilled World

As Will Li rouses himself from sleep, he walks over to "his" computer to see what he's missed overnight. Truthfully, the computer isn't really his: He owns rights to its usage but isn't allowed to change its hardware or software, or else he'd void his warranty or break the law. His computer is really only an access point, as all his data is in the cloud, yet another thing that's owned—with all the data in it—by a big corporation. Before Will can reach for the cloud, the system completes its mandatory scan of his computer for viruses and copyright infringement.

The price of media access has also spawned its own subculture of media pirates. They usually meet in person, sharing miniature portable terabyte flash drives packed with music, TV shows, movies, e-books, and more. The pirates often get their "warez" from people who collected old computers from trash heaps, recycling centers, and garage sales. They've even developed a code language to arrange meet-ups, but Will hardly keeps up with the ever-evolving lingo.

Leaning over his morning coffee, Will dreams of how nice it would be to have a personal agent, but he's heard most are double agents that also report back to the authorities and sell information to corporations. And he doesn't like the way FaceWall is collecting all the information on him whenever he uses it. He also can't afford to hire the technician it would require to help him set up the devices and access all the fragmented networks of media sites, search engines, and social applications online. Each has a tricky "right to information" form to sign. So he's reduced his online presence to a minimum, trying to limit himself to good old-fashioned e-mails and avoid social media.

However, Will needs to use FaceWall today to find something. He's forced to wait thirty seconds to let the mandatory ad play. It has his picture in it. CoffeeCo must have bought a recent photo that tagged him on a friend's wall. Will notices that his system slows down as the massive data file from the advertisement clogs up his bandwidth, but since the corporations pay more to guarantee themselves fast access, he endures the wait.

It's almost ironic to see a return to the days of loading screens since the amount of available bandwidth has only increased, but all that bandwidth is auctioned at sky-high prices or owned by a few companies. Finally finding the photo, Will learns he cannot delete it because CoffeeCo now owns it. Perhaps he should make sure no one ever uploads anything about him again, though that would be difficult. Most people seem to put up with these situations because they want to keep going online. Will assumes that from now on he'll get peppered with ads geared to the tastes that FaceWall has observed online—both for him and for all those other 40-year-olds who became unemployed when countries set up their own walled-off Internets, claiming that morality and national security demanded it.

Giving the situation further thought, Will starts to browse his friends' profiles, and finds that his sister Lorelei is earning extra money by selling her personal information to FaceWall, including links to his profile. Maybe that's how CoffeeCo found his photo. He'll ask her when they meet today to never do it again. You can never be quite sure of who's informing on you, only in this case it's not only the state but data-aggregating organizations.

Will remembers from history class how, in the 1960s, FBI Director J. Edgar Hoover had used his dossiers on the Kennedys to keep power. Now, FaceWall has even more comprehensive dossiers on everyone. Doing what he knows he shouldn't, Will reaches for a doughnut. Maybe he can sneak one without his insurance company's sensors registering it. At least Will made the right decision by paying extra for their privacy clause. Otherwise, his health data might have just been sold off to the highest bidder at an info auction. But, since he's not able to see the information himself, he can't be sure.

Will and his best friend, Spider, prefer to meet in person: There is less chance for any number of things happening. They remember how Spider was once duped by someone passing himself off as an online insurance representative to steal private information. The latest scam is reverse-identity theft. The thieves pose as old friends, using detailed avatars whose digital image and voice have been reconstructed from public profiles. Too bad the government killed the trusted identities program. Will shuts off the computer monitor, grabs his phone and his travel pass, and goes out past the security scanner.

After a wait, Lorelei pulls up, giggling about the whole-body security scan at the gate. "Hope they got a better picture this time." She's also worried that maybe the guards had found the incriminating photo of her online. She's already lost one job because of it, even though it was taken without her permission and out of context. They head off for their meal, but arrive just in time to see the last open table become occupied.

The Possible Futures of Networked Individuals

Although present technologies are still far from realizing either scenario in its entirety, each represents a potential evolution from current trajectories. The first scenario assumes a move toward more networked individualism based on continued technological progress and trust in computer and human networks—including the withering of boundaries.

The second scenario assumes more boundaries, more costs, more corporate concentration, and more surveillance. At present, the Western world is trending in the direction of the first scenario, but we would be naïve to think that the second scenario could not happen.

What we call the Triple Revolution—in social networks, in the Internet, and in mobile connectedness—will change but never end in the ongoing turn to a networked operating system. The foreseeable future holds the prospect that individuals will be able to act more independently with greater power to shape their lives, if they choose to do so and if the circumstances will enable them to do so.

Yet, the foreseeable future also contains the burden of knowing that people will have to work harder on their own to get their needs met. Tightly knit, permanent groups will continue to be stable cores for some, and social networks will play greater roles in all human activities. The work of networked individuals is never quite done—and the satisfactions of netweaving are always available.

Critical Thinking

1. What are the critical factors in our society that will determine where our actual future falls on the continuum between Rainie's and Wellman's utopia and dystopia? What will determine how those factors play out?

2. In reading the dystopian scenario two, which particular characteristic of this society troubled you the most? Why?

3. Rainie and Wellman refer to the "Triple Revolution," what is it? How is it related to the two extreme futures they portray?

Create Central

www.mhhe.com/createcentral

Internet References

Gary Kovacs: Tracking Our Online Trackers [TED Talk]
www.ted.com/talks/gary_kovacs_tracking_the_trackers.html

Marc Goodman: What Does the Future of Crime Look Like? [NPR Interview from TED Radio Hour]
www.npr.org/2013/09/13/215831944/what-does-the-future-of-crime-look-like

The Quantified Self: Data Gone Wild?
www.pbs.org/newshour/bb/science/july-dec13/quantifiedself_09-28.html

Tomorrow's World: A Guide to the Next 150 Years
www.bbc.com/future/story/20130102-tomorrows-world

Warning: Cover Up Your Webcam When Not in Use
http://techland.time.com/2013/06/20/warning-cover-up-your-webcam-when-not-in-use/?iid=obinsite

---

LEE RAINIE is the director of the Pew Research Center's Internet & American Life Project, a nonprofit, nonpartisan "fact tank" that studies the social impact of the Internet. Prior to that he was the managing editor for *U.S. News & World Report*. He is delivering the opening plenary keynote at WorldFuture 2012, the annual conference of *the World Future Society, in Toronto, Canada, July 27–29*. (*http://www.wfs.org/worldfuture-2012*).

BARRY WELLMAN directs the University of Toronto's NetLab, is a member of the Cities Centre and the Knowledge Media Design Institute, and is a cross-appointed member of the Faculty of Information. Wellman is a member of the Royal Society of Canada, chair-emeritus of both the Community and Information Technologies section and the Community and Urban Sociology section of the American Sociological Association, and a fellow of IBM Toronto's Centre for Advanced Studies.

Rainie, Lee and Wellman, Barry. As seen in *The Futurist*, July/August 2012; excerpted from *Networked: The New Social Operating System* by Lee Rainie and Barry Wellman (MIT Press 2012). © 2012 Massachusetts Institute of Technology. All rights reserved. (Christian Beermann and Tsahi Hayat co-authored the chapter.) Reprinted by permission of MIT Press and World Future Society.

Article   Prepared by: Daniel Mittleman, *DePaul*

What Facebook Knows

The company's social scientists are hunting for insights about human behavior. What they find could give Facebook new ways to cash in on our data—and remake our view of society.

Tom Simonite

Learning Outcomes

After reading this article, you will be able to:

- Understand the depth of personal information stored by businesses on the Internet.

- Understand how and why Google, Facebook, and other sites collect demographic and behavioral data.

- Understand how social networking data can be monetized at both the personal and aggregate level.

Cameron Marlow calls himself Facebook's "in-house sociologist." He and his team can analyze essentially all the information the site gathers.

Few Privacy Regulations Inhibit Facebook

Laws haven't kept up with the company's ability to mine its users' data.

If Facebook were a country, a conceit that founder Mark Zuckerberg has entertained in public, its 900 million members would make it the third largest in the world.

It would far outstrip any regime past or present in how intimately it records the lives of its citizens. Private conversations, family photos, and records of road trips, births, marriages, and deaths all stream into the company's servers and lodge there. Facebook has collected the most extensive data set ever assembled on human social behavior. Some of your personal information is probably part of it.

And yet, even as Facebook has embedded itself into modern life, it hasn't actually done that much with what it knows about us. Now that the company has gone public, the pressure to develop new sources of profit is likely to force it to do more with its hoard of information. That stash of data looms like an oversize shadow over what today is a modest online advertising business, worrying privacy-conscious Web users and rivals

such as Google. Everyone has a feeling that this unprecedented resource will yield something big, but nobody knows quite what.

Even as Facebook has embedded itself into modern life, it hasn't done that much with what it knows about us. Its stash of data looms like an oversize shadow. Everyone has a feeling that this resource will yield something big, but nobody knows quite what.

Heading Facebook's effort to figure out what can be learned from all our data is Cameron Marlow, a tall 35-year-old who until recently sat a few feet away from Zuckerberg. The group Marlow runs has escaped the public attention that dogs Facebook's founders and the more headline-grabbing features of its business. Known internally as the Data Science Team, it is a kind of Bell Labs for the social-networking age. The group has 12 researchers—but is expected to double in size this year. They apply math, programming skills, and social science to mine our data for insights that they hope will advance Facebook's business and social science at large. Whereas other analysts at the company focus on information related to specific online activities, Marlow's team can swim in practically the entire ocean of personal data that Facebook maintains. Of all the people at Facebook, perhaps even including the company's leaders, these researchers have the best chance of discovering what can really be learned when so much personal information is compiled in one place.

Facebook has all this information because it has found ingenious ways to collect data as people socialize. Users fill out profiles with their age, gender, and e-mail address; some people also give additional details, such as their relationship status and mobile-phone number. A redesign last fall introduced profile pages in the form of time lines that invite people to add historical information such as places they have lived and worked. Messages and photos shared on the site are often tagged with a precise location, and in the last two years Facebook has begun to track activity elsewhere on the Internet, using an addictive invention called the "Like" button. It appears on apps and websites outside Facebook and allows people to indicate with a click that they are interested in a brand, product, or piece of digital content. Since last fall, Facebook has also been able to collect data on users' online lives beyond its borders automatically: in certain apps or websites, when users listen to a song or read a news article, the information is passed along to Facebook, even if no one clicks "Like." Within the feature's first five months, Facebook catalogued more than five billion instances of people listening to songs online. Combine that kind of information with a map of the social connections Facebook's users make on the site, and you have an incredibly rich record of their lives and interactions.

"This is the first time the world has seen this scale and quality of data about human communication," Marlow says with a characteristically serious gaze before breaking into a smile at the thought of what he can do with the data. For one thing, Marlow is confident that exploring this resource will revolutionize the scientific understanding of why people behave as they do. His team can also help Facebook influence our social behavior for its own benefit and that of its advertisers. This work may even help Facebook invent entirely new ways to make money.

Contagious Information

Marlow eschews the collegiate programmer style of Zuckerberg and many others at Facebook, wearing a dress shirt with his jeans rather than a hoodie or T-shirt. Meeting me shortly before the company's initial public offering in May, in a conference room adorned with a six-foot caricature of his boss's dog spray-painted on its glass wall, he comes across more like a young professor than a student. He might have become one had he not realized early in his career that Web companies would yield the juiciest data about human interactions.

In 2001, undertaking a PhD at MIT's Media Lab, Marlow created a site called Blogdex that automatically listed the most "contagious" information spreading on weblogs. Although it was just a research project, it soon became so popular that Marlow's servers crashed. Launched just as blogs were exploding into the popular consciousness and becoming so numerous that Web users felt overwhelmed with information, it prefigured later aggregator sites such as Digg and Reddit. But Marlow didn't build it just to help Web users track what was popular online. Blogdex was intended as a scientific instrument to uncover the social networks forming on the Web and study how they spread ideas. Marlow went on to Yahoo's research labs to study online socializing for two years. In 2007 he joined Facebook, which he considers the world's most powerful instrument for studying human society. "For the first time," Marlow says, "we have a microscope that not only lets us examine social behavior at a very fine level that we've never been able to see before but allows us to run experiments that millions of users are exposed to."

Marlow's team works with managers across Facebook to find patterns that they might make use of. For instance, they study how a new feature spreads among the social network's users. They have helped Facebook identify users you may know but haven't "friended," and recognize those you may want to designate mere "acquaintances" in order to make their updates less prominent. Yet the group is an odd fit inside a company where software engineers are rock stars who live by the mantra "Move fast and break things." Lunch with the data team has the feel of a grad-student gathering at a top school; the typical member of the group joined fresh from a PhD or junior academic position and prefers to talk about advancing social science than about Facebook as a product or company. Several members of the team have training in sociology or social psychology, while others began in computer science and started using it to study human behavior. They are free to use some of their time, and Facebook's data, to probe the basic patterns and motivations of human behavior and to publish the results in academic journals—much as Bell Labs researchers advanced both AT&T's technologies and the study of fundamental physics.

It may seem strange that an eight-year-old company without a proven business model bothers to support a team with such an academic bent, but Marlow says it makes sense. "The biggest challenges Facebook has to solve are the same challenges that social science has," he says. Those challenges include understanding why some ideas or fashions spread from a few individuals to become universal and others don't, or to what extent a person's future actions are a product of past communication with friends. Publishing results and collaborating with university researchers will lead to findings that help Facebook improve its products, he adds.

Eytan Bakshy experimented with the way Facebook users shared links so that his group could study whether the site functions like an echo chamber.

For one example of how Facebook can serve as a proxy for examining society at large, consider a recent study of the notion that any person on the globe is just six degrees of separation from any other. The best-known real-world study, in 1967, involved a few hundred people trying to send postcards to a particular Boston stockholder. Facebook's version, conducted in collaboration with researchers from the University of Milan, involved the entire social network as of May 2011, which amounted to more than 10% of the world's population. Analyzing the 69 billion friend connections among those 721 million people showed that the world is smaller than we thought: four intermediary friends are usually enough to introduce anyone to a random stranger. "When considering another person in the world, a friend of your friend knows a friend of their friend, on average," the technical paper pithily concluded. That result may not extend to everyone on the planet, but there's good reason to believe that it and other findings from the Data Science Team are true to life outside Facebook. Last year the Pew Research Center's Internet & American Life Project found that 93% of Facebook friends had met in person. One of Marlow's researchers has developed a way to calculate a country's "gross national happiness" from its Facebook activity by logging the occurrence of words and phrases that signal positive or negative emotion. Gross national happiness fluctuates in a way that suggests the measure is accurate: it jumps during holidays and dips when popular public figures die. After a major earthquake in Chile in February 2010, the country's score plummeted and took many months to return to normal. That event seemed to make the country as a whole more sympathetic when Japan suffered its own big earthquake and subsequent tsunami in March

2011; while Chile's gross national happiness dipped, the figure didn't waver in any other countries tracked (Japan wasn't among them). Adam Kramer, who created the index, says he intended it to show that Facebook's data could provide cheap and accurate ways to track social trends—methods that could be useful to economists and other researchers.

Other work published by the group has more obvious utility for Facebook's basic strategy, which involves encouraging us to make the site central to our lives and then using what it learns to sell ads. An early study looked at what types of updates from friends encourage newcomers to the network to add their own contributions. Right before Valentine's Day this year a blog post from the Data Science Team listed the songs most popular with people who had recently signaled on Facebook that they had entered or left a relationship. It was a hint of the type of correlation that could help Facebook make useful predictions about users' behavior—knowledge that could help it make better guesses about which ads you might be more or less open to at any given time. Perhaps people who have just left a relationship might be interested in an album of ballads, or perhaps no company should associate its brand with the flood of emotion attending the death of a friend. The most valuable online ads today are those displayed alongside certain Web searches, because the searchers are expressing precisely what they want. This is one reason why Google's revenue is 10 times Facebook's. But Facebook might eventually be able to guess what people want or don't want even before they realize it.

Recently the Data Science Team has begun to use its unique position to experiment with the way Facebook works, tweaking the site—the way scientists might prod an ant's nest—to see how users react. Eytan Bakshy, who joined Facebook last year after collaborating with Marlow as a PhD student at the University of Michigan, wanted to learn whether our actions on Facebook are mainly influenced by those of our close friends, who are likely to have similar tastes. That would shed light on the theory that our Facebook friends create an "echo chamber" that amplifies news and opinions we have already heard about. So he messed with how Facebook operated for a quarter of a billion users. Over a seven-week period, the 76 million links that those users shared with each other were logged. Then, on 219 million randomly chosen occasions, Facebook prevented someone from seeing a link shared by a friend. Hiding links this way created a control group so that Bakshy could assess how often people end up promoting the same links because they have similar information sources and interests.

He found that our close friends strongly sway which information we share, but overall their impact is dwarfed by the collective influence of numerous more distant contacts—what sociologists call "weak ties." It is our diverse collection of weak ties that most powerfully determines what information we're exposed to.

That study provides strong evidence against the idea that social networking creates harmful "filter bubbles," to use activist Eli Pariser's term for the effects of tuning the information we receive to match our expectations. But the study also reveals the power Facebook has. "If [Facebook's] News Feed is the thing that everyone sees and it controls how information is disseminated, it's controlling how information is revealed to society, and it's something we need to pay very close attention to," Marlow says. He points out that his team helps Facebook understand what it is doing to society and publishes its findings to fulfill a public duty to transparency. Another recent study, which investigated which types of Facebook activity cause people to feel a greater sense of support from their friends, falls into the same category.

Facebook is not above using its platform to tweak users' behavior, as it did by nudging them to register as organ donors. Unlike academic social scientists, Facebook's employees have a short path from an idea to an experiment on hundreds of millions of people.

But Marlow speaks as an employee of a company that will prosper largely by catering to advertisers who want to control the flow of information between its users. And indeed, Bakshy is working with managers outside the Data Science Team to extract advertising-related findings from the results of experiments on social influence. "Advertisers and brands are a part of this network as well, so giving them some insight into how people are sharing the content they are producing is a very core part of the business model," says Marlow.

Facebook told prospective investors before its IPO that people are 50% more likely to remember ads on the site if they're visibly endorsed by a friend. Figuring out how influence works could make ads even more memorable or help Facebook find ways to induce more people to share or click on its ads.

Social Engineering

Marlow says his team wants to divine the rules of online social life to understand what's going on inside Facebook, not to develop ways to manipulate it. "Our goal is not to change the pattern of communication in society," he says. "Our goal is to understand it so we can adapt our platform to give people the experience that they want." But some of his team's work and the attitudes of Facebook's leaders show that the company is not above using its platform to tweak users' behavior. Unlike academic social scientists, Facebook's employees have a short path from an idea to an experiment on hundreds of millions of people.

In April, influenced in part by conversations over dinner with his med-student girlfriend (now his wife), Zuckerberg decided that he should use social influence within Facebook to increase organ donor registrations. Users were given an opportunity to click a box on their Timeline pages to signal that they were registered donors, which triggered a notification to their friends. The new feature started a cascade of social pressure, and organ donor enrollment increased by a factor of 23 across 44 states.

Marlow's team is in the process of publishing results from the last U.S. midterm election that show another striking example of Facebook's potential to direct its users' influence on one another. Since 2008, the company has offered a way for users to signal that they have voted; Facebook promotes that to their friends with a note to say that they should be sure to vote, too. Marlow says that in the 2010 election his group matched voter registration logs with the data to see which of the Facebook users who got nudges actually went to the polls. (He stresses that the researchers worked with cryptographically "anonymized" data and could not match specific users with their voting records.)

Sameet Agarwal figures out ways for Facebook to manage its enormous trove of data—giving the company a unique and valuable level of expertise.

This is just the beginning. By learning more about how small changes on Facebook can alter users' behavior outside the site, the company eventually "could allow others to make use of Facebook in the same way," says Marlow. If the American Heart Association wanted to encourage healthy eating, for example, it might be able to refer to a playbook of Facebook social engineering. "We want to be a platform that others can use to initiate change," he says.

Advertisers, too, would be eager to know in greater detail what could make a campaign on Facebook affect people's actions in the outside world, even though they realize there are limits to how firmly human beings can be steered. "It's not clear to me that social science will ever be an engineering science in a way that building bridges is," says Duncan Watts, who works on computational social science at Microsoft's recently opened New York research lab and previously worked alongside Marlow at Yahoo's labs. "Nevertheless, if you have enough data, you can make predictions that are better than simply random guessing, and that's really lucrative."

Doubling Data

Like other social-Web companies, such as Twitter, Facebook has never attained the reputation for technical innovation enjoyed by such Internet pioneers as Google. If Silicon Valley were a high school, the search company would be the quiet math genius who didn't excel socially but invented something indispensable. Facebook would be the annoying kid who started a club with such social momentum that people had to join whether they wanted to or not. In reality, Facebook employs hordes of talented software engineers (many poached from Google and other math-genius companies) to build and maintain its irresistible club. The technology built to support the Data Science Team's efforts is particularly innovative. The scale at which Facebook operates has led it to invent hardware and software that are the envy of other companies trying to adapt to the world of "big data."

In a kind of passing of the technological baton, Facebook built its data storage system by expanding the power of open-source software called Hadoop, which was inspired by work at Google and built at Yahoo. Hadoop can tame seemingly impossible computational tasks—like working on all the data Facebook's users have entrusted to it—by spreading them across many machines inside a data center. But Hadoop wasn't built with data science in mind, and using it for that purpose requires specialized, unwieldy programming. Facebook's engineers solved that problem with the invention of Hive, open-source software that's now independent of Facebook and used by many other companies. Hive acts as a translation service, making it possible to query vast Hadoop data stores using relatively

simple code. To cut down on computational demands, it can request random samples of an entire data set, a feature that's invaluable for companies swamped by data. Much of Facebook's data resides in one Hadoop store more than 100 petabytes (a million gigabytes) in size, says Sameet Agarwal, a director of engineering at Facebook who works on data infrastructure, and the quantity is growing exponentially. "Over the last few years we have more than doubled in size every year," he says. That means his team must constantly build more efficient systems.

One potential use of Facebook's data storehouse would be to sell insights mined from it. Such information could be the basis for any kind of business. Assuming Facebook can do this without upsetting users and regulators, it could be lucrative.

All this has given Facebook a unique level of expertise, says Jeff Hammerbacher, Marlow's predecessor at Facebook, who initiated the company's effort to develop its own data storage and analysis technology. (He left Facebook in 2008 to found Cloudera, which develops Hadoop-based systems to manage large collections of data.) Most large businesses have paid established software companies such as Oracle a lot of money for data analysis and storage. But now, big companies are trying to understand how Facebook handles its enormous information trove on open-source systems, says Hammerbacher. "I recently spent the day at Fidelity helping them understand how the 'data scientist' role at Facebook was conceived . . . and I've had the same discussion at countless other firms," he says.

As executives in every industry try to exploit the opportunities in "big data," the intense interest in Facebook's data technology suggests that its ad business may be just an offshoot of something much more valuable. The tools and techniques the company has developed to handle large volumes of information could become a product in their own right.

Mining for Gold

Facebook needs new sources of income to meet investors' expectations. Even after its disappointing IPO, it has a staggeringly high price-to-earnings ratio that can't be justified by the barrage of cheap ads the site now displays. Facebook's new campus in Menlo Park, California, previously inhabited by Sun Microsystems, makes that pressure tangible. The company's 3,500 employees rattle around in enough space for 6,600. I walked past expanses of empty desks in one building; another, next door, was completely uninhabited. A vacant lot waited nearby, presumably until someone invents a use of our data that will justify the expense of developing the space.

One potential use would be simply to sell insights mined from the information. DJ Patil, data scientist in residence with the venture capital firm Greylock Partners and previously leader of LinkedIn's data science team, believes Facebook could take inspiration from Gil Elbaz, the inventor of Google's AdSense ad business, which provides over a quarter of Google's revenue. He has moved on from advertising and now runs a fast-growing startup, Factual, that charges businesses to access large, carefully curated collections of data ranging from restaurant locations to celebrity body-mass indexes, which the company collects from free public sources and by buying private data sets. Factual cleans up data and makes the result available over the Internet as an on-demand knowledge store to be tapped by software, not humans. Customers use it to fill in the gaps in their own data and make smarter apps or services; for example, Facebook itself uses Factual for information about business locations. Patil points out that Facebook could become a data source in its own right, selling access to information compiled from the actions of its users. Such information, he says, could be the basis for almost any kind of business, such as online dating or charts of popular music. Assuming Facebook can take this step without upsetting users and regulators, it could be lucrative. An online store wishing to target its promotions, for example, could pay to use Facebook as a source of knowledge about which brands are most popular in which places, or how the popularity of certain products changes through the year.

Hammerbacher agrees that Facebook could sell its data science and points to its currently free Insights service for advertisers and website owners, which shows how their content is being shared on Facebook. That could become much more useful to businesses if Facebook added data obtained when its "Like" button tracks activity all over the Web, or demographic data or information about what people read on the site. There's precedent for offering such analytics for a fee: at the end of 2011 Google started charging $150,000 annually for a premium version of a service that analyzes a business's Web traffic.

Back at Facebook, Marlow isn't the one who makes decisions about what the company charges for, even if his work will shape them. Whatever happens, he says, the primary goal of his team is to support the well-being of the people who provide Facebook with their data, using it to make the service smarter. Along the way, he says, he and his colleagues will advance humanity's understanding of itself. That echoes Zuckerberg's often doubted but seemingly genuine belief that Facebook's job is to improve how the world communicates. Just don't ask yet exactly what that will entail. "It's hard to predict where we'll go, because we're at the very early stages of this science," says Marlow. "The number of potential things that we could ask of Facebook's data is enormous."

Critical Thinking

1. The article states that the manager in charge of mining all the personal data Facebook collects believes this will revolutionize the scientific understanding of why people behave as they do. Do you think this understanding will be a good or bad thing for the average Facebook user? For society in general? If we had a better understanding of why people behave as they do, what could we do with such knowledge?

2. Simonite writes, "Facebook might eventually be able to guess what people want or don't want even before they realize it." If so, how might this impact: Product marketing? Homeland security? Personal relationships?

3. Facebook was able to increase organ donations by a factor of 23 simply by permitting people to check a box saying they were organ donors and sharing that information with friends. Is Facebook's ability to manipulate behavior on this scale a good or bad thing? Why?

Create Central

www.mhhe.com/createcentral

Internet References

Could Facebook Get Squashed by a "Better Mousetrap?"
www.pbs.org/newshour/bb/business/jan-june12/makingsense_06-22.html

Me and My Data: How Much Do the Internet Giants Really Know?
www.theguardian.com/technology/2012/apr/22/
me-and-my-data-internet-giants

Malte Spitz: Your Phone Company Is Watching [TED Talk]
www.ted.com/talks/malte_spitz_your_phone_company_is_watching.html

When a Retailer Asks, 'Can I Have Your ZIP Code?' Just Say No
http://business.time.com/2013/07/11/when-retailer-asks-can-i-have-
your-zip-code-just-say-no/?iid=obinsite

Your TV Might Be Watching You
http://money.cnn.com/2013/08/01/technology/security/tv-hack/index.html

TOM SIMONITE is *Technology Review's* senior IT editor.

Article   Prepared by: Daniel Mittleman, *DePaul University*

Google's European Conundrum: When Does Privacy Mean Censorship?

Though Google is a U.S. company, its American rights don't transpose across the pond. A court case will determine whether Google has to comply with EU law, which could have far-reaching consequences for European users.

ZACK WHITTAKER

Learning Outcomes

After reading this article, you will be able to:

- Understand how data placed on the Internet is virally replicated in a manner that no one entity can control it, let alone erase it.

- Articulate how information available on the Internet impacts the trade-off of concerns between free speech rights and privacy rights.

- Know the risks of maintaining an online presence.

How Google and other American Internet companies operate in Europe could come down to a link that, depending on what side of the Atlantic Ocean you're on, should or should not be deleted.

A case heard Tuesday before the European Court of Justice (ECJ) hinges on a complaint submitted by a Spanish citizen who searched Google for his name and found a news article from several years earlier, saying his property would be auctioned because of failed payments to his social security contributions.

Spanish authorities argued that Google, other search engines, and other Web companies operating in Spain should remove information such as that if it is believed to be a breach of an individual's privacy. Google, however, believes that it should not have to delete search results from its index [http://www.reuters.com/article/2013/02/26/us-eu-googledataprotection-idUSBRE91P0A320130226] because the company didn't create it in the first place. Google argued that it is the publisher's responsibility and that its search engine is merely a channel for others' content.

The ECJ's advocate-general will publish its opinion on the case on June 25, with a judgment expected by the end of the year. The outcome of the hearing will affect not only Spain but also all of the 27 member states of the European Union.

In principle, this fight is about freedom of speech versus privacy, with a hearty dash of allegations of censorship mixed in. In reality, this could be one of the greatest changes to EU privacy rules in decades—by either strengthening the rules or negating them altogether.

The European view is simple: If you're at our party, you have to play by our rules. And in Europe, the "right to be forgotten" is an important one.

"Facebook and Google argue they are not subject to EU law as they are physically established outside the EU," a European Commission spokesperson told CNET. In new draft privacy law proposals, the message is, "as long as a company offers its goods or services to consumers on the EU territory, EU law must apply."

While Europe has some of the strongest data protection and privacy laws in the world, the U.S. doesn't. And while the U.S. has some of the strongest free speech and expression laws in the world, enshrined by a codified constitution, most European countries do not, instead favoring "fair speech" principles.

Google is also facing another legal twist: Spanish authorities are treating it like a media organization without offering it the full legal protection of one.

The European view is simple: If you're at our party, you have to play by our rules. And in Europe, the "right to be forgotten" is an important one.

Newspapers should be exempt from individual takedown requests to preserve freedom of speech, according to Spanish authorities, but Google should not enjoy the same liberties, despite having no editorial control and despite search results being determined by algorithms. Though Google is branded a "publisher" like newspapers, the search giant does not hold media-like protection from takedowns under the country's libel laws. This does not translate across all of Europe, however. Some European member states target newspapers directly and are held accountable through press regulatory authorities in a bid to balance freedom of speech and libel laws.

One of Spain's highest courts, the Agencia Espanola de Proteccion de Datos (AEPD), found in favor of the complainant in early 2011 and ruled that Google should delete the search result [http://online.wsj.com/article/SB1000142405274870339 6604576087573944344348.html]. This case is one of around 180 other ongoing cases in the country.

Google appealed the decision and the case was referred to the highest court in Europe, the ECJ, which will eventually determine if the search giant is the "controller" of the data or whether it is merely a host of the data.

The case will also decide on whether U.S.-based companies are subject to EU privacy law, which may mean EU citizens have to take their privacy cases to U.S. courts to determine whether Google is responsible for the damage caused by the "diffusion of personal information."

In a blog post on Tuesday [http://googlepolicyeurope .blogspot.com/2013/02/judging-freedom-of-expression-at .html], Bill Echikson, Google's "head of free expression," said the search giant "declined to comply" with a request by Spanish data protection authorities, as the search listing "includes factually correct information that is still publicly available on the newspaper's Web site."

"There are clear societal reasons why this kind of information should be publicly available. People shouldn't be prevented from learning that a politician was convicted of taking a bribe, or that a doctor was convicted of malpractice," Echikson noted.

"We believe the answer to that question is 'no'. Search engines point to information that is published online—and in this case to information that had to be made public, by law. In our view, only the original publisher can take the decision to remove such content. Once removed from the source webpage, content will disappear from a search engine's index."

EU's Latest Privacy Proposal: The "Right To Be Forgotten"

Should the ECJ find in favor of the Spanish complainant, it will see the biggest shakeup to EU privacy rules in close to two decades and would enable European citizens a "right to be forgotten."

In January 2011, the European Commission lifted the lid on draft proposals for a single one-size-fits-all privacy regulation for its 27 member states. One of the proposals was the "right to be forgotten," empowering every European resident the right to force Web companies as well as offline firms to delete or remove their data [http://www.cnet.com/8301-1009_3-57363585-83/new-eu-dataprotection-rules-due-this-week/] to preserve their privacy.

For Europeans, privacy is a fundamental right to all residents, according to Article 8 of the European Convention of Human Rights, in which it states [http://www.hri.org/docs/ECHR50 .html#C.Art8]: "Everyone has the right to respect for his private and family life, his home and his correspondence." It does however add a crucial exception. "There shall be no interference by a public authority with the exercise of this right except . . . for the protection of the rights and freedoms of others."

Because U.S.-based technology giants like Google, Facebook, and Twitter have users and in many cases a physical presence in Europe, they must comply with local laws. The "right to be forgotten" would force Facebook and Twitter to remove any data it had on you, as well as Google removing results from its search engine. It would also extraterritorially affect users worldwide outside the European Union who would also be unable to search for those removed search terms.

Such Web companies have said (and lobbied to that effect) [http://www.telegraph.co.uk/technology/news/9070019/EU-Privacy-regulations-subject-to-unprecedented-lobbying.html] that the "right to be forgotten" should not allow data to be removed or manipulated at the expense of freedom of speech. This, however, does not stop with republished material and other indexed content, and most certainly does not apply to European law enforcement and intelligence agencies.

Two Continents, Separated by "Free" and "Fair Speech"

The U.S. and the EU have never seen eye-to-eye on data protection and privacy. For Americans and U.S.-based companies, the belief is that crossover between freedom of speech and privacy overlaps in "a form of censorship," according to Google's lawyers [http://www.bbc.co.uk/news/technology-12239674] speaking during the Spanish court case.

In the U.S., you can freely say the most appalling words, so long as they don't lead to a crime or violence against a person or a group of people. In European countries such as the U.K. words can lead to instant arrest. Europe's laws allow for "fair speech" in order to prevent harassment, fear of violence, or even alarm and distress. It's a dance between the American tradition of protecting the individual and the European tradition of protecting society.

Google is fundamentally so very American in this regard. That said, Google already filters and censors its own search results at the behest of governments and private industry, albeit openly and transparently [http://www.google.com/ transparencyreport/]. Google will agree to delete links that violate copyrights under the Digital Millennium Copyright Act, which seeks to remove content from Google's search results that may facilitate copyright infringement.

Google also complies, when forced by a court, with numerous types of government requests, not limited to subpoenas, search warrants, and National Security Letters [http://www .zdnet.com/what-google-does-when-a-government-requests-your-data-7000010418/], or so-called 'gagging orders'. It also discloses those requests and when it complies with them. And it's a system not that dissimilar to what it's being asked to do in Europe.

Whose Jurisdiction Is Google Under: U.S., EU, or Both?

While Europe's privacy principles apply to the Web, it's unclear whether they apply to data "controllers" established outside of the European Union. But several European court cases have sided with local law. A German court found that Facebook fell under Irish law [http://www.bloomberg.com/news/2013-02-15/facebook-scores-win-in-legal-regime-dispute-with-germany.html] because the social networking company had a physical presence in Ireland, another EU member state. In Google's case, Spanish authorities are making a similar argument, claiming that Google is processing data in a European state and therefore EU law should apply.

Many American companies have voiced their objections to the proposed EU privacy law [http://www.zdnet.com/blog/london/european-draft-data-law-announced-what-you-need-to-know/2609], including Amazon, eBay, and Yahoo, according to a lobbying watchdog [http://www.lobbyplag.eu/#/compare/overview]. It could still take a year or two for the law to be ratified.

"Exempting non-EU companies from our data protection regulation is not on the table. It would mean applying double standards," said Europe's Justice Commissioner Viviane Reding, the top politician in Europe on data protection and privacy rules in the region, in an interview with the *Financial Times of London* [http://www.ft.com/intl/cms/s/0/903b3302-7398-11e2-bcbd-00144feabdc0.html#axzz2MCRmwDfo].

The new EU Data Protection Regulation, proposed by the European Commission and currently being debated in the European Parliament, will likely be voted on by June.

But this fight isn't as much about censorship as one might think. It's about a cultural difference between two continents and perspectives on what freedom of speech can and should be. It's also about privacy, and whether privacy or free speech is more important.

Critical Thinking

1. Explain why it is so difficult to completely remove information placed on the Internet.
2. Assuming it were technologically feasible to completely remove information from the Internet, should a public figure be permitted to selectively remove information from the Internet about himself or herself? Should a private person be permitted to do so? Should someone under 18 be permitted to do so? What about someone who had embarrassing information posted with their consent?
3. Should a potential employer be permitted to sift through old Internet information when making an employment decision? Should an existing employer be permitted to look and potentially terminate an employee? Should a potential spouse be able to look? Should a potential first date? If your answers are split between yes and no, what general policy should guide when a historical search is appropriate and when it is not?

Create Central

www.mhhe.com/createcentral

Internet References

California "Eraser Law" Lets Minors Remove Embarrassing Online Content
www.pbs.org/newshour/rundown/2013/09/california-eraser-law-lets-minors-remove-embarrassing-online-content.html

EU Report: The "Right To Be Forgotten" Is Technically Impossible . . . So Let's Do It Anyway
www.techdirt.com/articles/20121205/08425221239/eu-report-right-to-be-forgotten-is-technically-impossible-so-lets-do-it-anyway.shtml

Juan Enriquez: Your Online Life, Permanent as a Tattoo [TED Talk]
www.ted.com/talks/juan_enriquez_how_to_think_about_digital_tattoos.html

Reputation 3.0: The Internet Is Your Resume
www.forbes.com/sites/dorieclark/2013/07/19/reputation-3-0-the-internet-is-your-resume

Survey: One-Third of Youths Engage in Sexting
www.wired.com/threatlevel/2009/12/sexting-survey

Temporary Social Media
www.technologyreview.com/featuredstory/513731/temporary-social-media

---

ZACK WHITTAKER writes for ZDNet, CNET and CBS News. He is based in New York City.

Article

Prepared by: Daniel Mittleman, *DePaul University*

New Document Sheds Light on Government's Ability to Search iPhones

CHRIS SOGHOIAN AND NAOMI GILENS

Learning Outcomes

After reading this article, you will be able to:

- Understand how much personal information is embedded in the storage area of one's communcation and computing device.

- Recognize the tools that governments (and others) have to quickly and easily access information from communication devices.

- Recognize that U.S. Constitutional rights are limited at border crossings.

Cell phone searches are a common law enforcement tool, but up until now, the public has largely been in the dark regarding how much sensitive information the government can get with this invasive surveillance technique. A document submitted to court in connection with a drug investigation, which we recently discovered, provides a rare inventory of the types of data that federal agents are able to obtain from a seized iPhone using advanced forensic analysis tools. The list starkly demonstrates just how invasive cell phone searches are—and why law enforcement should be required to obtain a warrant before conducting them.

Last fall, officers from Immigration and Customs Enforcement (ICE) seized an iPhone from the bedroom of a suspect in a drug investigation. In a single data extraction session, ICE collected a huge array of personal data from the phone. Among other information, ICE obtained:

- call activity
- phone book directory information
- stored voicemails and text messages
- photos and videos
- apps
- eight different passwords
- 659 geolocation points, including 227 cell towers and 403 WiFi networks with which the cell phone had previously connected.

Before the age of smartphones, it was impossible for police to gather this much private information about a person's communications, historical movements, and private life during an arrest. Our pockets and bags simply aren't big enough to carry paper records revealing that much data. We would have never carried around several years' worth of correspondence, for example—but today, five-year-old emails are just a few clicks away using the smartphone in your pocket. The fact that we now carry this much private, sensitive information around with us means that the government is able to get this information, too.

The type of data stored on a smartphone can paint a near-complete picture of even the most private details of someone's personal life. Call history, voicemails, text messages and photographs can provide a catalogue of how—and with whom—a person spends his or her time, exposing everything from intimate photographs to 2 AM text messages. Web browsing history may include Google searches for Alcoholics Anonymous or local gay bars. Apps can expose what you're reading and listening to. Location information might uncover a visit to an abortion clinic, a political protest, or a psychiatrist.

In this particular case, ICE obtained a warrant to search the house, and seized the iPhone during that search. They then obtained a second, separate warrant based on probable cause before conducting a detailed search of the phone. However, even though ICE obtained a warrant for this cell phone search, courts are divided about whether a warrant is necessary in these circumstances, and no statute requires one. As a result, there are many circumstances where police contend they do not need a warrant at all, such as searches incident to arrest and at the U.S. border.

The police should not be free to copy the contents of your phone without a warrant absent extraordinary circumstances. However, that is exactly what is happening. Last year in California, for example, Governor Jerry Brown vetoed a common-sense bill that would have required the police to obtain a warrant before searching seized phones, despite the bill's broad bipartisan support in the state legislature.

Intrusive cell phone searches are becoming ever easier for law enforcement officers to conduct. Companies such as Cellebrite produce portable forensics machines that can download copies of an iPhone's "existing, hidden, and deleted phone data, including call history, text messages, contacts, images, and geotags" in minutes. This type of equipment, which allows the government to conduct quick, easy phone searches, is widely available to law enforcement agencies—and not just to federal agents.

While the law does not sufficiently protect the private data on smartphones, technology can at least provide some protection. All modern smartphones can be locked with a PIN or password, which can slow down, or in some cases, completely thwart forensic analysis by the police (as well as a phone thief or a prying partner). Make sure to pick a sufficiently long password: a 4 character numeric PIN can be cracked in a few minutes, and the pattern-based unlock screen offered by Android can be bypassed by Google if forced to by the government. Finally, if your mobile operating system offers a disk encryption option (such as with Android 4.0 and above), it is important to turn it on.

Critical Thinking

1. Read the *New York Times* and *The Atlantic Wire* web links at the end of this article about U.S. government searches at border crossings. Why do you think the government is granted more leeway at the border than Fourth Amendment protections against unwarranted search and seizure normally provide? Do you think this extra leeway is appropriate? Why?

2. Describe the difference between data and metadata in terms of the information stored on your cellphone. How can meta-data be used to build a profile of the owner of a cell phone?

Create Central

www.mhhe.com/createcentral

Internet References

The Border Is a Back Door for U.S. Device Searches
www.nytimes.com/2013/09/10/business/the-border-is-a-back-door-for-us-device-searches.html?pagewanted=all

Documents Reveal NSA Can Crack Online Encryption, "Last Bastion of Privacy"
www.pbs.org/newshour/bb/government_programs/july-dec13/surveillance_09-06.html

4 Things You Should Know About Metadata, Hackers and Privacy That Edward Snowden Would Never Tell You
www.forbes.com/sites/gregsatell/2013/08/03/4-things-you-should-know-about-metadata-hackers-and-privacy-that-edward-snowden-would-never-tell-you

Here's How Phone Metadata Can Reveal Your Affairs, Abortions, and Other Secrets
www.washingtonpost.com/blogs/the-switch/wp/2013/08/27/heres-how-phone-metadata-can-reveal-your-affairs-abortions-and-other-secrets

When It's at the Border, Your Data Is Fair Game—Even on Your Laptop
www.theatlanticwire.com/politics/2013/09/how-us-government-uses-border-crossing-avoid-privacy-restrictions/69251

Unit 4

UNIT

Prepared by: Daniel Mittleman, *DePaul University*

Personal Security

Security is the yang to privacy's yin. And our online security today is under siege. Global cybercrime is likely costing victims something over $100 billion a year.[1] And in 2013, cybercrime accounts for only about 53 percent of the known attacks on computer networks, with political hacktivism accounting for 37 percent, and a combination of cyber warfare and cyber espionage accounting for the final 10 percent.[2]

Our security is at risk from cybercrime because the economic, social, and civic fabric of our lives has moved to the virtual and become more tightly coupled with these networks and data repositories. Our modern Internet-based society is dominated by several types of complementary networks and data repositories, many of them coexisting on the Internet. Among those data repositories are the vast collections of information held by Google, Apple, Facebook, LinkedIn, Amazon, eBay, and others about our personal surfing, posting, and shopping habits. Also potentially accessible out there in more secured spaces are our credit card and banking information, our credit histories, our medical histories, and government data such as property holdings, license and registration data, criminal and traffic history, and voter registration records. The rare exception among us who has largely stayed offline is impacted nevertheless by institutional data placed online outside of that person's control. Therefore, it is reasonable to conclude that all of us run the risk of getting hurt.

Beyond our personal data that is stored on the Internet cloud are institutional and public data. The aforementioned medical, insurance, and credit information is held for the most part by private companies doing the best job they can (we hope) to successfully steward our data. Further, many banks, retail stores, and other institutions employ networked security cameras to track the comings and goings of their patrons. Beyond that are the police and criminal databases often referred to during cop shows on TV. And there exist databases and active networks used to manage civic security cameras, and public works such as water and power distribution. And our national security infrastructure makes use of networks (sometimes, but not always, separate and more secure than the Internet) to undertake their mission. This includes, but is not limited to, work by Homeland Security departments, the military, and the various government spy agencies.

None of these networks is one hundred percent secure. Many, likely most, of these networks are under regular attack—though security protocols automatically block the common and more amateur attacks. There have been multiple reports of late, however, of more skilled and determined attacks on our public networks from groups within China and, perhaps, Iran.[3,4,5]

The U.S. security forces as well, apparently, have been engaged in cyber attacks of their own. Many will remember the Stuxnet virus, thought to target Iran's nuclear weapons program. One report notes that Iran replaced about 1,000 centrifuges in late 2009 or early 2010, perhaps as a result of the attack. As it happens, our "electrical power grid is easier to break into than any nuclear enrichment facility."

With the realization in 2013 that the U.S. government has been collecting domestic telephone and Internet data, concern has focused on the potential vulnerability to everyday Americans from the government holding this information. But large Internet and communication companies possess as much—perhaps more—information about our online activities. And many of these companies, due to license agreements we agree to, maintain rights to make use of this data in a variety of ways. Google's vast database of our web browsing and related history contains far more detailed personal interests and behaviors than any government could know.[6] And Facebook is aiming to capture every one of everyone's relationships with objects, organizations, and each other.[7] What are the implications of having such personal and complete information about almost all of us sitting in corporate databases?

What is a reasonable person to make of all of this? We can communicate with almost anyone almost anywhere on the planet at almost no cost. The wealth of the world is available on Amazon or eBay for those with credit cards. Google, Wikipedia, and an ocean of other sites provide information in abundance and at a speed that would have seemed like science fiction a generation ago. Yet thieves get hold of digitally stored personal information. Our digital records are disintegrating even as we digitize more and more of them. The government compiles massive databases about terrorism and catches the innocent in its nets. Disruption of the global communications network could be catastrophic, as financial markets and global supply chains collapse. And one, if not several, governments are sabotaging nuclear centrifuges of their enemies. One strives for the equanimity of Neil Postman: "Technology giveth and technology taketh away."

Notes

1. See: http://cacm.acm.org/magazines/2013/3/161196-cybercrime-its-serious-but-exactly-how-serious/fulltext, and http://www.mcafee.com/us/resources/reports/rp-economic-impact-cybercrime.pdf

2. See: http://hackmageddon.com/category/security/cyber-attacks-statistics

3. S. Gorman, J. Barnes, 'Iran Blamed for Cyberattacks,' *Wall Street Journal,* October 13, 2012.

4. E. Nakashima, 'China Testing Cyber-attack Capabilities, Report Says,' *Washington Post,* March 7, 2012.

5. J. Winter, J. Kaplan, 'Washington Confirms Chinese Hack Attack on White House Computer,' FoxNews.com (accessed 10/13/12 at http://www.foxnews.com/tech/2012/10/01/washington-confirms-chinese-hack-attack-on-white-house-computer/#ixzz29D5gQjKp)

6. James Gleick, 'How Google Dominates Us,' *The New York Review of Books,* August 13, 2011.

7. Tom Simonite, "What Facebook Knows," *Technology Review,* July/August 2012.

Article   Prepared by: Daniel Mittleman, *DePaul University*

Hacking the Lights Out

Computer viruses have taken out hardened industrial control systems. The electrical power grid may be next.

Every facet of the modern electrical grid is controlled by computers. It is our greatest example of physical infrastructure interlinked with electronics.

The Stuxnet virus that infected Iran's nuclear program showed just how vulnerable machines could be to a well-crafted electronic virus. The grid shares many of the vulnerabilities that Stuxnet exposed; being larger, its vulnerabilities are, if anything, more numerous. Although a sophisticated attack could bring down a large chunk of the U.S. electrical grid, security is being ramped up.

DAVID M. NICOL

Learning Outcomes

After reading this article, you will be able to:

- Articulate what the concepts of cyber espionage and cyber warfare are.

- Understand the risks of and consequences from, a cyber attack on American infrastructure such as a utility plant or water treatment facility.

Last year word broke of a computer virus that had managed to slip into Iran's highly secure nuclear enrichment facilities. Most viruses multiply without prejudice, but the Stuxnet virus had a specific target in its sights—one that is not connected to the Internet. Stuxnet was planted on a USB stick that was handed to an unsuspecting technician, who plugged it into a computer at a secure facility. Once inside, the virus spread silently for months, searching for a computer that was connected to a prosaic piece of machinery: a programmable logic controller, a special-purpose collection of microelectronics that commonly controls the cogs of industry—valves, gears, motors and switches. When Stuxnet identified its prey, it slipped in, unnoticed, and seized control.

The targeted controllers were attached to the centrifuges at the heart of Iran's nuclear ambitions. Thousands of these centrifuges are needed to process uranium ore into the highly enriched uranium needed to create a nuclear weapon. Under normal operating conditions, the centrifuges spin so fast that their outer edges travel just below the speed of sound. Stuxnet bumped this speed up to nearly 1,000 miles per hour, past the point where the rotor would likely fly apart, according to a December report by

the Institute for Science and International Security. At the same time, Stuxnet sent false signals to control systems indicating that everything was normal. Although the total extent of the damage to Iran's nuclear program remains unclear, the report notes that Iran had to replace about 1,000 centrifuges at its Natanz enrichment facility in late 2009 or early 2010.

Stuxnet demonstrates the extent to which common industrial machines are vulnerable to the threat of electronic attack. The virus targeted and destroyed supposedly secure equipment while evading detection for months. It provides a dispiriting blueprint for how a rogue state or terrorist group might use similar technology against critical civilian infrastructure anywhere in the world.

Unfortunately, the electrical power grid is easier to break into than any nuclear enrichment facility. We may think of the grid as one gigantic circuit, but in truth the grid is made from thousands of components hundreds of miles apart acting in unerring coordination. The supply of power flowing into the grid must rise and fall in lockstep with demand. Generators must dole their energy out in precise coordination with the 60-cycle-per-second beat that the rest of the grid dances to. And while the failure of any single component will have limited repercussions to this vast circuit, a coordinated cyberattack on multiple points in the grid could damage equipment so extensively that our nation's ability to generate and deliver power would be severely compromised for weeks—perhaps even months.

Considering the size and complexity of the grid, a coordinated attack would probably require significant time and effort to mount. Stuxnet was perhaps the most advanced computer virus ever seen, leading to speculation that it was the work of either the Israeli or U.S. intelligence agencies—or both. But Stuxnet's code is now available on the Internet, raising the chance that a rogue group could customize it for an attack on a new target. A less technologically sophisticated group such as al Qaeda probably does not have the expertise to inflict significant damage to the grid at the moment, but black hat hackers for hire in China or the former Soviet Union might. It is beyond time we secured the country's power supply.

The Break-In

A year ago I took part in a test exercise that centered on a fictitious cyberattack on the grid. Participants included representatives from utility companies, U.S. government agencies and the military. (Military bases rely on power from the commercial grid, a fact that has not escaped the Pentagon's notice.) In the test scenario, malicious agents hacked into a number of transmission substations, knocking out the specialized and expensive devices that ensure voltage stays constant as electricity flows across long high-power transmission lines. By the end of the exercise half a dozen devices had been destroyed, depriving power to an entire Western state for several weeks.

Computers control the grid's mechanical devices at every level, from massive generators fed by fossil fuels or uranium all the way down to the transmission lines on your street. Most of these computers use common operating systems such as Windows and Linux, which makes them as vulnerable to malware as your desktop PC is. Attack code such as Stuxnet is successful for three main reasons: these operating systems implicitly trust running software to be legitimate; they often have flaws that admit penetration by a rogue program; and industrial settings often do not allow for the use of readily available defenses.

Even knowing all this, the average control system engineer would have once dismissed out of hand the possibility of remotely launched malware getting close to critical controllers, arguing that the system is not directly connected to the Internet. Then Stuxnet showed that control networks with no permanent

connection to anything else are still vulnerable. Malware can piggyback on a USB stick that technicians plug into the control system, for example. When it comes to critical electronic circuits, even the smallest back door can let an enterprising burglar in.

Consider the case of a transmission substation, a waypoint on electricity's journey from power plant to your home. Substations take in high-voltage electricity coming from one or more power plants, reduce the voltage and split the power into multiple output lines for local distribution. A circuit breaker guards each of these lines, standing ready to cut power in case of a fault. When one output line's breaker trips, all of the power it would have carried flows to the remaining lines. It is not hard to see that if all the lines are carrying power close to their capacity, then a cyberattack that trips out half of the output lines and keeps the remaining ones in the circuit may overload them.

These circuit breakers have historically been controlled by devices connected to telephone modems so that technicians can dial in. It is not difficult to find those numbers; hackers invented programs 30 years ago to dial up all phone numbers within an exchange and make note of the ones to which modems respond. Modems in substations often have a unique message in their dial-up response that reveals their function. Coupled with weak means of authentication (such as well-known passwords or no passwords at all), an attacker can use these modems to break into a substation's network. From there it may be possible to change device configurations so that a danger condition that would otherwise open a circuit breaker to protect equipment gets ignored.

New systems are not necessarily more secure than modems. Increasingly, new devices deployed in substations may communicate with one another via low-powered radio, which does not stop at the boundaries of the substation. An attacker can reach the network simply by hiding in nearby bushes with his computer. Encrypted Wi-Fi networks are more secure, but a sophisticated attacker can still crack their encryption using readily available software tools. From here he can execute

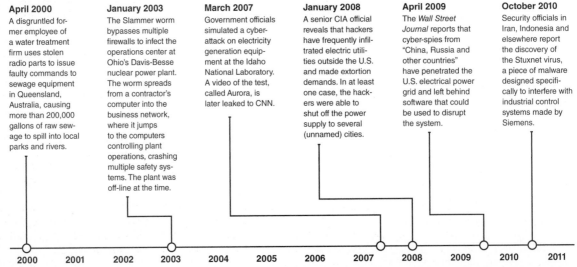

Digital Attacks, Physical Harm   As industrial machinery goes online, the potential for wreaking havoc grows. Intrusions over the past decade show that the grid is not the only vulnerability—anything with a microchip can be a target.

April 2000
A disgruntled former employee of a water treatment firm uses stolen radio parts to issue faulty commands to sewage equipment in Queensland, Australia, causing more than 200,000 gallons of raw sewage to spill into local parks and rivers.

January 2003
The Slammer worm bypasses multiple firewalls to infect the operations center at Ohio's Davis-Besse nuclear power plant. The worm spreads from a contractor's computer into the business network, where it jumps to the computers controlling plant operations, crashing multiple safety systems. The plant was off-line at the time.

March 2007
Government officials simulated a cyberattack on electricity generation equipment at the Idaho National Laboratory. A video of the test, called Aurora, is later leaked to CNN.

January 2008
A senior CIA official reveals that hackers have frequently infiltrated electric utilities outside the U.S. and made extortion demands. In at least one case, the hackers were able to shut off the power supply to several (unnamed) cities.

April 2009
The *Wall Street Journal* reports that cyber-spies from "China, Russia and other countries" have penetrated the U.S. electrical power grid and left behind software that could be used to disrupt the system.

October 2010
Security officials in Iran, Indonesia and elsewhere report the discovery of the Stuxnet virus, a piece of malware designed specifically to interfere with industrial control systems made by Siemens.

2000 2001 2002 2003 2004 2005 2006 2007 2008 2009 2010 2011

a man-in-the-middle attack that causes all communication between two legitimate devices to pass through his computer or fool other devices into accepting his computer as legitimate. He can craft malicious control messages that hijack the circuit breakers—tripping a carefully chosen few to overload the other lines perhaps or making sure they do not trip in an emergency.

Once an intruder or malware sneaks in through the back door, its first step is usually to spread as widely as possible. Stuxnet again illustrates some of the well-known strategies. It proliferated by using an operating system mechanism called autoexec. Windows computers read and execute the file named AUTO-EXEC.BAT every time a new user logs in. Typically the program locates printer drivers, runs a virus scan or performs other basic functions. Yet Windows assumes that any program with the right name is trusted code. Hackers thus find ways to alter the AUTOEXEC.BAT file so that it runs the attackers' code.

Attackers can also use clever methods that exploit the economics of the power industry. Because of deregulation, competing utilities share responsibility for grid operation. Power is generated, transmitted and distributed under contracts obtained in online auctions. These markets operate at multiple timescales—one market might trade energy for immediate delivery and another for tomorrow's needs. A utility's business unit must have a constant flow of real-time information from its operations unit to make smart trades. (And vice versa: operations need to know how much power they need to produce to fulfill the business unit's orders.) Here the vulnerability lies. An enterprising hacker might break into the business network, ferret out user names and passwords, and use these stolen identities to access the operations network.

Other attacks might spread by exploiting the small programs called scripts that come embedded in files. These scripts are ubiquitous—PDF files routinely contain scripts that aid in file display, for example—but they are also a potential danger. One computer security company recently estimated that more than 60 percent of all targeted attacks use scripts buried in PDF files. Simply reading a corrupted file may admit an attacker onto your computer.

Consider the hypothetical case where a would-be grid attacker first penetrates the Website of a software vendor and replaces an online manual with a malicious one that appears exactly like the first. The cyberattacker then sends an engineer at the power plant a forged e-mail that tricks the engineer into fetching and opening the booby-trapped manual. Just by going online to download an updated software manual, the unwitting engineer opens his power plant's gates to the Trojan horse. Once inside, the attack begins.

Search and Destroy

An intruder on a control network can issue commands with potentially devastating results. In 2007 the Department of Homeland Security staged a cyberattack code-named Aurora at the Idaho National laboratory. During the exercise, a researcher posing as a malicious hacker burrowed his way into a network connected to a medium-size power generator. Like all generators, it creates alternating current operating at almost exactly 60 cycles per second. In every cycle, the flow of electrons starts out moving in one direction, reverses course, and then returns

to its original state. The generator has to be moving electrons in exactly the same direction at exactly the same time as the rest of the grid.

During the Aurora attack, our hacker issued a rapid succession of on/off commands to the circuit breakers of a test generator at the laboratory. This pushed it out of sync with the power grid's own oscillations. The grid pulled one way, the generator another. In effect, the generator's mechanical inertia fought the grid's electrical inertia. The generator lost. Declassified video shows the hulking steel machine shuddering as though a train hit the building. Seconds later steam and smoke fill the room.

Industrial systems can also fail when they are pushed beyond their limits—when centrifuges spin too fast, they disintegrate. Similarly, an attacker could make an electric generator produce a surge of power that exceeds the limit of what the transmission lines can carry. Excess power would then have to escape as heat. Enough excess over a long enough period causes the line to sag and eventually to melt. If the sagging line comes into contact with anything—a tree, a billboard, a house—it could create a massive short circuit.

Protection relays typically prevent these shorts, but a cyberattack could interfere with the working of the relays, which means damage would be done. Furthermore, a cyberattack could also alter the information going to the control station, keeping operators from knowing that anything is amiss. We have all seen the movies where crooks send a false video feed to a guard.

Control stations are also vulnerable to attack. These are command and control rooms with huge displays, like the war room in *Dr. Strangelove*. Control station operators use the displays to monitor data gathered from the substations, then issue commands to change substation control settings. Often these stations are responsible for monitoring hundreds of substations spread over a good part of a state.

Data communications between the control station and substations use specialized protocols that themselves may have vulnerabilities. If an intruder succeeds in launching a man-in-the-middle attack, that individual can insert a message into an exchange (or corrupt an existing message) that causes one or both of the computers at either end to fail. An attacker can also try just injecting a properly formatted message that is out of context—a digital non sequitur that crashes the machine.

Attackers could also simply attempt to delay messages traveling between control stations and the substations. Ordinarily the lag time between a substation's measurement of electricity flow and the control station's use of the data to adjust flows is small—otherwise it would be like driving a car and seeing only where you were 10 seconds ago. (This kind of lack of situational awareness was a contributor to the Northeast Blackout of 2003.)

Many of these attacks do not require fancy software such as Stuxnet but merely the standard hacker's tool kit. For instance, hackers frequently take command over networks of thousands or even millions of ordinary PCs (a botnet), which they then instruct to do their bidding. The simplest type of botnet attack is to flood an ordinary Website with bogus messages, blocking or slowing the ordinary flow of information. These "denial of service" attacks could also be used to slow traffic moving between the control station and substations.

Botnets could also take root in the substation computers themselves. At one point in 2009 the Conficker botnet had

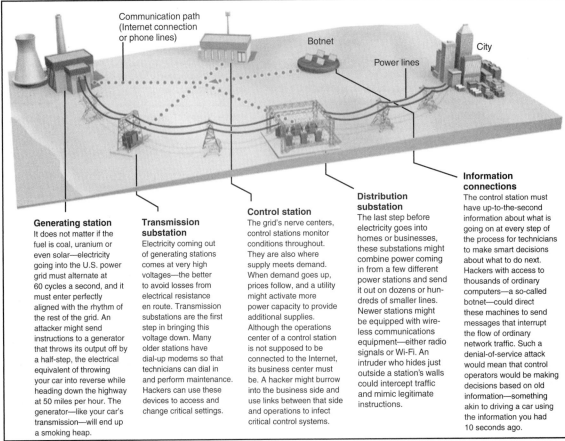

Communication path (Internet connection or phone lines)

Botnet

Power lines

City

Generating station
It does not matter if the fuel is coal, uranium or even solar—electricity going into the U.S. power grid must alternate at 60 cycles a second, and it must enter perfectly aligned with the rhythm of the rest of the grid. An attacker might send instructions to a generator that throws its output off by a half-step, the electrical equivalent of throwing your car into reverse while heading down the highway at 50 miles per hour. The generator—like your car's transmission—will end up a smoking heap.

Transmission substation
Electricity coming out of generating stations comes at very high voltages—the better to avoid losses from electrical resistance en route. Transmission substations are the first step in bringing this voltage down. Many older stations have dial-up modems so that technicians can dial in and perform maintenance. Hackers can use these devices to access and change critical settings.

Control station
The grid's nerve centers, control stations monitor conditions throughout. They are also where supply meets demand. When demand goes up, prices follow, and a utility might activate more power capacity to provide additional supplies. Although the operations center of a control station is not supposed to be connected to the Internet, its business center must be. A hacker might burrow into the business side and use links between that side and operations to infect critical control systems.

Distribution substation
The last step before electricity goes into homes or businesses, these substations might combine power coming in from a few different power stations and send it out on dozens or hundreds of smaller lines. Newer stations might be equipped with wireless communications equipment—either radio signals or Wi-Fi. An intruder who hides just outside a station's walls could intercept traffic and mimic legitimate instructions.

Information connections
The control station must have up-to-the-second information about what is going on at every step of the process for technicians to make smart decisions about what to do next. Hackers with access to thousands of ordinary computers—a so-called botnet—could direct these machines to send messages that interrupt the flow of ordinary network traffic. Such a denial-of-service attack would mean that control operators would be making decisions based on old information—something akin to driving a car using the information you had 10 seconds ago.

Holes in the Grid. The modern electrical grid involves an intricate balance between the amount of energy needed by society and the amount generated at power plants. Dozens of components orchestrate the flow of electrons over distances of hundreds of miles, aligning the alternating currents and making sure no single component gets stretched beyond its limits. Any one of these parts might suffer from the attention of malicious actors. Here are some of the most troublesome choke points and the ways they might be compromised.

Source: (Diagram © George Retseck)

insinuated itself into 10 million computers; the individuals, as yet unknown, who control it could have ordered it to erase the hard drives of every computer in the network, on command. A botnet such as Conficker could establish itself within substations and then have its controller direct them simultaneously to do anything at any time. According to a 2004 study by researchers at Pennsylvania State University and the National Renewable Energy Laboratory in Golden, Colo., an attack that incapacitated a carefully chosen minority of all transmission substations—about 2 percent, or 200 in total—would bring down 60 percent of the grid. Losing 8 percent would trigger a nationwide blackout.

What to Do

When microsoft learns of a potential security liability in its Windows software, it typically releases a software patch. Individual users and IT departments the world over download the patch, update their software and protect themselves from the threat. Unfortunately, things are not that simple on the grid.

Whereas the power grid uses the same type of off-the-shelf hardware and software as the rest of the world, IT managers at power stations cannot simply patch the faulty software when bugs crop up. Grid control systems cannot come down for three hours every week for maintenance; they have to run continuously. Grid operators also have a deep-rooted institutional conservatism. Control networks have been in place for a long time, and operators are familiar and comfortable with how they work. They tend to avoid anything that threatens availability or might interfere with ordinary operations.

In the face of a clear and present danger, the North American Electric Reliability Corporation (NERC), an umbrella body of grid operators, has devised a set of standards designed to protect critical infrastructure. Utilities are now required to identify their critical assets and demonstrate to NERC-appointed auditors that they can protect them from unauthorized access.

Yet security audits, like financial audits, cannot possibly be exhaustive. When an audit does go into technical details, it does so only selectively. Compliance is in the eye of the auditor.

The most common protection strategy is to employ an electronic security perimeter, a kind of cybersecurity Maginot line. The first line of defense is a firewall, a device through which all electronic messages pass. Each message has a header indicating where it came from, where it is going, and what protocol is used to interpret the message. Based on this information, the firewall allows some messages through and stops others. An auditor's job is partly to make sure the firewalls in a utility are configured properly so that they do not let any unwanted traffic in or out. Typically the auditors would identify a few critical assets, get a hold of the firewall configuration files, and attempt to sort through by hand the ways in which a hacker might be able to break through the firewall.

Firewalls, though, are so complex that it is difficult for an auditor to parse all the myriad possibilities. Automated software tools might help. Our team at the University of Illinois at Urbana-Champaign has developed the Network Access Policy Tool, which is just now being used by utilities and assessment teams. The software needs only a utility's firewall configuration files—it does not even have to connect to the network. Already it has found a number of unknown or long-forgotten pathways that attackers might have exploited.

The DOE has come out with a roadmap that lays out a strategy for enhancing grid security by 2015. (A revision due this year extends this deadline to 2020.) One focus: creating a system that recognizes an intrusion attempt and reacts to it automatically. That would block a Stuxnet-like virus as soon as it jumped from the USB stick. But how can an operating system know which programs are to be trusted?

One solution is to use a one-way hash function, a cryptographic technique. A hash function takes a fantastically huge number—for example, all the millions of 1s and 0s of a computer program, expressed as a number—and converts it to a much smaller number, which acts as a signature. Because programs are so large, it is highly unlikely that two different ones would result in the same signature value. Imagine that every program that wants to run on a system must first go through the hash function. Its signature then gets checked against a master list; if it does not check out, the attack stops there.

The DOE also recommends other security measures, such as physical security checks at operator workstations (think radio chips in identification badges). It also highlights the need to exert tighter control over communication between devices inside the network. The 2007 Aurora demonstration involved a rogue device tricking a generator's network into believing it was sending authoritative commands. These commands eventually led to the destruction of the generator.

These worthwhile steps will require time and money and effort. If we are going to achieve the DOE roadmap to a more secure grid in the next decade, we are going to have to pick up the pace. Let us hope we have even that much time.

References

Roadmap to Secure Control Systems in the Energy Sector. Jack Eisenhauer et al. Energetics Incorporated, January 2006. www.oe.energy.gov/csroadmap.htm

Security of Critical Control Systems Sparks Concern. David Geer in *IEEE Computer,* Vol. 39, No. 1, pages 20–23; January 2006.

Trustworthy Cyber Infrastructure for the Power Grid. Multiuniversity research project funded by the U.S. Department of Energy. www.tcipg.org

What Is the Electric Grid, and What Are Some Challenges It Faces? U.S. Department of Energy. www.eia.doe.gov/energy_in_brief/power_grid.cfm

Scientific American Online For an extended look at the history of electronic attacks on physical structures, visit ScientificAmerican.com/jul2011/lights-out

Critical Thinking

1. Use the Internet to research the Stuxnet virus. Who is thought to have been responsible for it?

2. The author mentions a type of cyber-attack known as at Trojan horse. Use the Internet to read about the Trojan horse attack. While you're at it, where was the first Trojan horse described?

3. The author uses the phrase "clear and present danger." Use the Internet to learn who first used it and in what context. Is the phrase being misused in the article?

4. Think about technology biting back. Is there a simpler solution to protecting the grid than those proposed? Again, use the Internet to do some research.

Create Central

www.mhhe.com/createcentral

Internet References

Avi Rubin: All Your devices Can Be Hacked [TED Talk] www.ted.com/talks/avi_rubin_all_your_devices_can_be_hacked.html

Examining Cyber Security with Homeland Security Secretary Janet Napolitano www.pbs.org/newshour/bb/science/jan-june13/cybersecurity_02-15.html

Want To Take Down a Web Site? This Service Will Do It for Just $10. www.washingtonpost.com/blogs/the-switch/wp/2013/08/26/want-to-take-down-a-web-site-this-service-will-do-it-for-just-10

DAVID M. NICOL is director of the Information Trust Institute and a professor in the department of electrical and computer engineering at the University of Illinois at Urbana-Champaign. He has worked as a consultant for the U.S. Department of Homeland Security and Department of Energy.

Article   Prepared by: Daniel Mittleman, *DePaul University*

A Beginner's Guide to Building Botnets—with Little Assembly Required

For a few hundred dollars, you can get tools and 24/7 support for Internet crime.

SEAN GALLAGHER

Learning Outcomes

After reading this article, you will be able to:

- Recognize that an entire market of low-cost and easy-to-access software and services exists.

- Understand the scope and scale of cybercrime in terms of both the types of crime there are and the size of attack that is possible.

Have a plan to steal millions from banks and their customers but can't write a line of code? Want to get rich quick off advertising click fraud but "quick" doesn't include time to learn how to do it? No problem. Everything you need to start a life of cybercrime is just a few clicks (and many more dollars) away.

Building successful malware is an expensive business. It involves putting together teams of developers, coordinating an army of fraudsters to convert ill-gotten gains to hard currency without pointing a digital arrow right back at you. So the biggest names in financial botnets—Zeus, Carberp, Citadel, and SpyEye, to name a few—have all at one point or another decided to shift gears from fraud rings to crimeware vendors, selling their wares to whoever can afford them.

In the process, these big botnet platforms have created a whole ecosystem of software and services in an underground market catering to criminals without the skills to build it themselves. As a result, the tools and techniques used by last years' big professional bank fraud operations, such as the "Operation High Roller" botnet that netted over $70 million last summer, are available off-the-shelf on the Internet. They even come with full technical support to help you get up and running.

The customers of these services often plan more for the short term than the long game played by the big cyber-crime rings. They have very different goals. Botnet infrastructures can be applied in lots of ways for different sorts of profit—cash,

information, or political gain. There are many ways to make money off botnets beyond outright theft, such as using them to steal advertising clicks, generate spam e-mails for a paying client, or renting out bots for denial-of-service attacks. And the same basic principles used to distribute botnets have been creeping up in more targeted attacks to steal intellectual property or to spread the malware used in the recent "wiper" attack on South Korean banks and broadcasters.

So how easy is it to get into the botnet business? Well, Ars decided to find out. Given the surprising availability of botnet building blocks online, I set out to build a shopping list to understand how everything is bought and sold within this black market. It all started with checking sources through a few Web searches then making trips into Web forums I dared visit only with a virtual machine and Google Translator's help. All I had to do was paste in "botnet" in Cyrillic, and I was on my way down the rabbit hole.

To assemble your list for some of the simplest get-rich-quick schemes, all you need is about $600, a little spare time, and no compunctions about breaking laws to make a profit. I didn't deploy an Ars-enal of botnet destruction in the end, but I absolutely could have. That may be the scariest lesson here.

It Looks Like You're Trying to Build a Botnet . . .

There are no personal shoppers to help walk you through the underground marketplaces to identify what fits a particular criminal scheme—though there may be plenty of people willing to give you paid advice on how to get started. With absolutely no budget for bitcoins, I got my start with some help from Max Goncharov, a security researcher for Trend Micro who specializes in following the Russian underground marketplaces for online fraud services. Goncharov came to Washington, DC in late March for a Trend Micro press briefing, and he laid out some of the basic things that go into a beginner fraudster's software and services shopping cart: botnets, malware-spreading tools, and hacking for hire. (Goncharov detailed some of these services in a paper published late last year and presented during this press road show.) Goncharov's suggested setup came with a $595 price tag for the first month of operations and a monthly cost of $225 to sustain the operation.

Of course, that price is for a particular type of botnet. It isn't representative of everything that's running wild on the Internet today. It also assumes total noob-hood. For those seeking to do something a little less overtly criminal than stealing credit card numbers or committing wire fraud, there are less expensive options. With a little sweat equity, you can pull off a workable botnet for a fraction of that price. If you're willing to try it without the benefits that come from paying professionals—like software updates, monitoring services, and 24/7 technical support—you can cut the cost back even further.

With my rough estimate in place, it was time to actually start some research of my own. Hello overseas VPN connection, Google Translator, and Google.ru—time for the underground hacker marketplace.

The Marketplace of (Bad) Ideas

The "underground" forums do more than just give would-be criminals access to a level of service that might make some enterprise software companies look bad. They also act as a sort of hiring hall for people with very specific skills (like hacking webmail accounts) or botnets of their own ready to do a paying customer's bidding. On these barely underground sites, hacker wares are made available to anyone willing to pay. Current versions of Zeus and SpyEye botnet software are for sale, or you can find the last version cracked by someone for cheap or free.

Many of the sites run under the thin veneer of "security" discussion boards. But they're often paid for by advertisements for the tools sought by a certain class of cyber-criminal: botnet-herders and the service provider ecosystem that has sprung up around them. These are largely the small and medium businesses of cybercrime, following a well-worn approach to making money. If you cast a big enough net, you're bound to catch some fish.

The botnet herders' standard business plan is to "use exploit kits, and then run a phishing campaign or some sort of campaign against massive numbers of people with hopes that someone is going to click on a link and get the exploit to drop a botnet or banking trojan onto their machine," said Nicholas J. Percoco, senior vice-president of Trustwave and head of the company's SpiderLabs penetration testing and security research team. "Once they've done that, it goes down the path of them monitoring them when they do banking transactions, or the botnet may be involved in spam or distributed denial of service attacks. Or maybe it's a sort of Swiss Army knife botnet that can do many different things depending on what that botnet herder decides, or what he makes it available to do for people who want to utilize his or her botnet."

No matter what the racket, Percoco told Ars, the equation for botnet herders is the same. "From a criminal's perspective, they're looking at massive numbers of attacks to achieve their financial goals."

They're also looking at massive turnover. When a piece of malware like a botnet lands on thousands of PCs, "it may hit the radar of an antivirus company pretty quickly," Percoco noted. That means time and money spent on finding new victims, deploying patches and updates, paying for new exploits, and generally continuing the game of "whack-a-mole" with antivirus companies and other organizations—as the mole.

Building a Botnet Shopping List

I did some additional research afterward to check Goncharov's math, and I also looked at some alternative approaches. The underground software market for hacking, fraud, and botnet tools has matured to the point where developers provide most of what you'd expect from legitimate software and online service providers—maybe even more. There's full support for the paid services, including 24/7 voice support in some cases, in a business where positive word of mouth in forums is the best (and often only) advertising. And there's no shortage of "consultants" to help you get started.

Botnet software itself is an important part of the whole equation, but it's only a fraction of first-month startup costs—and one that's fungible if you're willing to invest some of your own sweat equity in the setup (or dispense with the "legitimate" route and use a cracked version without software support). Just like any Internet business, launching a financial fraud botnet—or any kind of long-running botnet endeavor—requires a sustainable business plan. You need to know your target market, ensure distribution, keep your installed base a step ahead of the competition, and keep your business processes secure.

Here's a typical botnet-herder's startup shopping list:

A "Bulletproof" VPN

Before you start building a bot army of incredible magnitude, you need—just as with any other hacking endeavor of questionable legality—to hide yourself from prying eyes. That means using some sort of tool to avoid monitoring by your ISP, law enforcement, and other cybercriminals. Generally speaking, the best way is a virtual private network.

As confessed LulzSec member Cody Kretsinger found out, not all VPN providers are created equal. He used a service called HideMyAss.com, a VPN and proxy service run by UK-based Privax Ltd. Unfortunately, he didn't read the company's privacy and legal policies, and they gave up his logs when law enforcement came knocking. "Bulletproof" VPN services are ones that claim to be shielded from law enforcement requests because of their location or logging practices. Many of these services have disclaimers about "abuse" of the services, but the fact is that they take a number of anonymous forms of payment (CryptoVPN, for example, accepts Liberty Reserve, Bitcoin, and a number of other similar anonymous payment services). At worst, these services may just cancel your account if it attracts too much trouble.

A typical "bulletproof" VPN service, such as CryptoVPN runs about $25 a month. If you're thinking long-term, you can sign-up for $200 a year. However, it's best not to think long-term if you're botnet-herding; it may behoove you to change services every now and then to keep your profile low.

Budget Botnet Shopper's Price: $25/month.

A "Bulletproof" Host

Once you've got your network secured, you need some place to host your botnet's command and control network and all of the other assorted badness needed to launch a massive assault on the unsuspecting world. For those without the skills, time, or desire to simply go hack someone else's server every couple of weeks, that means buying a dedicated or virtual dedicated server from someone who doesn't care what you're doing—lest your botnet's nerve center be wiped during a security sweep or seized by law enforcement.

There are many kinds of "bulletproof" hosts catering to various kinds of customers. Most of them buy space in data centers around the world in places with either weak data privacy laws or plain disregard for what other countries' laws say. This provides a sort of insurance policy for their customers, Goncharov said. At a minimum, the data on the servers won't be given up to law enforcement.

Some are smaller hosting companies such as Hostim VSE, a Romanian hosting company with a Russian language website more targeted at protecting pornographers, pirates, and other targets of DMCA takedown requests. Hostim VSE publicly denounces botnetters and financial fraudsters to prevent attention from local law enforcement. It describes "bulletproof hosting" as "hosting resistant to complaints and other types of attacks on competitors. When placed on a standard website hosting, your site can receive complaints from competitors under the guise of copyright holders. In consequence of this, most other hosting providers disable your site until the circumstances [change]. We also review all such complaints, check its validity, conduct a site audit, demand [the accuser] to produce documents confirming the rights, and otherwise deal with all to settle the conflict, and only then disable the client's site."

All of this, the company says with a wink, takes a lot of time and human resources, and as a small company there may be some delays before it gets around to it. In other words, "don't worry—we're inefficient." Hostim VSE's dedicated servers start at $39/month with additional charges for more bandwidth. The company also, ironically, provides DDoS protection and other support services. But prices for its services will rise dramatically if you're attracting too much attention or using too much bandwidth.

For really hard-core criminal undertakings, there are the more specialized underground "bulletproof" hosting services that are run specifically for malware owners. These offer hosting at a significant markup in exchange for looking the other way. These operations generally don't maintain webpages. They advertise strictly in underground forums and do business over ICQ, Jabber, and other instant messaging.

Mihai Ionut Paunescu, the 28-year old Romanian behind underground host powerhost.ro, was caught in December by Romanian authorities. His servers were home to the Gozi financial malware command and control network. Paunescu kept tabs on exactly what sort of business his users were up to and charged accordingly. In some cases, the rates reached thousands per month, averaging better than a 100-percent margin on the servers he managed.

Of course, many of these hosting companies provide support (in some cases, 24-hour voice support via phone or Skype) and help with configuring Apache and MySQL on dedicated hosts for customers who are generally clueless about such things.

Budget Botnet Shopper's Price: $50/month, plus spot "consulting."

Bulletproof Domains and "Fast Flux"

In order for your bots to reach your host reliably, you need some domain names—fully qualified domain names that allow you to have full control over the domain name service (DNS). You'll want a bunch so you can avoid making yourself obvious in the DNS logs of networks that get infected.

You'll also want to register those domains with a registrar that's not going to roll on you and shut you down on the first complaint of abuse. You need someone who will shield your identity from the prying eyes of security firms and law enforcement. In other words, you want a bulletproof registrar. Preferably, it's one that accepts payments via Western Union or some other anonymous service.

Of course, it's never a bad idea to have some additional protection to make sure that you cover your trail completely by using a "fast flux" scheme. This hides your servers' true location by assigning the DNS addresses to a rapidly changing set of proxies. Fast flux providers will take your domains—or even register them for you—and then assign host names to a collection of their own bots. These in turn pass traffic between your bots and your server. By using a short "time to live" for the host "A" name records in the DNS server, fast flux systems create hundreds of potential communication paths for the bots.

Fast flux service is costly. An advertisement on one forum recently offered to support five DNS name servers for customers starting at $800. So for most starting botnet operations getting their feet wet, just registering a few domain names may be enough to begin with.

Budget Botnet Shopper's Price: $50 for five domains.

Your Choice of Botnet/C&C Platform

The current editions of botnet-building frameworks are sometimes sold by their developers for premium prices. Carberp was sold by its developers prior to their recent arrest for a whopping $40,000 as a kit, while the current Zeus toolkit sold for about $400 when it first hit the market. But the market pays what the market can bear, and most first-timers can find less expensive options that are easier to sustain.

Do-it-yourselfers who don't care about things like patches and full support can find "cracked" versions of some of these toolkits (or ways to disable their licensing code) for free.

There's also an option to pick up older but still supported versions on the aftermarket. Zeus' source code was released to the world last year, sort of turning it into "open source," so you can now purchase supported versions of it for $125, plus $15 per month for updates to the code and $25 for monthly 24/7 new customer support. That could include everything from helping a noob fix a misconfigured server to doing a whole walkthrough of configuring the PHP scripts and MySQL backends for the system over Skype. You could always just use one of those YouTube guides, though, and save some money.

Budget Botnet Shopper's Price: $125, plus $40/month for support.

Web Attack "Injector" Kits

The Zeus botnet's market dominance has created a whole additional ecosystem of software add-ons to make its bots do various things. A big part of that market is "injectors"—the add-on modules that tell the bot what to watch for in browser activity and what code to inject into the browser when it visits targeted websites.

There are financial botnet injectors that insert Web code into banking sites. These injectors try to grab your personal information to hijack your account, make wire transfer withdrawals, or even change the values presented in your online statement to conceal all of it.

Other types of injectors could be used for things like click-fraud—changing the links that users click on to direct them to different websites, while sending a referral code to a Web advertising provider to collect the pay-per-click. Some new botnets have been configured to simply generate clicks in the background on webpages without the computer user seeing them, creating ad revenue without the user scratching his head about why he ended up on a Russian porn site instead of the car insurance site he was trying to visit.

Beginners can buy injector packs for a set of banks through marketplaces and pay for direct support to help install, tune and customize them. In some cases, these require some server setup as well to properly harvest the data collected. It sounds complicated, but there are people happy to help you figure it all out for a small fee.

Budget Botnet Shopper's Price: $80, plus $8/month for support.

An Exploit Tool or Service

In order to take command of victims' PCs, a bot herder needs a reliable way of defeating the basic security provided by operating systems, browsers, and e-mail anti-virus scanners. That usually means relying on an "exploit pack" or some other crafted application exploit.

The modus operandi of most bot herders is to use Web links as the delivery method for their malware, sending out streams of spam to potential victims in the hope that someone will fall for their social engineering. One click leads to a webpage set up to drop a package of nastiness on them. There are ready-made exploit packs, loaded with code written specifically for the purpose of planting malware on victim's PCs that can be purchased and installed on a Web server or "rented" as a service.

Botnet builders can rent capacity on these services or outright buy them. A Phoenix exploit kit (like the one used to seed the recent Bamital botnet), can be purchased for $120, plus another $38 per month for patches and technical support, according to Goncharov. BlackHole, another market leader in exploits, offers its latest and greatest as a leased service for $50 a day, with extra fees for traffic overages. BlackHole also comes with an Oracle-like annual license for those who want to deploy on their own server. That costs $1,500 per year, with various add-on functionality fees.

Budget Botnet Shopper's Price: $120 for the kit, plus $38/month for support.

Crypters and Dropper Builders

The problem with just pushing a Zeus bot in its raw form out to targets through an exploit is that the Zeus bot is bound to be detected by antivirus software because of its signature. To prevent that, botnet-herders turn to "dropper" malware that disguises the bot trojan, delivering it in encrypted form to disguise the file signature of the trojan and its associated files.

Creating a "dropper" requires the services of a malware "crypter." Some are sold as straight software, with added services to see if the signatures of built droppers have been picked up by antivirus companies' databases. Others are sold purely as a service, with timer-based licenses, and may include the antivirus signature check as a built-in service.

There are even crypter services now available on the Web, delivered as a service. One such service offers dropper-building at the rate of $7 per "sample."

Another key to not getting caught is "antisandbox" code that detects if the malware has been dropped onto a sandboxed system or virtual machine—such as those used by digital forensics experts and security analysts. If the code detects that it's been deposited inside such a system, it can prevent the botnet trojan from being deployed and giving up the nature of the code it carries. Antisandbox code is a feature of some crypters.

If you want to save some money—and aren't particularly concerned about whether your bot gets picked up after a while by antivirus scans—there are sites offering "cracked" crypter kits for free.

Budget Botnet Shopper's Price: $20/month for crypter and accessory licenses.

Special Delivery: Spam and Social Engineering Services

But wait! You still have to deliver the exploit link to drop your botnet package on your unsuspecting (or possibly suspecting) victims. How do you get them to click on that link? The traditional route is by blasting semi-convincing spam messages and hoping people are dumb enough to click on a link in them to see a video, download a document, or reconfirm their PayPal information.

That typically means buying a spam blast, often from another botnet operator. Some spam-masters have moved their focus to social networks and charge not per message but per hit. You can spam out to social networks and over SMS with clickjack links using "borrowed" credentials or leave it to the professionals to do it for you for around a buck per thousand targets.

But that's the old-fashioned way. The new-fashioned way is to use "spear-phish" attacks that use social information about the target in some way that convinces them to click the link, either through a social network message in a compromised account or an e-mail that appears to be from a friend. If you want to make it even more convincing, you can always pay someone to hack a victim's e-mail address to get access to their account and contacts. Then it's as simple as posing as the victim to fool all their friends.

For beginners, spam remains the best bet. It can be used to hit a variety of potential targets and it's relatively cheap: cheap spamming services can run as little as $10 per 1 million e-mail addresses, with better services based on stolen customer databases running five to ten times as much.

Budget Botnet Shopper's Price: $50 for an initial blast to qualified addresses.

Economies of Scale

Using our budget shopper prices, that adds up to about $576 for the first month of operation.

None of these purchases guarantee success, obviously, and it could take multiple spam attempts and help from other specialists to finally establish that botnet you've dreamed of. Even then, the payoffs are not necessarily that big. There's a glut of botnets already out there and botnet herders may be up against a short window before detection.

On the upside, it's an easy game to buy into—unlike the bigger, more enterprise-scale cyber-crime rings behind big corporate data breaches. While the whales of the cybercrime game may share some of the basic technology approaches with their smaller cousins, they have more in common with the intellectual property stealing "Advanced Persistent Threat" (APT) hackers alleged to be associated with the Chinese military (though they may surpass them in skill). Trend Micro Chief Technology Officer Raimund Genes said during the DC briefing that he thought the recent alleged Chinese APT attacks had been uncovered largely because they lacked the finesse of Eastern European cybercrime rings.

The bigger financial hacking organizations—which are a small number of organizations of hundreds or perhaps even thousands of people—operate in their own closed forums, sometimes on "darknets," where you can only gain access by being invited. While there's some use of botnets by the major cyber-crime rings, they tend to want to protect their investments in the more specialized, targeted attack tools they use. Botnet use is sparse in that space. "Once they get access to the environment," Percoco said, "they then deploy custom pieces of malware that are sometimes written from scratch, brand new, never been utilized before—and they plant them on specific systems within the environment."

As a result, the data breaches caused by these targeted hacks can go on for months, even years before being detected.

A study released by Percoco's team at Trustwave in February found that the average targeted attack went more than 210 days before it was detected. And this detection was usually because of a customer complaint or notification by law enforcement or a payment processor, not because antivirus software detected the hack. At some companies, the hacks lasted more than three years without being detected, all while millions of credit card transactions and other data were being pumped back to the hackers.

Botnet operators generally go big or go home in their attacks. But the tools they use can just as easily be applied to the long game if they're used in a targeted fashion and they apply some of the lessons learned by the big-time hacking organizations. "Swiss Army knife" botnets and remote administration tools can be used as part of a poor man's APT by those who are willing to take the time to do the research and social engineering to get their malware in the right place. And just because Zeus and other botnets are a known threat doesn't mean they can't be used in stealth. According to the site ZeusTracker, the average detection rate for Zeus binaries by antivirus software is only 38 percent. And that's for **known** Zeus botnets.

So take heart, would-be botnetter. With the market saturated with tools, a community of several thousand known botnet operators, and new ways to profit emerging every day, your first botnet could bear a return on investment hundreds of times larger than what you put in. You don't need to know the first thing about coding. Though a lack of morality wouldn't hurt either.

Critical Thinking

1. Given the editors of this reader (or of Ars Technica) are not training hackers, why do you think this article was written and why does it appear in this reader? What are the principal lessons a non-hacker should take away from this article?
2. If there is a known online marketplace for cybercrime software and services, why do you think it is that the authorities simply don't shut it down?

Create Central

www.mhhe.com/createcentral

Internet References

The Geeks at the Frontlines
www.rollingstone.com/feature/the-geeks-on-the-frontlines#i.14fl1oq1e28f09

James Lyne: Everyday Cybercrime—and What You Can Do about It [TED Talk]
www.ted.com/talks/james_lyne_everyday_cybercrime_and_what_you_can_do_about_it.html

Rise of Domestic Drones Draws Questions about Privacy, Limiting Use
www.pbs.org/newshour/bb/science/jan-june13/drones_04-18.html

Shodan: The Scariest Search Engine on the Internet
http://money.cnn.com/2013/04/08/technology/security/shodan/index.html?iid=EL

Article   Prepared by: Daniel Mittleman, *DePaul University*

Network Insecurity

Are We Losing the Battle against Cyber Crime?

JOHN SEABROOK

Learning Outcomes

After reading this article, you will be able to:

- Understand what cybercrime is, as differentiated from traditional crime.

- Understand what cybercrime is, as differentiated from hacktivism, and cyber espionage.

- Be familiar with specific terminology of cybercrime used by Seabrook including: botnet, DDoS, phishing, spear phishing, key logger, malware, and rootkit.

Richard McFeely, of the F.B.I., is a former insurance adjuster from Unionville, in eastern Pennsylvania horse country. He has a friendly face, meaty hands, and a folksy speaking style that doesn't seem very F.B.I.-like. "Call me Rick," he said, when I met him at his office, in Washington, coming around his wide desk and gesturing toward the soft furniture in the front part of the room.

McFeely, who is fifty-one, and whose official title is executive assistant director ("E.A.D.," in office shorthand), oversees about sixty per cent of F.B.I. operations, including the Cyber Division: some one thousand agents, analysts, forensic specialists, and computer scientists. The bureau has made several high-profile takedowns in recent years, including the dismantling of the Coreflood botnet, a network of millions of infected "zombie" computers, or bots, controlled by a Russian hacking crew.

"But we are just touching the tip of the surface in terms of what companies and what government agencies are at the most risk," McFeely said, shaking his big head ruefully. "We simply don't have the resources to monitor the mammoth quantity of intrusions that are going on out there." Shawn Henry, McFeely's predecessor at the F.B.I., told me, "When I started in my career, in the late eighties, if there was a bank robbery, the pool of suspects was limited to the people who were in the vicinity at the time. Now when a bank is robbed the pool of suspects is limited to the number of people in the world with access to a five-hundred-dollar laptop and an Internet connection. Which today is two and a half billion people." And instead of stealing just one person's credit card, you can steal from

millions of people at the same time. This may have happened when, in 2011, PlayStation's gaming network was hacked and its members' credit-card data compromised.

"It's not the eighties," Tony Stark sneers, in "Iron Man 3." "No one says 'hack' anymore." Hacking used to mean hippie technologists who wanted to set information free. Now hackers can be organized criminal gangs, working out of the former Soviet bloc, who steal financial information; or state-affiliated spies in China, who are carting away virtual truckloads of intellectual property; or saboteurs in Iran or in North Korea who are trying to disrupt or destroy critical infrastructure—not to mention all the small-scale criminals downloading hacking tools and launching attacks because this shit is cool and you can't get caught.

General Keith Alexander, who is the head of the N.S.A. and of the U.S. Cyber Command, has called the loss of American industrial secrets and intellectual property to cyber espionage "the greatest transfer of wealth in history." Plans for the F-35 jet fighter, source code from Google, and details about Coca-Cola's 2009 bid to buy China Huiyuan Juice Group have been stolen. The *Times* and the *Wall Street Journal* both revealed in January that Chinese hackers penetrated their networks last year, apparently in order to gather intelligence about upcoming stories on Chinese officials. Until recently, the U.S. has been reluctant to publicly accuse China of spying, but, in March, Tom Donilon, President Obama's national-security adviser, spoke of "cyber intrusions emanating from China on an unprecedented scale." This month, the Pentagon released a report that bluntly accused the Chinese military of cyber espionage. China denies these accusations.

China is by no means our only cyber-security problem. Organized criminal gangs, loosely affiliated with nation states, constitute an entirely new category of threat. As the world moves online, traditional boundaries break down, and whether it will ever be possible to secure the Internet is an open question. McFeely, his voice rising plaintively, said, "The cyber bad guys have evened the playing field! In the past, we knew it was the traditional big players who were spying on us. Now you get these small countries that are trying to gain a competitive advantage in some industry. So they can go and hire a hacking group, specifically target a company, and steal years and years of R. & D."

In October, Leon Panetta, the Defense Secretary at the time, warned that "an aggressor nation or extremist group could gain control of critical switches and derail passenger trains, or trains loaded with lethal chemicals," resulting in a "cyber Pearl Harbor." Privacy advocates criticized the statement as scare-mongering, suspecting that Panetta's ulterior motive was to increase government oversight of the Internet. Approximately eighty-five per cent of the critical infrastructure in the U.S. is privately held, and the government's authority over it is limited. The Cyber Security Act of 2012, which would have asked companies to comply with basic security regulations, died in the Senate last year. Republicans thought that the regulations would be too expensive and would entail too much government oversight.

The Department of Homeland Security reported a hundred and ninety-eight attacks on critical U.S. infrastructure in fiscal year 2012; there were just nine attacks in 2009. These included the penetration of twenty-three oil and natural-gas pipeline operators and six attacks on nuclear power plants. Last year, hackers also broke into an unclassified network in the White House Military Office. In all these cases, the intruders seemed more interested in snooping than in sabotage, though they could return, with more sinister intentions.

A large part of the nation's financial infrastructure is also under siege. The most furious wave of assaults began in September, when almost fifty major U.S. banks suffered "distributed denial of service" (DDoS) attacks, in which botnets—which can be controlled from afar with remote-access tools, known as RATs—directed high volumes of traffic to the banks' Web sites, causing them to run slowly or to crash altogether.

In many cases, the F.B.I. knows where cyber attacks originate, and in some cases it knows who the attackers are. Much of this information is gathered by the National Cyber Investigative Joint Task Force, an interagency group, based in an undisclosed location near Washington. But, even when hackers are identified, law enforcement is often powerless to confront them. "If you look at the typical attacks on a bank," McFeely said, "most of the attacks aren't coming from within the U.S. What's the stomach of our policymakers here to conduct a unilateral operation on foreign soil?

"I get sick to my stomach when I see that stuff," McFeely went on. "We literally watch our intellectual property leave the country. But, if we do stop it, we lose sight of the rest of it." The bureau would end up revealing its sources and methods to the enemy, while the hackers would simply move on to another target. "So it's a huge conundrum for us. Could the U.S. government do something about these attacks that the financial sector has been undergoing for over a year? Of course we could. The question is, what are the triggers that are going to cause us to take action and what will the impact be?"

From the earliest days of the Internet, the basic approach to network security has been to play defense. The idea is to secure the perimeter of a network with firewalls and intrusion-prevention systems that keep "blacklists" of suspect bits of code, and rely on algorithms which detect suspicious patterns; the algorithms are constantly updated as new threats emerge. Tom Kellermann, a vice-president of Trend Micro, a

cyber-security firm based in Cupertino, California, calls this approach "the citadel paradigm." It depends heavily on antivirus software and users' diligent updating of it. "You keep the crown jewels on the inside, and you build electronic walls and a moat around them," he told me. "It's like the Federal Reserve in lower Manhattan, where the gold is kept." This type of strategy works well when the attacks are opportunistic and random: the intruders are simply searching for an easy way in.

In recent years, however, the citadel paradigm has been battered by so-called "targeted attacks," in which the adversary goes after a particular government agency, company, or individual, with a specific goal in mind. This kind of determined adversary often uses a relatively sophisticated e-mail scam known as "spear phishing." Earlier phishing attacks tended to be clunky and scattershot, like the bogus-looking e-mails purportedly from Google asking you to verify your log-on information, or Nigerian banking scams, or the "Help, I've been robbed in Dublin, can you wire money to Western Union" e-mails supposedly from a friend but actually from a con artist who has hacked your friend's e-mail account. The flimflam was easy to sniff out, generally because the spelling was atrocious (bad guys apparently don't use spell-checkers). Toying with these hapless thieves—"I have wired a thousand dollars to the local police station, you can collect your reward there"—used to be good sport.

But a spear-phishing e-mail is tailored especially for you. Not long ago, the National Association of Manufacturers received an e-mail purportedly from a reporter at Bloomberg who was working on a story about the group, with an Excel spreadsheet contained in an enclosure. In fact, Chinese hackers had spoofed the reporter's e-mail address, and the enclosure contained espionage-related "malware": malicious code. Social networks make it much easier for hackers to impersonate friends and colleagues. "Here are the numbers we spoke about at last night's party"—the one you posted pictures of on Facebook. Downloading the attachment silently installs the malware, without your noticing; later, you may wonder why your computer's fan is always on (it's because the hacker is using your machine's extra computing power). Now you've got a RAT in your machine, which can capture your passwords, credit-card numbers, and banking information, and can turn on your computer's microphone and camera. (Around this magazine's offices, people have started putting Post-it notes over their Mac's little Cyclops-eyed camera.) Your machine is now part of a botnet (in China, bots are called "meaty chickens"), and can be used to launch denial-of-service attacks or send out spam.

RATs also work on smartphones, turning them into ideal spying and tracking devices; you bug yourself, basically. No one is safe. A computer (and therefore any network) can be infected if you simply open an e-mail or visit the wrong Web site. And anyone can be hacked. Even RSA, the maker of the SecurID tokens that are supposed to keep intruders off networks, got hacked when an employee clicked on an enclosure in a spear-phishing e-mail with the subject line "2011 Recruitment Plan," ostensibly from beyond.com, a career-advancement Web site, and inadvertently installed malware on his computer.

The hackers then captured passwords from that computer and used them to gain access to other machines on the network and steal some of RSA's data, which, in turn, allowed them to hack RSA's clients using duplicates of the now compromised security tokens. RSA subsequently offered to replace or monitor all of its tokens, which, as of 2009, numbered forty million. The same spear-phishing attack affected more than seven hundred and fifty other companies, including about a fifth of the Fortune 100. Dmitri Alperovitch, the co-founder and chief technology officer of CrowdStrike, a private security firm, summed all this up for me by saying, "The idea that any company in the world is going to be able to protect itself against an intelligence service or an armed military unit of another country is, quite frankly, ridiculous."

There are simply too many ways for an attacker to get into your computer now. If you log on to the office network with a smartphone, or if you carry a laptop between work and home (a workplace trend known as B.Y.O.D., for "bring your own device," although I heard security people say that it means "bring your own disaster"), you make it very easy for intruders to enter the office network. "In fact, some of the biggest espionage cases we're working on right now involve the home-to-work commuting thing," McFeely told me. "The company can have great security within its own walls, but as soon as it transits out you're at the mercy of the weakest link in the chain." With Wi-Fi hot spots, which can be easy to tap into, popping up everywhere, and with ever more network-enabled devices entering both the office and the home—smart TVs, smart front-door locks—intruders have a panoply of ways to break into your life. Several years ago, Best Buy was discovered to be selling digital picture frames that had been infected with malware.

"Up until four years ago, we kind of had a handle on this shit," Tom Kellermann says. "Virus scanning and encryption and firewalls were doing a pretty good job. But the latest attack kits are bypassing those perimeter defenses, which is why this paradigm has to shift."

I spent a day inside the citadel, with Google's security team, at the company's headquarters, in Mountain View, California. As part of its mission to organize the world's information, Google tries to provide its users with a secure way to access it. Google doesn't guarantee that it will protect its customers from cyber criminals and spies, but it has devised a number of ways of alerting users to suspicious patterns that its security algorithms pick up. The company has been unusually forthcoming about attacks. In January, 2010, for example, Google announced that it had fallen victim to an attack that came to be known as Operation Aurora. (At least twenty other companies, including Adobe, Intel, and Yahoo, were hit, too, but Google was the first to make the information public.) Subsequent analysis by cyber-security experts suggested that hackers affiliated with the Chinese government were behind the attack, and that they had exploited a vulnerability in Internet Explorer to get onto Google's network and steal some of its source code. Google's chief legal officer, David Drummond, wrote that "we have evidence to suggest that a primary goal of the attackers was accessing the Gmail accounts of Chinese human-rights activists." Although only two Gmail accounts were compromised

in the attack, Drummond said that the ensuing investigation revealed that the accounts of dozens of Gmail users in the U.S., China, and Europe who are advocates of human rights in China appeared to have been routinely accessed by third parties.

Sergey Brin, one of Google's co-founders, told me that he invests a lot of time in keeping his security team motivated. "Corporate security teams are often low in morale," he said last October, at a conference in Arizona. (Brin, dressed in Lycra cycling duds, was sporting Google Glass, Google's computing eyewear; sometimes I couldn't tell whether he was talking to me or to the screen inside the lens.) He continued, "In big corporations, people don't understand what security people do, for the most part, and no one pays attention to them unless something goes wrong. Frankly, a lot of companies aren't that interested in security. They say they care, but they really don't; they are vulnerable, they can't do that much about it, and they know it. They're just waiting for something big to happen." Brin meets with the security team every Friday, to review the week's catalogue of threats. Because Google and its users are attacked thousands of times each day, there is usually much to discuss.

The team at Google is led by Eric Grosse, a software engineer who came from Bell Labs, and includes Linus Upson, who oversees security for Google's browser, Chrome; Matt Cutts, who handles Web spam; Niels Provos, who leads Google's anti-malware efforts; and Shane Huntley, who works on targeted threats, which include state-sponsored espionage. The citadel paradigm works better in some of these areas than in others. Google's anti-spam efforts are the brightest spot in its security landscape; spam is exactly the sort of mass, opportunistic attack that the defensive strategy was designed for. Web spam, which clogged up search-engine results, and unsolicited e-mails advertising prescription drugs, penis-enlargement methods, and casinos, which threatened to sink the Internet in the early two-thousands, have been all but eliminated by Google's anti-spam algorithms. "We like to say the spammers have the numbers, we have the math," Cutts told me.

Grosse and I discussed passwords, often the weakest link in the security chain. The recent takeover of the Associated Press's Twitter account by Syrian hackers, which caused a momentary hundred-and-fifty-point drop in the Dow, is an example of the kind of havoc a stolen password can bring about. "My goal is to get rid of passwords completely," Grosse said. "Perhaps you will still have a password but it wouldn't be a prime line of defense." In the short term, however, more passwords, not fewer, seems to be the solution. "We rolled out this two-step verification"—using two passwords, essentially. "The biggest problem is people can't be expected to remember two hundred passwords. I mean, I have two hundred passwords, and they're all different and they're all strong."

"How do you remember them?" I asked.

"I have to write them down."

"But then that piece of paper could be stolen."

"Yeah, but if your adversary is somebody on the other side of the ocean he can't get the piece of paper you have in a safe at home. If you're trying to guard against your roommate, then you need a new roommate." With the two-step process, you register your mobile number, and when you enter your first password, Google texts a unique code to your phone, and then you enter that.

For Upson, who works on securing Chrome, the principal threat is what's known as a "zero-day exploit": a kind of vulnerability, either in an operating system or in an application such as Flash, Quicktime, or Chrome itself, through which intruders can sneak into a computer. (Because the exploit is either unknown to the software vender, or has not yet been patched, it is said to have zero days of remediation.) Exploits can sell for hundreds of thousands of dollars on the black market. Upson told me that Chrome updates itself automatically to fix known exploits, rather than requiring the user to do it. But if an adversary does find his way into your machine through an unpatched hole, he said, "you are better off just throwing your computer away and starting again with a new one, because there are so many places for the malware to hide." That's especially true if the hacker uses a "rootkit," a type of malicious software that can conceal itself from the antivirus software that is supposed to detect it, making cleaning your machine extremely difficult.

One of the Eastern European crews' favorite ploys, Provos told me, is to masquerade as an anti-malware company. "You go to your computer and your screen flashes and you get this dialogue box that says, 'We found all this malware on your computer and you are really in deep trouble, but don't despair, if you pay forty dollars right now you can download this security solution.' So now the malware authors have got forty dollars and they also have complete control of your computer." The latest wrinkle in this style of attack is "ransomware"—a program that encrypts your hard drive and sends you a message that appears to come, for example, from the F.B.I.'s Cyber Division, saying that it has detected child pornography or pirated software on your computer and instructing you where to send money, in order to unencrypt your data.

State-sponsored political espionage is perhaps the most difficult challenge the Google team faces. Chinese targets include the so-called "five poisons": the Falun Gong, Taiwan, the democracy movement, and Uighur and Tibetan separatists; even the Dalai Lama's computers were hacked. But China isn't alone in practicing cyber espionage. Oppressive regimes from Syria to Bahrain use the latest cyber-surveillance tools, many of them made by Western companies, to spy on dissidents. Finfisher spyware, for example, made by Gamma International, a U.K.-based firm, can be used to monitor Wi-Fi networks from a hotel lobby, hack cell phones and P.C.s, intercept Skype conversations, capture passwords, and activate cameras and microphones. Egyptian dissidents who raided the office of Hosni Mubarak's secret police after his overthrow found a proposal from Gamma offering the state Finfisher hardware, software, and training for about four hundred thousand dollars.

Shane Huntley told me, "Our analysis shows that if you are engaged in democracy movements or talking about human rights there is a much greater than fifty-per-cent chance that you are going to be the subject of a targeted attack." He added, "We found that a range of high-level U.S. officials were also having their accounts hijacked" by spear-phishing schemes. "The breadth and depth is kind of amazing."

"It's clear now that relying on traditional tools like antivirus alone is not sufficient for defense," Eric Grosse said. Today, he said, the various social-engineering attacks, like spear phishing, "are actually quite good at tricking and ensnaring victims." To counter these threats, he went on, "dynamic defenses that evolve almost instantaneously" are required. "For example, attackers who use compromised Web sites to deliver phishing pages now often have to shift the location of their sites within a matter of minutes to avoid being caught by software that blocks them."

Adam Meyers, who is the head of intelligence for Crowd-Strike, the security firm, walked me through a hypothetical corporate-espionage attack coming from China. Meyers, who is tall, techy, and wears four small earrings in his left ear (three in the lobe and one higher up, in the cartilage), began by noting that many patterns of corporate espionage bear a suspicious resemblance to China's five-year plans for modernizing the country's infrastructure. The scenario he conjured up involved China's South Sea Fleet, one of three fleets that make up the naval branch of the People's Liberation Army, or P.L.A. The Chinese navy is known to be interested in expanding its capabilities from green-water activities—near to shore—and building up a blue-water, or deep-sea, presence. To do that, it needs to advance its satellite communications, boat building, robotics, and other technologies.

"So the P.L.A. naval officer says to his intelligence forces, 'Here's the five-year plan,'" Meyers said. "He's not using the military's élite hacking crews, because he doesn't want this traced back to the military. But there are plenty of crews for hire that are only loosely affiliated with the government, so he uses one of those. He says, 'Get me everything you can on these technologies.' So they go out and start their operation.

"The first thing they need to do is get access. That starts with open-source intelligence collection—same way you'd start a story, I imagine. They find out who the key people are at the tech companies they're interested in, and do a Google search. They get people, facilities, potentially who the company's software vendors are, and what kind of security software they run. They get the jargon they can use to start crafting an attack. And if they can't get access to you they will find out who your partners are and get access to them. It's all about exploiting a trust relationship.

"Then they run all the names through social media—Facebook, Twitter, LinkedIn—and map your personal relationships." The spear-phishing e-mail "could be a weaponized press release," Meyers continued. "If it's *The New Yorker* I'm after, I send your P.R. people an e-mail saying, 'Hey, we've got evidence your reporters are paying people for stories, we're going to go to press with this in the next twelve hours'—and attach the link. Chances are you are going to click on it." Attacks follow marketing guidelines on what day and time is best to send out e-mails that people will open. "Like Tuesday, late morning. Or they'll send something on a Friday, before a three-day weekend, because they know all the Americans are going away. Memorial Day is a big one. Then they've got until Tuesday before anyone even thinks of doing work"—giving them plenty of time to nose around the network.

Meyers showed me an e-mail that one of CrowdStrike's customers had received from a Chinese hacking crew, with the identifying information redacted:

Dear Sir, I am writing to you to ask you for some information about [BLANK]. Our company plan to purchase five sets of [BLANK]. We are now ask for quote on this product. . . . Looking for your reply.

Below was an attachment with the header "Details About Requirement."

Not particularly convincing, I said, noting the poor grammar.

"Yeah," Meyers replied, "but if you're a sales guy and you see this come in the middle of the first week of the first quarter, and the guy plans to purchase five, and this is a million-dollar product—that's a five-million-dollar deal. So you open it up, it triggers a bug, and your Adobe Reader crashes. But the adversary controls the flow of that crash. As it goes down, he installs the malware. So now they're in. They establish a back door and then start looking at your system to see what tools you are running."

In targeted attacks, the intruders generally know exactly what they are looking for, and can use your search tools to navigate around not just your computer but the office network. It's easy to move around, because most networks are built like Mentos, "crunchy on the outside, but soft and chewy in the middle," Meyers said, meaning that the networks lack strong internal security. "They install a key logger, dump your passwords, turn on the microphone, turn on the camera. Then they push down a different type of malware, so while the security guys are high-fiving and having a cup of coffee, the second malware is established and the hackers are still in. And, worse, we think we've stopped the problem. Then they push down tools that allow them to move laterally across the network. When they find what they're looking for, they'll compress it, and encrypt it, and exfiltrate it. And they'll leave a back door behind to make sure they can come back in the future."

If the old paradigm was the citadel, the new paradigm, Tom Kellermann, of Trend Micro, contends, is the prison. "You're not trying to build the Federal Reserve, you're trying to build Rikers Island. Instead of trying to keep the bad guys out, you keep them in, or you let them in the basement where you keep your Rottweilers, and you make life miserable for them while they are in, so they won't want to come back."

What would a cyber prison look like? To get a better idea, I spoke with Shawn Henry. With his shaved head and Bruce Willis tough-guy demeanor, Henry is the G-man from central casting. Having retired as the E.A.D. overseeing the F.B.I.'s Cyber Division last year, he is now a senior executive at CrowdStrike (where he continues to work with the former deputy head of the Cyber Division, Steven Chabinsky, whom he brought to the company). Part of his job is to impress clients with the urgency and the scope of their cyber-security problem. His fierce-looking eyes squint into a grim future as he conjures up cyber threats, and our lack of readiness for them. "When the electronic equivalent of planes crashing into buildings occurs," he said, "and the lights go out, I guarantee you the public will be up in arms."

CrowdStrike, which has an office in Crystal City, Virginia, is one of a new generation of security companies, such as Fire-Eye, Damballa, and Mandiant, that offer clients a variety of active strategies—security and intelligence-gathering tools that bring the fight to the attacker in your system. "The old performance measure was, Can you keep a determined adversary off your network," Henry told me. "The new measure of success needs to be, How soon after they get access can you I.D. them, so you can take immediate action."

In one instance, which Dmitri Alperovitch, of CrowdStrike, cited approvingly to me, the government of Georgia lured a Russian hacker, who had been breaking into government ministries and banks for more than a year, to a machine that planted spyware on the hacker's computer and used his Webcam to take his picture; the photographs were published in a government report. "The private sector needs to be empowered to take that kind of action," Alperovitch said.

But that kind of action, which is generally referred to as "hacking back," is illegal in the U.S. The same broad-reaching laws, grouped under the 1984 federal Computer Fraud and Abuse Act, or C.F.A.A., that the government uses to go after people like Aaron Swartz—the twenty-six-year-old activist who downloaded millions of articles from the JSTOR database—also limit private companies' powers to take offensive action. However, the C.F.A.A. is notoriously vague and out of date. "There are gray areas," Alperovitch told me. "What if the hackers stole malware that you had planted inside your network, and infected themselves? Is that illegal?"

Could those same gray areas allow the government to hack you? During Henry's time at the F.B.I., the agency developed malware and spyware for possible use in criminal investigations. In 2001, the F.B.I. confirmed the existence of Magic Lantern, a type of spyware that comes in an e-mail attachment. At the time, the agency denied that the spyware had been deployed. But in 2007 the F.B.I. obtained a court order to use a similar program, called a "computer and Internet protocol address verifier," or CIPAV, which works much the way that RATs do, secretly monitoring a computer's use remotely.

At CrowdStrike, Henry might not need to obtain a court order to use malware, depending on how it is deployed. However, he said that he has no intention of violating the C.F.A.A. "We don't hack back," he said. "We don't take actions that are illegal. I've been enforcing the C.F.A.A. for fifteen years, and I've put a lot of people in prison for violation of that law. So we're not doing that. But," he went on, "there are a variety of things we are able to do from a deceptive standpoint that don't involve putting malicious code on hackers' machines. Feeding them misinformation, giving them the wrong trade secrets. You can't give them the wrong plans for a plane, or the wrong drug, because people die. But if it's business plans, tactical information, it's different."

Orin Kerr, a professor at George Washington University and an expert in computer-crime law, argues that back-hacking could easily get out of control. He also told me, "It's hard to know if you are targeting the right person. It's easy to disguise your location online, so it's easy to create a false impression that someone else was behind the attack." But Stewart Baker, the former head of cyber policy for the Department of Homeland Security, maintains that in certain cases hacking back should be within a victim's rights. "If you had a motorcycle in your garage, and your neighbor stole it, and you could see a trail of oil leading from your garage to his garage, you're going to go get it back," he said. "And I don't think a court of law would convict you of trespassing. So, if you hack my intellectual property, shouldn't I be able to get it back?"

Most hacking crews have characteristic digital signatures, cryptography keys, and methodologies of attack, and all that information could be used to identify them, and possibly arrest them. But the information is rarely shared between the public and the private sectors. When the F.B.I. detects a cyber-security breach at a company, agents show up at the door with guns and badges and inform the company of the break-in, but they don't reveal who the intruders were, or what they were looking for, because that information might compromise the F.B.I.'s sources and methods. And when a private company discovers a security breach on its own (on average, more than two hundred days after the initial intrusion), it generally doesn't share the information either with the F.B.I. or with the public, fearing the impact on its partners, investors, and customers. Even private companies operating critical infrastructure sometimes decline to cooperate with government investigations of cyber attacks on their facilities. "Some of these companies are government contractors—they work with us!" McFeely told me. "That doesn't seem right."

Alperovitch said, "Everyone is focused on malware in the security industry. But malware isn't really the problem. Organizations think they have a malware problem; in reality they have an adversary problem. Someone is coming after them for a reason. People say attribution is impossible, but there are two fallacies with that. If you are doing multiple attacks, over years, the possibility of attribution goes up. And the second thing is we bemoan the lack of privacy that we have online, but that makes it harder for an adversary to operate in cyberspace without leaving a huge digital footprint as well."

Adam Meyers, CrowdStrike's intelligence director, showed me a picture of a Chinese hacker who had penetrated one of its client's networks. CrowdStrike used the hacker's unique cryptography key to trace him back to a Chinese university, where it was able to identify him by name, and then find his picture on a social network.

Alperovitch pointed at the young man, who was wearing a tie and a short-sleeved dress shirt and leaning on a large rock with three Chinese symbols on it. "This makes it personal," he said.

A second picture, also taken from the hacker's social-network page, showed the man in military gear, posing with a squadron of other, similarly clad men.

"Looks just like P.L.A., right?" Meyers said. "We thought we'd hit gold." But, on closer inspection of the uniforms, it turned out that the men were dressed for paintball.

Looming darkly over this almost Mordorian cyber threatscape is the prospect of cyber war—a future conflict fought with weaponized code that can do physical damage to infrastructure,

and potentially kill people. So far, the only nations known to have deployed such code are the U.S. and Israel. Working together, the two countries produced the Stuxnet worm and, reportedly, Flame, a high-grade espionage tool. Stuxnet, discovered in 2010 but deployed as early as 2007, was designed to attack Iran's nuclear facilities by exploiting multiple zero-day vulnerabilities in Microsoft's Windows; it reportedly destroyed about a thousand of the centrifuges used to enrich uranium, by causing them to spin out of control. Iran is believed to have retaliated by launching many of the 2012 DDoS attacks on U.S. banks and by infecting the oil company Saudi Aramco with a virus that damaged tens of thousands of its computers, with the aim of impeding the flow of oil.

"This has the whiff of August, 1945," Michael Hayden, the former C.I.A. and N.S.A. director, said of Stuxnet, at an event at George Washington University in February. "It's a new class of weapon, a weapon never before used." A cyber arms race is getting under way, and it is escalating, as the tools needed to deploy weaponized cyber attacks spread around the world. (In March, General Alexander, of the U.S. Cyber Command, told the House Armed Services Committee that he's establishing forty new cyber teams, including thirteen dedicated to offensive attacks.) Whether that conflict will be "hot" or "cold" is hard to say, because virtually all the government's cyber operations against other countries are classified (neither the U.S. nor Israel has taken responsibility for Flame), cloaked in the same secrecy as our drone attacks. David Rothkopf, of *Foreign Policy,* recently characterized cyber conflict as a "cool war," writing, "It is a little warmer than cold because it seems likely to involve almost constant offensive measures that, while falling short of actual warfare, regularly seek to damage or weaken rivals or gain an edge through violations of sovereignty and penetration of defenses." In any case, the Department of Defense recently announced a fivefold increase in our national cyber forces.

And yet, dire though matters appear to be, the American public doesn't seem particularly alarmed by our cyber-security problem. Danger is everywhere and also nowhere; being invisible, cyber crime is easy to put out of your mind. In this respect, at least, it is nothing like terrorism, which feeds on bloody spectacles, martyred bombers, and public mayhem. The cyber threat is faceless and creeps in on little cat feet. You know that, like death, it's coming, but all you can do is hope that someone will fix it before it comes for you.

There is nostalgia in the voices of security people when they speak about the "good old days" of the nineteen-nineties, when the gravest threat to network security came from computer viruses. "Wasn't it nice?" Raimund Genes, Trend Micro's chief technology officer, said recently, waxing nostalgic about Melinda, the 1999 computer virus, which, along with the "I Love You" virus, of 2000, marked the end of the age of viruses and the dawn of cyber crime. "A virus was highly visible, and everyone knew something was wrong with the system. And the virus was just done for fun. There was no commercial interest in creating viruses."

Tom Kellermann told me, "Guys like me—I'm not enjoying this anymore. It's like I'm a forest ranger, and back in the day I used to have to deal with forest fires that were accidentally set by campers, and now I have to deal with fires that are set by arsonists." He added, "I'm looking at worse shit, crazier crap every day, running on four hours' sleep, only ever seeing part of the puzzle, and everyone I know in the government who deals with this is completely frazzled. There's a multiplicity of actors, in a free-fire zone. I'm so tired of people saying China this and China that. If it was just China, then at least we could create international norms and use diplomacy and other mechanisms that have been viable for hundreds of years."

So is there any solution to our cyber problem? Every advance in connectivity and mobility seems to increase the possibilities for crime.

"We're completely fucked," Kellermann said. "I bought a new car yesterday. And the guy says, 'Hey, man, do you know you can turn on a Wi-Fi hot spot in your car?' I said, 'What the?' He said, 'Yeah, it's constantly on, bro, so all you need to do is have any of your passengers synch their devices to it, and you can get high-speed Internet while you are driving!' I said, 'Are you fucking kidding me? Where is it? Turn it off!'"

Critical Thinking

1. In what fundamental ways does cybercrime differ from traditional crime that makes cybercrime a threat our security experts express worry about?
2. Seabrook says, "From the earliest days of the Internet, the basic approach to network security has been to play defense." Discuss what playing offense and defense means in this context? What are examples from the article of each? What are the pros and cons of each approach?

Create Central

www.mhhe.com/createcentral

Internet References

Cyber Crime: Nailing the Botnet

www.businessworld.in/news/finance/cyber-crime:-nailing-the-botnet/924848/page-1.html

Cyber Thieves Steal $45 Million [PBS NewsHour.]

www.pbs.org/newshour/extra/daily_videos/cyber-thieves-steal-45-million

U.S. and China Leaders Debate Cyber Security [PBS NewsHour.]

www.pbs.org/newshour/extra/daily_videos/u-s-and-china-leaders-debate-cyber-security

Unit 5

UNIT

Prepared by: Daniel Mittleman, *DePaul University*

Social Media and Commerce

Most of us by the time we reach college (or in Western Civ. during freshman year) learn that the history of economics can be divided into several eras: agricultural age; industrial age; and information age. Each age is characterized by a key scarce resource; accumulation of that resource is the basis for wealth. In an agricultural economy, the basis for wealth is arable land. While land alone won't provide wealth—one needs access to labor and tools to work the land—it is the scarce and core necessary enabler for the creation of wealth.

In the industrial age (late 18th to the late 20th century), land became less important. Wealth was created by building factories to produce quantities of items for sale. But factories were expensive to build, and raw materials were required to make finished goods. The scarce resource that drove wealth in this economy was capital: money or credit to acquire buildings, equipment, and materials.

The information age (mid-20th century to perhaps the beginning of the 21st century) was brought about by mass adoption of computing technologies. It became possible to accumulate vast wealth by building software tools and databases to access and organize information better than others. The scarce resource that drove this economy was information, and the knowledge to use it effectively.

Several commentators have suggested that the information age was short lived; that we are moving into a new age already. But few have captured just what differentiates this new age from the information age. Clearly information is no longer a scarce resource. All of us can Google almost any information we need. Most of us are bombarded with way too much information on a daily basis in the form of e-mail, text messages, tweets, and Facebook status updates. Few of us are able to find the time to consume more than a small fraction of the information we would find interesting or useful. So, if information is no longer scarce, what is it that is scarce?

Google's value proposition may provide a clue. Yes, Google provides us with information. But so do Yahoo, Microsoft, Apple, and others. What Google does is provide us with this information within a user experience intended to minimize our attention resources. That is, it is not the information that is scarce; rather it is our time and our ability to focus on, parse though, and prioritize all the information being pushed our way. When Google helps us with that, we come back for more. And most of us will happily accept their ads on the page if we perceive real value from their services. Occasionally, we might even click on an ad.

Google's search engine prioritizes results of our searches guessing at which pages will be most useful. Google's Gmail filters our incoming e-mail messages guessing at which ones

are important. Google Maps and Earth help us navigate the physical world—and even make shopping recommendations if we request them. Google Docs, Pixlr, and YouTube (all Google products) help us organize multimedia resources in the cloud. In each case, the tool provides information, but more importantly, it organizes, filters, and prioritizes to permit us to consume information using less attention resources.

While the label has not yet caught on, James Gleick might well be calling our current era the Attention Age.[2] Gleick notes that Google defines its mission as "to organize the world's information." In this sense, Google appears to be trying to build links among all data—everything, everywhere—to enable you to find what you need (or let Google suggest what you need) simply by asking.

Facebook's value proposition may be strikingly parallel to Google's. If Google is trying to capture and catalog all of the world's information so that it can parse and effectively deliver to you exactly the information you need, Facebook seems to be trying to capture and catalog the relationships among all of the people in the world. How it will monetize knowledge of these relationships is only beginning to become clear.

Amazon.com's growth into a retail giant can be characterized by excellence on multiple dimensions. One, they have taken a long view of a supply chain, running at a loss over their first six years of operations, not because of poor sales or management, but because they reinvested would-be profits into supply-chain infrastructure. They built large automated warehouse and distribution facilities, with far greater capacity than they needed at the time. Because of this long-term investment they can now deliver product faster, cheaper, and more reliably than almost anyone else. Faster, better, and cheaper is hard to beat.

Two, they have focused on customer personalization. Amazon has invested in ecommerce technology in the same manner they invested in supply-chain technology. By doing so, they have crafted a site effectively individualized to every shopper. Unless you have taken action (such as blocking cookies) to mask your identity from Amazon, their website will build you a customized homepage based on their knowledge of your past purchases and browsing behaviors. They constantly strive to improve their algorithms to provide a better shopping experience (better for both Amazon and you in the sense you see product you are interested in).

And three, they have been ambitious in moving into new retail markets while not locking into any particular business acquisition strategy. They have bought retailers and folded the stores into Amazon's brand; they have bought retailers and permitted them to continue as their own independent brand; they have partnered with established retailers serving as storefront and/or distribution channel for the partnership. Each model has been employed when deemed optimal. And this has enabled Amazon to grow inventory well beyond the books and digital media that were the bread and butter of their salad years. (Sorry, I couldn't resist that wordplay.)

In 2007, Amazon brought in 62 percent of its revenue from book and media sales, and 38 percent from everything else. In 2012, the most recent year available, the ratio flipped: Amazon brought in 33 percent of its revenue from books and media, 63 percent from other product, and 4 percent from Internet services. And over the same years this flip occurred, Amazon also grew to be the number one book seller in the United States, passing Barnes & Noble and bankrupting Borders.[1]

Amazon is now aiming to conquer the online grocery marketplace by ramping up their AmazonFresh brand and leveraging their supply-chain expertise to succeed where others have failed. Given the solid foundation they have built and the patience they have shown, they might just succeed.

Notes

1. See: http://www.fonerbooks.com/booksale.htm; http://www.fool.com/investing/general/2013/05/09/the-huge-opportunities-ahead-for-amazoncom.aspx; http://mashable.com/2012/07/26/amazon-beating-google-shopping

2. James Gleick, "How Google Dominates Us," *The New York Review of Books*, August 18, 2011.

Article Prepared by: Daniel Mittleman, *DePaul University*

Social Media: Why It Will Change the World

Richard Stacy

Learning Outcomes

After reading this article, you will be able to:

- Understand why "trust is changing."
- Understand why "business models are changing."
- Understand why "information itself is changing."

It is tempting to look at platforms such as Facebook and Twitter and see them as mildly irritating teenagers that have yet to grow up, develop adult sensibilities and start conforming to the realities of the real world. Many journalists, judges and politicians take this view I believe. It is rather less comfortable to imagine Facebook and Twitter as the vanguard of something that is going to remake the world and change its realities. But social media is going to do this and outlined below are the reasons.

For 600 years we have lived in a world where distributing information was expensive and our approach to managing information was therefore restrictive. Information was a scare and precious resource because the channels it had to live within made it so. News was edited down into 30 second segments, marketing was edited down into 30 second ads and trust was imprisoned within institutionalized mediators (news organizations, banks, universities, encyclopaedias). The big shift has happened because social media liberates information from restrictive means of distribution—it has meant that information has become free in both a monetary sense and a mobility sense—and this is why lots of things are going to change.

Why Trust Is Changing

We live in a society where most of the available trust lives in institutions—brands, banks, governments, universities. The reason we do this goes back to Gutenberg and his printing press. Before Gutenberg, it was harder to trust. People either had to rely upon individual experience or upon forms of tradition and practice, most of which had their roots in forms of oral culture. Gutenberg created a print culture and what this did was allow us to trust things which lay outside of the narrow boundaries of personal experience (as well as questioning our trust in the hitherto established traditions and practices). In effect, printing made it possible to start to build reputation amongst audiences of people. Put another way, printing allowed us to add scale to trust. The catch was that the tools needed to do this—the tools of publication—were expensive and thus could only live within the hands of institutions (or rather institutions such as the media, evolved in order to exploit the opportunity these tools presented).

But now that the tools of publication are no longer expensive, trust is leaking out of institutions and it is shifting into processes. Wikipedia is the classic example. We don't trust its entries because we trust the institution of Wikipedia, as we do with the institution that is Encyclopaedia Britannica. We trust its individual entries only in-so-far as we trust the process that has produced them. We used to trust a news story because we trusted the institution from which it came. And because of the cost restrictions inherent in the medium this institution had to operate within, a news organisation created trust by editing down what it presented as the truth. It therefore shields us from much of the available information, or crunches it down into an 'interpretation' of what we should think. When the cost restrictions are removed what happens is that news stops being a finished product and becomes a raw material and we can start to apply a process-based assessment to how we define its truth. Rather than seek to define the truth, or accuracy, of any particular bit of information by excluding what we consider untrue (or not worthy of publication), we can assess where any individual bit of information sits in relation to the whole dataset of relevant information. It is an approach I call the probability curve of news. We can see what information sits at the margins and what sits within the mainstream and the reason we can do this is because we can access and process the whole dataset. We don't have to edit things away in order to squeeze the truth (or a version thereof) into 800 words or 30 seconds. We don't need an editor, we need a processor. News organizations that realize how to deal with news as a raw material will survive in some form. Those that don't will die.

But it is not just news, let us take banking. A bank is simply an institutionalized mediator of trust. It sits in the middle between people who have money and people who want it. Creating the trust necessary for these people to transact between themselves was difficult and this is the problem that banking was set up to solve. If you are lending money, you don't have to trust the borrowers, you just have to trust the bank. But now we have peer-to-peer lending and what these lenders provide is a process that allows you to trust individual borrowers: trust has shifted from an opaque institution to a transparent process.

Why Marketing and Corporate Reputation Is Changing

Marketing may seem like a rather marginal issue in terms of changing the world, but we live in a consumer society where the advertising dollar drives the world of media and therefore subsidizes much of the information currently in circulation. Social media liberates advertisers (brands) from the requirement to talk to audiences. Marketing has always been based on the assumption that we talk to consumers or customers as though they were an audience, but this was because the only channels we have had to reach them were audience-based channels. Social media doesn't 'do' audiences: it connects individuals or small groups. Facebook was designed to help geeks get girlfriends, and you don't need an audience of girlfriends. Facebook was not designed as a marketing platform, although it is trying to turn itself into such in order to be relevant to the marketing dollar (or is that in order to continue to make the marketing dollar relevant?) and sustain a market capitalization that currently sits around US$60 billion.

Most brands have not figured this out yet. Instead they see the challenge as building audiences within social media, so that social media can thus continue to work as a vehicle for audience-based approaches: hence the obsession with generating likes and followers. But I say if you want to reach a lot of people, get an ad don't get a Facebook page. Traditional media is a high reach, but low engagement game, whereas social media is a low reach but high engagement game. It comes down to what I call The Three Per Cent Rule. This states that you are only ever going to reach three per cent (and usually much less) of your audience via social media. This is fine, provided you then do something with this three per cent that creates value. The value challenge in this space is not about channel and message, it is about behavior identification and response. You don't target consumers or customers, these people identify themselves via their behavior, which is frequently about asking questions or complaining. You create value on account of how you respond to this behavior and pushing content at them, no matter how 'engaging' you think it might be, is almost never going to be the right response. Until organizations recognize that there are now two worlds—the world of the audience and the world of the individual—which require totally different approaches, they are never going to be able to operate effectively within the social digital space.

Why Business Models Are Changing

Craig Newmark (he of Craigslist) has said probably the most sensible and insightful thing about money and business models in the social digital space. Given that Craigslist was eating the lunch of the multi-billion dollar classified advertising market, he was asked why he was not a billionaire. He simply said "I don't need that much money." Now Craig may have meant that personally, he didn't need piles of cash, but what he equally could have meant was that it didn't take that much money to run Craigslist. Classified advertising is only a multi-billion dollar business because it needs to sustain the multi-billion dollar cost of the distribution model that is newspaper printing. Craigslist is just a good idea, some geeks and some server space—not expensive or scarce commodities (except the good idea bit).

As the publishing industry is finding, when you cross the digital divide you cannot take the money with you. The reason for this is that the costs don't come with you either, unless you continue to drag them with you via the need to subsidize expensive distribution technologies. It is very easy to make money in the digital space, just not with business models dragged from the old space.

Facebook currently has the opposite of this problem. Like Craigslist, Facebook is just a good idea, geeks and server space. Facebook's problem is that the Wall Street boys who had to put a valuation on it dragged a model with them from the old space. The number of Facebook users is an order of magnitude greater than any regular audience for a traditional media platform. Crunch these sort of numbers through any variant of the old media platform model and the valuation number that therefore comes out is either enormous or vast. As a result, Facebook's value was set accordingly high as was its requirement to generate a level of revenue. Despite the fact that this revenue was not apparent at the time, the logic of the model the Wall Street boys applied would dictate that this was simply because Facebook had yet to work out how to realize its revenue potential. What has never really occurred to anybody is that perhaps the model is wrong. Perhaps we need a Craig Newmark type of model that looks at Facebook not in terms of what it can make as a traditional media platform, but what it costs to deliver the service its users want (not the service advertisers want): the cost of the geeks and the server space, plus a premium for having the good idea. After all, the revenue assumptions of traditional media platforms are based on costs of delivering the service—but because the cost of distribution technologies has been high this has determined the revenue per user equation.

Ultimately, the real business issue here is one of scale. When social media touches a business model, what happens is that scale starts to leak out of it. The music business is a good example, having been one of the first to become dis-intermediated by social media. The music business has been shipping scale at a rate of knots for some years now. You don't have new big bands any more, or if you do, they don't last more than a year or two. Smallness has proliferated and the space has shattered into thousands of niches because you don't need money (scale) to distribute music. Music itself has become a utility: you don't own it as a product, you simply rent access to it. Dealing with a world where the scale advantages are disappearing is probably the biggest business challenge that social media deals up.

Taking an example from the consumer goods sector, Procter & Gamble is successful because it uses its scale to negotiate advantageous terms in renting space within expensive information distribution channels. It is the world's largest advertiser. When the channels become free, where is the scale advantage? The answer lies in the concept of utility and commodity. Modern marketing is based on the idea of taking what is essentially a commodity product produced at volume and persuading consumers that it is unique, special and therefore premium. The scale advantage this conferred is being eroded, but advantages still remain, just not within the realms of marketing and branding. Mass production still offers scale advantages—although the fact that China is everyone's factory undermines this to an extent—as does the ability to negotiate terms with retailers or suppliers. There now has to be a compelling reason to be big, because it is now much easier to be small. Social media is putting scale back into a box labelled utility and commodity, which actually is where it lives best.

Why Information Itself Is Changing

While social media tends towards the small, there is one thing that has become big as a result, and this is data. We now all live within a thousand datasets, each one of which is like a compass bearing on our identity. This fact is overturning all our concepts of privacy, data protection and the significance of information. Edward Snowden's recent exposure of the way governments spy on citizens is small beer compared to the implications inherent in the ability of algorithms to identify behaviors based on information which people want to make public. There is no such thing as inconsequential information any more: all information has a consequence. Google says that we can be anonymous, but this is a bit like saying driving is 100 per cent safe, right up until the moment you have a car crash. Indeed, we

can all swim in a sea of Google anonymity right up until the moment the data fisherman gets us on the hook. That's the way Big Data works. Social media may well challenge institutions and deliver greater power into the hands of consumers and citizens, but Big Data could be used to redress the balance. Either way—the world is going to change as a result.

Critical Thinking

1. Stacy equates trust to "building reputation." How does "building reputation" change with the advent of social media? Are there examples of this phenomenon other than the ones mentioned in the article?
2. What is a business model? Why are business models changing because of social media? What are examples of new business models evolving due to social media other than the ones mentioned in the article?
3. Why does Stacy argue that information itself is changing? What are implications of information itself changing on our work, social, entertaining, and community participation activities?

Create Central

www.mhhe.com/createcentral

Internet References

Google's Schmidt and Cohen Discuss Promise and Pitfalls of the Digital Future
    www.pbs.org/newshour/bb/science/jan-june13/digitalage_05-02.html

How Connecting 7 Billion to the Web Will Transform the World
    www.pbs.org/newshour/rundown/2013/05/in-new-digital-age-google-leaders-see-more-possibilities-to-connect-the-worlds-7-billion.html

Net Benefits: How to Quantify the Gains That the Internet has Brought to Consumers
    www.economist.com/news/finance-and-economics/21573091-how-quantify-gains-internet-has-brought-consumers-net-benefits

Rachel Botsman: The Case for Collaborative Consumption [TED Talks]
    www.ted.com/talks/rachel_botsman_the_case_for_collaborative_consumption.html

Zuckerberg Explains Facebook's Plan to Get Entire Planet Online
    www.wired.com/business/2013/08/mark-zuckerberg-internet-org

Article   Prepared by: Daniel Mittleman, *DePaul University*

How Google Dominates Us

JAMES GLEICK

Learning Outcomes

After reading this article, you will be able to:

- Understand how Google, Facebook, and other sites collect demographic and behavioral data about their users.

- Understand the trade-offs between advantages and risks of sharing information on social networks.

- Understand how you pay to visit the most popular websites through the sale of your preferences to advertisers.

- Articulate Google's business model and, in particular, the model of making money by giving away service for free.

Tweets Alain de Botton, philosopher, author, and now online aphorist:
    The logical conclusion of our relationship to computers: expectantly to type "what is the meaning of my life" into Google.

You can do this, of course. Type "what is th" and faster than you can find the *e* Google is sending choices back at you: what is the *cloud?* what is the *mean?* what is the *american dream?* what is the *illuminati?* Google is trying to read your mind. Only it's not your mind. It's the World Brain. And whatever that is, we know that a twelve-year-old company based in Mountain View, California, is wired into it like no one else.

Google is where we go for answers. People used to go elsewhere or, more likely, stagger along not knowing. Nowadays you can't have a long dinner-table argument about who won the Oscar for that Neil Simon movie where she plays an actress who doesn't win an Oscar; at any moment someone will pull out a pocket device and Google it. If you need the art-history meaning of "picturesque," you could find it in *The Book of Answers,* compiled two decades ago by the New York Public Library's reference desk, but you won't. Part of Google's mission is to make the books of answers redundant (and the reference librarians, too). "A hamadryad is a wood-nymph, also a poisonous snake in India, and an Abyssinian baboon," says the narrator of John Banville's 2009 novel, *The Infinities.* "It takes a god to know a thing like that." Not anymore.

The business of finding facts has been an important gear in the workings of human knowledge, and the technology has just been upgraded from rubber band to nuclear reactor. No wonder there's some confusion about Google's exact role in that—along with increasing fear about its power and its intentions.

Most of the time Google does not actually *have* the answers. When people say, "I looked it up on Google," they are committing a solecism. When they try to erase their embarrassing personal histories "on Google," they are barking up the wrong tree. It is seldom right to say that anything is true "according to Google." Google is the oracle of redirection. Go there for "hamadryad," and it points you to Wikipedia. Or the Free Online Dictionary. Or the Official Hamadryad Web Site (it's a rock band, too, wouldn't you know). Google defines its mission as "to organize the world's information," not to possess it or accumulate it. Then again, a substantial portion of the world's printed books have now been copied onto the company's servers, where they share space with millions of hours of video and detailed multilevel imagery of the entire globe, from satellites and from its squadrons of roving street-level cameras. Not to mention the great and growing trove of information Google possesses regarding the interests and behavior of, approximately, everyone.

When I say Google "possesses" all this information, that's not the same as owning it. What it means to own information is very much in flux.

In barely a decade Google has made itself a global brand bigger than Coca-Cola or GE; it has created more wealth faster than any company in history; it dominates the information economy. How did that happen? It happened more or less in plain sight. Google has many secrets but the main ingredients of its success have not been secret at all, and the business story has already provided grist for dozens of books. Steven Levy's new account, *In the Plex,* is the most authoritative to date and in many ways the most entertaining. Levy has covered personal computing for almost thirty years, for *Newsweek* and *Wired* and in six previous books, and has visited Google's headquarters periodically since 1999, talking with its founders, Larry Page and Sergey Brin, and, as much as has been possible for a journalist, observing the company from the inside. He has been able to record some provocative, if slightly self-conscious, conversations like this one in 2004 about their hopes for Google:

"It will be included in people's brains," said Page. "When you think about something and don't really know much about it, you will automatically get information."

"That's true," said Brin. "Ultimately I view Google as a way to augment your brain with the knowledge of the world. Right now you go into your computer and type a phrase, but you can imagine that it could be easier in the future, that you can have just devices you talk into, or you can have computers that pay attention to what's going on around them. . . ."

. . . Page said, "Eventually you'll have the implant, where if you think about a fact, it will just tell you the answer."

In 2004, Google was still a private company, five years old, already worth $25 billion, and handling about 85 percent of Internet searches. Its single greatest innovation was the algorithm called PageRank, developed by Page and Brin when they were Stanford graduate students running their research project from a computer in a dorm room. The problem was that most Internet searches produced useless lists of low-quality results. The solution was a simple idea: to harvest the implicit knowledge already embodied in the architecture of the World Wide Web, organically evolving.

The essence of the Web is the linking of individual "pages" on websites, one to another. Every link represents a recommendation—a vote of interest, if not quality. So the algorithm assigns every page a rank, depending on how many other pages link to it. Furthermore, all links are not valued equally. A recommendation is worth more when it comes from a page that has a high rank itself. The math isn't trivial—PageRank is a probability distribution, and the calculation is recursive, each page's rank depending on the ranks of pages that depend . . . and so on. Page and Brin patented PageRank and published the details even before starting the company they called Google.

Most people have already forgotten how dark and unsignposted the Internet once was. A user in 1996, when the Web comprised hundreds of thousands of "sites" with millions of "pages," did not expect to be able to search for "Olympics" and automatically find the official site of the Atlanta games. That was too hard a problem. And what was a search supposed to produce for a word like "university"? AltaVista, then the leading search engine, offered up a seemingly unordered list of academic institutions, topped by the Oregon Center for Optics.

Levy recounts a conversation between Page and an AltaVista engineer, who explained that the scoring system would rank a page higher if "university" appeared multiple times in the headline. Alta Vista seemed untroubled that the Oregon center did not qualify as a major university. A conventional way to rank universities would be to consult experts and assess measures of quality: graduate rates, retention rates, test scores. The Google approach was to trust the Web and its numerous links, for better and for worse.

PageRank is one of those ideas that seem obvious after the fact. But the business of Internet search, young as it was, had fallen into some rigid orthodoxies. The main task of a search engine seemed to be the compiling of an index. People naturally thought of existing technologies for organizing the world's information, and these were found in encyclopedias and dictionaries. They could see that alphabetical order was about to become less important, but they were slow to appreciate how dynamic and ungraspable their target, the Internet, really was. Even after Page and Brin flipped on the light switch, most companies continued to wear blindfolds.

The Internet had entered its first explosive phase, boom and then bust for many ambitious startups, and one thing everyone knew was that the way to make money was to attract and retain users. The buzzword was "portal"—the user's point of entry, like Excite, Go.com, and Yahoo—and portals could not make money by rushing customers into the rest of the Internet. "Stickiness," as Levy says, "was the most desired metric in websites at the time." Portals did not want their search functions to be *too good.* That sounds stupid, but then again how did Google intend to make money when it charged users nothing? Its user interface at first was plain, minimalist, and emphatically free of advertising—nothing but a box for the user to type a query, followed by two buttons, one to produce a list of results and one with the famously brash tag "I'm feeling lucky."

The Google founders, Larry and Sergey, did everything their own way. Even in the unbuttoned culture of Silicon Valley they stood out from the start as originals, "Montessori kids" (per Levy), unconcerned with standards and proprieties, favoring big red gym balls over office chairs, deprecating organization charts and formal titles, showing up for business meetings in roller-blade gear. It is clear from all these books that they believed their own hype; they believed with moral fervor in the primacy and power of information. (Sergey and Larry did not invent the company's famous motto—"Don't be evil"—but they embraced it, and now they may as well own it.)

As they saw it from the first, their mission encompassed not just the Internet but all the world's books and images, too. When Google created a free e-mail service—Gmail—its competitors were Microsoft, which offered users two megabytes of storage of their past and current e-mail, and Yahoo, which offered four megabytes. Google could have trumped that with six or eight; instead it provided 1,000—a *giga*byte. It doubled that a year later and promised "to keep giving people more space forever."

They have been relentless in driving computer science forward. Google Translate has achieved more in machine translation than the rest of the world's artificial intelligence experts combined. Google's new mind-reading type-ahead feature, Google Instant, has "to date" (boasts the 2010 annual report) "saved our users over 100 billion keystrokes and counting." (If you are seeking information about the Gobi Desert, for example, you receive results well before you type the word "desert.")

Somewhere along the line they gave people the impression that they didn't care for advertising—that they scarcely had a business plan at all. In fact it's clear that advertising was fundamental to their plan all along. They did scorn conventional marketing, however; their attitude seemed to be that Google would market itself. As, indeed, it did. Google was a verb and a meme. "The media seized on Google as a marker of a new form of behavior," writes Levy.

Endless articles rhapsodized about how people would Google their blind dates to get an advance dossier or how they would type in ingredients on hand to Google a recipe or use a telephone number to Google a reverse lookup. Columnists shared their self-deprecating tales of Googling themselves. . . . A contestant on the TV show *Who Wants to Be a Millionaire?* arranged with his brother to tap Google during the Phone-a-Friend lifeline. . . . And a fifty-two-year-old man suffering chest pains Googled "heart attack symptoms" and confirmed that he was suffering a coronary thrombosis.

Google's first marketing hire lasted a matter of months in 1999; his experience included Miller Beer and Tropicana and his proposal involved focus groups and television commercials. When Doug Edwards interviewed for a job as marketing manager later that year, he understood that the key word was "viral." Edwards lasted quite a bit longer, and now he's the first Google insider to have published his memoir of the experience. He was, as he says proudly in his subtitle to *I'm Feeling Lucky,* Google employee number 59. He provides two other indicators of how early that was: so early that he nabbed the e-mail address doug@google.com; and so early that Google's entire server hardware lived in a rented "cage."

Less than six hundred square feet, it felt like a shotgun shack blighting a neighborhood of gated mansions. Every square inch was crammed with racks bristling with stripped-down CPUs [central processing units]. There were twenty-one racks and more than fifteen hundred machines, each sprouting cables like Play-Doh pushed through a spaghetti press. Where other cages were right-angled and inorganic, Google's swarmed with life, a giant termite mound dense with frenetic activity and intersecting curves.

Levy got a glimpse of Google's data storage a bit later and remarked, "If you could imagine a male college freshman made of gigabytes, this would be his dorm."

Not anymore. Google owns and operates a constellation of giant server farms spread around the globe—huge windowless structures, resembling aircraft hangars or power plants, some with cooling towers. The server farms stockpile the exabytes of information and operate an array of staggeringly clever technology. This is Google's share of the cloud (that notional place where our data live) and it is the lion's share.

How thoroughly and how radically Google has already transformed the information economy has not been well understood. The merchandise of the information economy is not information; it is attention. These commodities have an inverse relationship. When information is cheap, attention becomes expensive. Attention is what we, the users, give to Google, and our attention is what Google sells—concentrated, focused, and crystallized.

Google's business is not search but advertising. More than 96 percent of its $29 billion in revenue last year came directly from advertising, and most of the rest came from advertising-related services. Google makes more from advertising than all the nation's newspapers combined. It's worth understanding precisely how this works. Levy chronicles the development of the advertising engine: a "fantastic achievement in building a money machine from the virtual smoke and mirrors of the Internet." In *The Googlization of Everything (and Why We Should Worry),* a book that can be read as a sober and admonitory companion, Siva Vaidhyanathan, a media scholar at the University of Virginia, puts it this way: "We are not Google's customers: we are its product. We—our fancies, fetishes, predilections, and preferences—are what Google sells to advertisers."

The evolution of this unparalleled money machine piled one brilliant innovation atop another, in fast sequence:

1. Early in 2000, Google sold "premium sponsored links": simple text ads assigned to particular search terms. A purveyor of golf balls could have its ad shown to everyone who searched for "golf" or, even better, "golf balls." Other search engines were already doing this. Following tradition, they charged according to how many people saw each ad. Salespeople sold the ads to big accounts, one by one.

2. Late that year, engineers devised an automated self-service system, dubbed AdWords. The opening pitch went, "Have a credit card and 5 minutes? Get your ad on Google today," and suddenly thousands of small businesses were buying their first Internet ads.

3. From a short-lived startup called Go To (by 2003 Google owned it) came two new ideas. One was to charge per click rather than per view. People who click on an ad for golf balls are more likely to buy them than those who simply see an ad on Google's website. The other idea was to let advertisers bid for keywords—such as "golf ball"—against one another in fast online auctions. Pay-per-click auctions opened a cash spigot. A click meant a *successful* ad, and some advertisers were willing to pay more for that than a human salesperson could have known. Plaintiffs' lawyers seeking clients would bid as much as fifty dollars for a single click on the keyword "mesothelioma"—the rare form of cancer caused by asbestos.

4. Google—monitoring its users' behavior so systematically—had instant knowledge of which ads were succeeding and which were not. It could view "click-through rates" as a measure of ad quality. And in determining the winners of auctions, it began to consider not just the money offered but the appeal of the ad: an effective ad, getting lots of clicks, would get better placement.

   Now Google had a system of profitable cycles in place, positive feedback pushing advertisers to make more effective ads and giving them data to help them do it and giving users more satisfaction in clicking on ads, while punishing noise and spam. "The system enforced Google's insistence that advertising shouldn't be a transaction between publisher and advertiser but a three-way relationship that also included the user," writes Levy. Hardly an equal relationship, however. Vaidhyanathan sees it as exploitative: "The Googlization of everything entails the harvesting, copying, aggregating, and ranking of information about and contributions made by each of us."

   By 2003, AdWords Select was serving hundreds of thousands of advertisers and making so much money that Google was deliberately hiding its success from the press and from competitors. But it was only a launching pad for the next brilliancy.

5. So far, ads were appearing on Google's search pages, discreet in size, clearly marked, at the top or down the right side. Now the company expanded its platform outward. The aim was to develop a form of artificial intelligence that could analyze chunks of text—websites, blogs, e-mail, books—and match them with keywords. With two billion Web pages already in its index and with its close tracking of user behavior, Google had exactly

the information needed to tackle this problem. Given a website (or a blog or an e-mail), it could predict which advertisements would be effective.

This was, in the jargon, "content-targeted advertising." Google called its program AdSense. For anyone hoping to—in the jargon—"monetize" their content, it was the Holy Grail. The biggest digital publishers, such as *The New York Times,* quickly signed up for AdSense, letting Google handle growing portions of their advertising business. And so did the smallest publishers, by the millions—so grew the "long tail" of possible advertisers, down to individual bloggers. They signed up because the ads were so powerfully, measurably productive. "Google conquered the advertising world with nothing more than applied mathematics," wrote Chris Anderson, the editor of *Wired.* "It didn't pretend to know anything about the culture and conventions of advertising—it just assumed that better data, with better analytical tools, would win the day. And Google was right." Newspapers and other traditional media have complained from time to time about the arrogation of their content, but it is by absorbing the world's advertising that Google has become their most destructive competitor.

Like all forms of artificial intelligence, targeted advertising has hits and misses. Levy cites a classic miss: a gory *New York Post* story about a body dismembered and stuffed in a garbage bag, accompanied on the *Post* website by a Google ad for plastic bags. Nonetheless, anyone could now add a few lines of code to their website, automatically display Google ads, and start cashing monthly checks, however small. Vast tracts of the Web that had been free of advertising now became Google partners. Today Google's ad canvas is not just the search page but the entire Web, and beyond that, great volumes of e-mail and, potentially, all the world's books.

Search and advertising thus become the matched edges of a sharp sword. The perfect search engine, as Sergey and Larry imagine it, reads your mind and produces the answer you want. The perfect advertising engine does the same: it shows you the ads you want. Anything else wastes your attention, the advertiser's money, and the world's bandwidth. The dream is virtuous advertising, matching up buyers and sellers to the benefit of all. But virtuous advertising in this sense is a contradiction in terms. The advertiser is paying for a slice of our limited attention; our minds would otherwise be elsewhere. If our interests and the advertisers' were perfectly aligned, they would not need to pay. There is no information utopia. Google users are parties to a complex transaction, and if there is one lesson to be drawn from all these books it is that we are not always witting parties.

Seeing ads next to your e-mail (if you use Google's free e-mail service) can provide reminders, sometimes startling, of how much the company knows about your inner self. Even without your e-mail, your search history reveals plenty—as Levy says, "your health problems, your commercial interests, your hobbies, and your dreams." Your response to advertising reveals even more, and with its advertising programs Google began tracking the behavior of individual users from one Internet site to the next. They observe our every click (where they can) and they measure in milliseconds how long it takes us to decide. If they didn't, their results wouldn't be so uncannily effective. They have no rival in the depth and breadth of their data mining. They make statistical models for everything they know, connecting the small scales with the large, from queries and clicks to trends in fashion and season, climate and disease.

It's for your own good—that is Google's cherished belief. If we want the best possible search results, and if we want advertisements suited to our needs and desires, we must let them into our souls.

The Google corporate motto is "Don't be evil." Simple as that is, it requires parsing.

It was first put forward in 2001 by an engineer, Paul Buchheit, at a jawboning session about corporate values. "People laughed," he recalled. "But I said, 'No, *really.*'" (At that time the booming tech world had its elephant-in-the-room, and many Googlers understood "Don't be evil" explicitly to mean "Don't be like Microsoft"; i.e., don't be a ruthless, take-no-prisoners monopolist.)

Often it is misquoted in stronger form: "Do no evil." That would be a harder standard to meet.

Now they're mocked for it, but the Googlers were surely sincere. They believed a corporation should behave ethically, like a person. They brainstormed about their values. Taken at face value, "Don't be evil" has a finer ring than some of the other contenders: "Google will strive to honor all its commitments" or "Play hard but keep the puck down."

"Don't be evil" does not have to mean transparency. None of these books can tell you how many search queries Google fields, how much electricity it consumes, how much storage capacity it owns, how many streets it has photographed, how much e-mail it stores; nor can you Google the answers, because Google values its privacy.

It does not have to mean "Obey all the laws." When Google embarked on its program to digitize copyrighted books and copy them onto its servers, it did so in stealth, deceiving publishers with whom it was developing business relationships. Google knew that the copying bordered on illegal. It considered its intentions honorable and the law outmoded. "I think we knew that there would be a lot of interesting issues," Levy quotes Page as saying, "and the way the laws are structured isn't really sensible."

Who, then, judges what is evil? "Evil is what Sergey says is evil," explained Eric Schmidt, the chief executive officer, in 2002.

As for Sergey: "I feel like I shouldn't impose my beliefs on the world. It's a bad technology practice." But the founders seem sure enough of their own righteousness. ("'Bastards!' Larry would exclaim when a blogger raised concerns about user privacy," recalls Edwards. "'Bastards!' they would say about the press, the politicians, or the befuddled users who couldn't grasp the obvious superiority of the technology behind Google's products.")

Google did some evil in China. It collaborated in censorship. Beginning in 2004, it arranged to tweak and twist its algorithms and filter its results so that the native-language Google.cn would omit results unwelcome to the government. In the most notorious example, "Tiananmen Square" would produce sightseeing guides but not history lessons. Google figured out what to censor by checking China's approved search engine, Baidu, and by accepting the government's supplementary guidance.

Yet it is also true that Google pushed back against the government as much as any other American company. When results were blocked, Google insisted on alerting users with a notice at the bottom of the search page. On balance Google clearly believed (and I think it was right, despite the obvious self-interest) that its presence benefited the people of China by increasing information flow and making clear the violation of transparency. The adventure took a sharp turn in January 2010, after organized hackers, perhaps with government involvement, breached Google's servers and got access to the e-mail accounts of human rights activists. The company shut down Google.cn and now serves China only from Hong Kong—with results censored not by Google but by the government's own ongoing filters.

So is Google evil? The question is out there now; it nags, even as we blithely rely on the company for answers—which now also means maps, translations, street views, calendars, video, financial data, and pointers to goods and services. The strong version of the case against Google is laid out starkly in *Search & Destroy,* by a self-described "Google critic" named Scott Cleland. He wields a blunt club; the book might as well been have been titled *Google: Threat or Menace?!* "There is evidence that Google is not all puppy dogs and rainbows," he writes.

Google's corporate mascot is a replica of a Tyrannosaurus Rex skeleton on display outside the corporate headquarters. With its powerful jaws and teeth, T-Rex was a terrifying predator. And check out the B-52 bomber chair in Google Chairman Eric Schmidt's office. The B-52 was a long range bomber designed to deliver nuclear weapons.

Levy is more measured: "Google professed a sense of moral purity . . . but it seemed to have a blind spot regarding the consequences of its own technology on privacy and property rights." On all the evidence Google's founders began with an unusually ethical vision for their unusual company. They believe in information—"universally accessible"—as a force for good in and of itself. They have created and led teams of technologists responsible for a golden decade of genuine innovation. They are visionaries in a time when that word is too cheaply used. Now they are perhaps disinclined to submit to other people's ethical standards, but that may be just a matter of personality. It is well to remember that the modern corporation is an amoral creature by definition, obliged to its shareholder financiers, not to the public interest.

The Federal Trade Commission issued subpoenas in June in an antitrust investigation into Google's search and advertising practices; the European Commission began a similar investigation last year. Governments are responding in part to organized complaints by Google's business competitors, including Microsoft, who charge, among other things, that the company manipulates its search results to favor its friends and punish its enemies. The company has always denied that. Certainly regulators are worried about its general "dominance"—Google seems to be everywhere and seems to know everything and offends against cherished notions of privacy.

The rise of social networking upends the equation again. Users of Facebook choose to reveal—even to flaunt—aspects of their private lives, to at least some part of the public world.

Which aspects, and which part? On Facebook the user options are notoriously obscure and subject to change, but most users share with "friends" (the word having been captured and drained bloodless). On Twitter, every remark can be seen by the whole world, except for the so-called "direct message," which former Representative Anthony Weiner tried and failed to employ. Also, the Library of Congress is archiving all tweets, presumably for eternity, a fact that should enter the awareness of teenagers, if not members of Congress.

Now Google is rolling out its second attempt at a social-networking platform, called Google+. The first attempt, eighteen months ago, was Google Buzz; it was an unusual stumble for the company. By default, it revealed lists of contacts with whom users had been chatting and e-mailing. Privacy advocates raised an alarm and the FTC began an investigation, quickly reaching a settlement in which Google agreed to regular privacy audits for the next twenty years. Google+ gives users finer control over what gets shared with whom. Still, one way or another, everything is shared with the company. All the social networks have access to our information and mean to use it. Are they our friends?

This much is clear: We need to decide what we want from Google. If only we can make up our collective minds. Then we still might not get it.

The company always says users can "opt out" of many of its forms of data collection, which is true, up to a point, for savvy computer users; and the company speaks of privacy in terms of "trade-offs," to which Vaidhyanathan objects:

Privacy is not something that can be counted, divided, or "traded." It is not a substance or collection of data points. It's just a word that we clumsily use to stand in for a wide array of values and practices that influence how we manage our reputations in various contexts. There is no formula for assessing it: I can't give Google three of my privacy points in exchange for 10 percent better service.

This seems right to me, if we add that privacy involves not just managing our reputation but protecting the inner life we may not want to share. In any case, we continue to make precisely the kinds of trades that Vaidhyanathan says are impossible. Do we want to be addressed as individuals or as neurons in the world brain? We get better search results and we see more appropriate advertising when we let Google know who we are. And we save a few keystrokes.

Critical Thinking

1. What is the overwhelming source of Google's revenue? Why do you think Google invests so heavily in products separate from their principal revenue sources? Why do you think Google offers so many of their products for free? Do you think this business model is sustainable? Do you think it would work for other companies today? Why or why not?

2. Gleick says "what it means to own information is very much in flux." What do you think it means to own information? Does Google own your information? Does Facebook? Do they possess your information? Do they have the right to make decisions about how to use it? Sell (or license) it? Show it to the government? Deprive you of access to it? Delete it?

3. Much is made of Google's PageRank algorithm, what is it? Consider Gleick's description of PageRank and how it displaced AltaVista's simpler search algorithm. How has PageRank technology impacted us beyond simply making Google the leading search engine?

Create Central

www.mhhe.com/createcentral

Internet References

Google Chairman: 6 Predictions for Our Digital Future
www.cnn.com/2013/04/23/tech/web/eric-schmidt-google-book/index.html

Seeing the World in a Different Way through Digital Maps
http://video.pbs.org/video/2298428370

2012: A Year in Google Searches [PBS NewsHour.]
www.pbs.org/newshour/extra/daily_videos/2012-a-year-in-google-searches

The Untold Story of Google's Quest to Bring the Internet Everywhere—By Balloon
www.wired.com/gadgetlab/2013/08/googlex-project-loon

Article   Prepared by: Daniel Mittleman, *DePaul University*

AmazonFresh is Jeff Bezos' Last Mile Quest for Total Retail Domination

Amazon upended retail, but CEO Jeff Bezos—*Who just bought the* Washington Post *for $250 million*—Insists it's still "day one." What comes next? A relentless pursuit of cheaper goods and faster shipping. The competition is already gasping for breath.

J. J. McCorvey

Learning Outcomes

After reading this article, you will be able to:

- Understand the differential advantages Amazon has created to gain dominance in the marketplace.

- Understand the issues driving the creation of an Internet sales tax and why Amazon, the biggest retailer of them all, is in favor of this tax.

The first thing you notice about Jeff Bezos is how he strides into a room.

A surprisingly diminutive figure, clad in blue jeans and a blue pinstripe button-down, Bezos flings open the door with an audible whoosh and instantly commands the space with his explosive voice, boisterous manner, and a look of total confidence. "How are you?" he booms, in a way that makes it sound like both a question and a high-decibel announcement.

Each of the dozen buildings on Amazon's Seattle campus is named for a milestone in the company's history—Wainwright, for instance, honors its first customer. Bezos and I meet in a six-floor structure known as Day One North. The name means far more than the fact that Amazon, like every company in the universe, opened on a certain date (in this case, it's July 16, 1995). No, Day One is a central motivating idea for Bezos, who has been reminding the public since his first letter to shareholders in 1997 that we are only at Day One in the development of both the Internet and his ambitious retail enterprise. In one recent update for shareholders he went so far as to assert, with typical I-know-something-you-don't flair, that "the alarm clock hasn't even gone off yet." So I ask Bezos: "What exactly does the rest of day one look like?" He pauses to think, then exclaims, "We're still asleep at that!"

He's a liar.

Amazon is a company that is anything but asleep. Amazon, in fact, is an eyes-wide-open army fighting—and winning—a battle that no one can map as well as its general. Yes, it is still the ruthless king of books—especially after Apple's recent loss in a book price-fixing suit. But nearly two decades after its real day one, the e-commerce giant has evolved light-years from being just a book peddler. More than 209 million active customers rely on Amazon for everything from flat-panel TVs to dog food. Over the past five years, the retailer has snatched up its most sophisticated competition—shoe seller Zappos and Quidsi, parent of such sites as Diapers.com, Soap.com, Wag.com, and BeautyBar.com. It has purchased the robot maker Kiva Systems, because robots accelerate the speed at which Amazon can assemble customer orders, sometimes getting it down to 20 minutes from click to ship. Annual sales have quadrupled over the same period to a whopping $61 billion. Along the way, incidentally, Amazon also became the world's most trusted company. Consumers voted it so in a recent Harris Poll, usurping the spot formerly held by Apple.

Amazon has done a lot more than become a stellar retailer. It has reinvented, disrupted, redefined, and renovated the global marketplace. Last year, e-commerce sales around the world surpassed $1 trillion for the first time; Amazon accounted for more than 5% of that volume. This seemingly inevitable shift has claimed plenty of victims, with more to come. Big-box retailers like Circuit City and Best Buy bore the brunt of Amazon's digital assault, while shopping-mall mainstays such as Sears and JCPenney have also seen sales tank. Malls in general, which once seemed to offer some shelter from the online pummeling, have been hollowed out. By Green Street Advisors' estimate, 10% of the country's large malls will close in the next decade. It has become painfully clear that the chance to sift through bins of sweaters simply isn't enough of a draw for shoppers anymore. "It has been this way in retail forever," says Kevin Sterneckert, a research VP at Gartner who focuses on shopping trends, and who lays out a strategy that should blow nobody's mind: "If you don't innovate and address who your customers are, you become irrelevant." And now that means fending off threats from every phone, tablet, and laptop on the planet.

Amazon's increasing dominance is now less about what it sells than how it sells. And that portends a second wave of change that will further devastate competitors and transform retail again. It's not just "1-Click Ordering" on Amazon's mobile app, which is tailor-made for impulse buying. It's not just the company's "Subscribe & Save" feature, which lets customers schedule regular replenishments of essentials like toilet paper and deodorant. It's not just Amazon's "Lockers" program, in which huge metal cabinets are installed at 7-Elevens and Staples in select cities, letting customers securely pick up packages at their convenience instead of risking missed (or stolen) deliveries.

No, it's all this, plus something more primal: speed. Bezos has turned Amazon into an unprecedented speed demon that can give you anything you want. Right. Now. To best understand Amazon's aggressive game plan—and its true ambitions—you need to begin with Amazon Prime, the company's $79-per-year, second-day delivery program. "I think Amazon Prime is the best bargain in the history of shopping," Bezos tells me, noting that the service now includes free shipping on more than 15 million items, up from the 1 million it launched with in 2005. Prime members also gain access to more than 40,000 streaming Instant Video programs and 300,000 free books in the Kindle Owners' Lending Library. As annoying as this might be to Netflix, it is not intended primarily as an assault on that business. Rather, Bezos is willing to lose money on shipping and services in exchange for loyalty. Those 10 million Prime members (up from 5 million two years ago, according to *Morningstar*) are practically addicted to using Amazon. The average Prime member spends an astounding $1,224 a year on Amazon, which is $700 more than a regular user. Members' purchases and membership fees make up more than a third of Amazon's U.S. profit. And memberships are projected to rise 150%, to 25 million, by 2017.

Robbie Schwietzer, VP of Prime, is more candid than his boss when explaining Prime's true purpose: "Once you become a Prime member, your human nature takes over. You want to leverage your $79 as much as possible," he says. "Not only do you buy more, but you buy in a broader set of categories. You discover all the selections we have that you otherwise wouldn't have thought to look to Amazon for." And what you buy at Amazon you won't buy from your local retailer.

Prime is phase one in a three-tiered scheme that also involves expanding Amazon's local fulfillment capabilities and a nascent program called AmazonFresh. Together, these pillars will remake consumers' expectations about retail. Bezos seems to relish the coming changes. "In the old world, you could make a living by hoping that your customer didn't know whether your price was actually competitive. That's a very"—Bezos pauses for a second to rummage for the least insulting word—"tenuous strategy in the new world. [Now] you can't convince

people you have the low price; you actually have to have the low price. You can't persuade people that your delivery speeds are fast; you actually have to have fast delivery speeds!" With that last challenge, he erupts in a thunderous laugh, throwing his cleanly depilated head so far back that you can see the dark fillings on his upper molars. He really does seem to know something the rest of us don't. We're still asleep, he says? The alarm clock at Amazon went off hours ago. Whether the rest of the retail world has woken up yet is another question.

Amazon's 1-million-square-foot Phoenix fulfillment center produces a steady and syncopated rhythm. It is the turn of mechanical conveyor belts, the thud of boxes hitting metal, the beeping of forklifts moving to and fro, and the hum of more than 100 industrial-size air conditioners whirring away. This is the sound of speed—a sonic representation of what it takes to serve millions of customers scattered across the globe.

In centers like this one, of which there are 89 globally (with more to come), Amazon has built the complex machinery to make sure a product will ship out in less than 2.5 hours from the time a customer clicks place your order. From that click, a set of algorithms calculates the customer's location, desired shipping speed, and product availability; it then dispatches the purchase request to "pickers" on duty at the nearest fulfillment center. The system directs the new order to the picker who is closest on the floor to that product, popping up with a bleep on the picker's handheld scanner gun. These men and women roam the sea of product shelves with carts, guided by Amazon's steady hand to the precise location of the product on the color-coded shelves. The picker gathers the item and puts it into a bin with other customer orders. And from there, the item zooms off on a conveyor belt to a boxing station, where a computer instructs a worker on what size box to grab and what items belong in that box. After the packer completes an order, the word success lights up in big green letters on a nearby computer screen. Then the package goes back on a conveyor, where the fastest delivery method is calculated by scanning the box, which is then kicked down a winding chute to the appropriate truck.

The process is efficient, but still lower tech than it could be. Although Amazon shelled out $775 million last year for those orange Kiva robots, it says it's still "evaluating" how to deploy the bots, and they're nowhere to be seen here. "Fulfillment by Amazon" is still a very human endeavor—and the company's creativity thrives within that limitation. A team at the Phoenix center is constantly thinking of ways to chip away at the 2.5-hour processing time. For instance, when products arrive from Amazon's vendors and the 2 million third-party merchants who sell their goods on the site, workers now scan them into Amazon's inventory system (again, with a handheld gun) instead of entering the details manually. Also, products have been stowed on shelves in what otherwise might appear to be a random way—for example, a single stuffed teddy bear might be next to a college biology book—because it reduces the potential distance a worker must trek between popular products that might be ordered together. Small tweaks like these have an impact: In the past two years, Amazon has reduced the time it took to move a product by a quarter. During the past holiday season, the company processed 306 items per second worldwide.

Amazon-Proof Retail

How one store merges digital and physical

If anyone can design a brick-and-mortar store for an e-commerce world, it should be Nadia Shouraboura. She used to be Amazon's VP of global supply chain and fulfillment technology and has since created Hointer, a fully automated store run on software algorithms and machinery. She calls it a "microwarehouse" that marries digital's instant gratification with in-store benefits. "In apparel, this will win," she predicts. It works like this:

Step 1. Search
A customer enters the spare store, where there's only one of every product in view. She pulls up the Hointer app, scans the QR code on a pair of jeans she likes, and enters her size.

Step 2. Deliver
Within 30 seconds of scanning the code, a pair of jeans in her size travels through a chute and lands in her dressing room. She can scan as many items as she likes.

Step 3. Refine
Inside the dressing room, she tries on the jeans, but they're too baggy. So she chucks them down another chute and selects a smaller size from the app.

Step 4. Purchase
The jeans fit! She pays on her phone or swipes her card at a kiosk, and leaves the store with her purchase. No sales clerk necessary.

These centers aren't just about warehouse speed, though: They're also about proximity. Over the past several years, Bezos has poured billions into building them in areas closer and closer to customers. The Phoenix warehouse, one of four in the region, serves a metro area of nearly 4 million. Robbinsville, New Jersey, is roughly one hour from 8 million New Yorkers. Patterson, California, is an hour and a half from 7 million people living in the San Francisco Bay Area. Three locations in Texas—Coppell, Haslet, and Schertz—will serve not only the nearly 9 million citizens of the Dallas and San Antonio metro areas but also the other 17 million or so customers in the state (and possibly neighboring states too) who live only a few hundred miles away.

"What you see happening," Bezos explains, "is that we can have inventory geographically near major urban populations. If we can be smart enough—and when I say 'smart enough,' I mean have the right technology, the right software systems, machine-learning tools—to position inventory in all the right places, over time, your items never get on an airplane. It's lower cost, less fuel burned, and faster delivery."

The holy grail of shipping—same-day delivery—is tantalizingly within reach. Amazon already offers that service in select cities, what it calls "local express" delivery, but the big trick is

to do it nationally. And the crucial element of this ambitious plan is revealed by something wonkier than a bunch of buildings. It is something only an accountant could see coming: a cunning shift in tax strategy.

If you were a competitor who knew what to listen for, you'd practically hear the Jaws theme every time Bezos said the word taxes. For years, Amazon fervently avoided establishing what is called a "tax nexus"—that is, a large-enough physical presence—in states that could potentially force it to collect sales tax from its customers, something brick-and-mortar and mom-and-pop stores had long argued would finally remove Amazon's unfair pricing advantage. In states that dared to challenge Amazon, the company would quickly yank operations. The scrutiny even extended to its sale of products by other merchants. "We had to be very careful, even with the third-party business, about not incurring tax-nexus stuff," recalls John Rossman, a former Amazon executive and current managing director at Alvarez and Marsal, a Seattle-based consulting firm.

But Amazon has since changed its mind. It determined that the benefits of more fulfillment centers—and all the speed they'll provide—will outweigh the tax cost they'll incur. So it began negotiating with states for tax incentives. South Carolina agreed to let the company slide without collecting sales tax until 2016, in exchange for bringing 2,000 jobs to the state. In California, Amazon was given a year to start collecting taxes in exchange for building three new warehouses. And at the end of 2011, Amazon even threw its support behind a federal bill that would mandate all online retailers with sales of more than $1 million to collect tax in states in which they sold to customers. In 2012 alone, Amazon spent $2.5 million lobbying for issues that included what's known as the Marketplace Fairness Act—the same law, essentially, it had once moved heaven and earth to eradicate. The bill recently cleared the U.S. Senate and awaits passage in the House.

"The general perception is companies thinking, Oh, great, finally a level playing field," Rossman says. "But other retailers are going to regret the day. Sales tax was one of the few things impeding Amazon from expanding. Now it's like wherever Amazon wants to be, whatever Amazon wants to do, they are going to do it."

There's yet another weapon in Amazon's offensive, and it's ready for rollout. It's called AmazonFresh, a grocery delivery service that has long been available only in Seattle. The site has a selection of 100,000 items, and from my hotel room in that city on a recent Saturday at 11 a.m., I gave it a try. I clicked on chips, bananas, apples, yogurt, and a case of bottled water—along with a DVD of Silver Linings Playbook and a Moleskine reporter's notebook. After checking out and paying the $10 delivery fee, I requested my goods to arrive during the 7 p.m. to 8 p.m window. At 7:15 that evening, De, my AmazonFresh delivery woman, showed up in the lobby. She helped carry my bags up the elevator and to my hotel room, and tried several times to refuse a $5 tip for the trouble I put her through in the name of research. It was simple, easy—and for Amazon competitors, very threatening.

De and the Kiva robots are central to what Amazon sees as the future of shopping: whatever you want, whenever you want it, wherever you want it, as fast as you demand it. AmazonFresh is expected to expand soon to 20 more urban markets—including some outside America. Los Angeles became the second AmazonFresh market, this past June, and customers there were offered something the folks in Seattle must wish they got: a free trial of Prime Fresh, the upgrade version of Amazon Prime, which provides free shipping of products and free delivery of groceries for orders over $35. Subscribers will pay an annual fee of $299. Considering that grocery delivery otherwise costs between $8 and $10 each time (depending on order size), the subscription covers itself after about 30 deliveries—which busy families will quickly exceed.

Bezos, in his cagey, friendly way, seems more excited about my Fresh experience than he is about describing Fresh's future. He seems almost surprised that the service worked so well at a hotel, given that it was designed for home delivery. "Thank you!" he shouts. After peppering me with questions on how, precisely, the delivery went down, he finally gets around to addressing the service's business purpose.

"We'd been doing a very efficient job with our current distribution model for a wide variety of things," Bezos says. "Diapers? Fine, no problem. Even Cheerios. But there are a bunch of products that you can't just wrap up in a cardboard box and ship 'em. It doesn't work for milk. It doesn't work for hamburger." So he developed a service that would work—not because he suddenly wanted to become your full-service grocer but because of how often people buy food.

AmazonFresh is actually a Trojan horse, a service designed for a much greater purpose. "It was articulated [in the initial, internal pitch to Bezos] that this would work with the broader rollout of same-day delivery," says Tom Furphy, a former Amazon executive who launched Fresh in 2007 and ran it until 2009. Creating a same-day delivery service poses tremendous logistical and economic hurdles. It's the so-called last-mile problem—you can ship trucks' worth of packages from a warehouse easily enough, but getting an individual package to wind its way through a single neighborhood and arrive at a single consumer's door isn't easy. The volume of freight and frequency of delivery must outweigh the costs of fuel and time, or else this last mile is wildly expensive. You can't hire a battalion of Des unless they earn their keep. So by expanding grocery delivery, Amazon hopes to transform monthly customers to weekly—or even thrice-weekly—customers. And that, in turn, will produce the kind of order volume that makes same-day delivery worth investing in. "Think of the synergy between Prime, same-day delivery, and Fresh," says Furphy. "When all of those things start working in concert, it can be a very beautiful thing."

AmazonFresh is arguably the last link in Bezos's big plan: to make Amazon the dominant servicer—not just seller—of the entire retail experience. The difference is crucial. Third-party sellers, retailers large and small, now account for 40% of Amazon's product sales. Amazon generally gets up to a 20% slice of each transaction. Those sellers are also highly incentivized to use Fulfillment by Amazon (known as FBA). Rather than shipping their products themselves after a sale is made on the Amazon site, these retailers let Amazon do the heavy lifting, picking and packing at places like the Phoenix center. For the sellers, an FBA agreement grants them access to Prime shipping speeds, which can help them win new customers and can allow them to sell at slightly higher prices. For Amazon, FBA increases sales, profits, and the likelihood that any shopper can find any item on its website.

The burgeoning AmazonFresh transportation network will help expand these numbers. In Los Angeles and Seattle, a fleet of Fresh trucks delivers everything from full-course meals to chocolate from local merchants. The bright green branded trucks—with polite drivers in branded uniforms—let Amazon personify its brand, giving it the same kind of trustworthy familiarity that fueled the rise of UPS in the 1930s. "If you have all kinds of fly-by-night operations coming to your door, people don't like that," says Yossi Sheffi, professor and director of the MIT Center for Transportation and Logistics. "It's different with someone in a U.S. Postal Service or FedEx uniform. Those brands inspire confidence."

As Amazon evolves into a same-day delivery service, its active transportation fleet could become yet another competitive advantage. By supplementing its long-term relationships with UPS and FedEx with its own Fresh trucks, Amazon may well be able to deliver faster than retailers that depend entirely on outside services. "Pretty soon, if you're a retailer with your online business, you're going to be faced with a choice," says Brian Walker, a former analyst at Forrester Research who is now with Hybris, a provider of e-commerce software. "You're not going to be able to match Amazon, so you're going to have to consider partnering with them and leveraging their network."

This shift could even turn Amazon into a competitor to UPS and FedEx, the long-standing duopoly of next-day U.S. shipping. "If Amazon could do it at enough scale, they could offer shipping at a great value and still eke out some margin," says Walker. "In classic Amazon fashion, they could leverage the infrastructure they've built for themselves, take a disruptive approach to the pricing, and run it as an efficiency play."

Amazon has been down this road before. Its Web Services began as an efficient, reliable back end to handle its own web operations—then became so adept that it now provides digital services for an enormous range of customers, including Netflix and, reportedly, Apple. It's not impossible to imagine Amazon doing the same with shipping. Last year, the company cut its shipping costs as a percentage of sales from 5.4% to 4.5%. As it builds more distribution centers, installs more lockers, and builds out its fleet, Amazon is likely to drive those efficiency costs down even further.

So is Amazon Freight Services Bezos's next mission? When I ask, the laugh lines vanish from his face as if someone flipped a switch on his back. He contends that same-day delivery is too expensive outside of urban markets and that it only makes sense for Amazon to deliver its own products within the Fresh program. In China, he explains, Amazon does in fact deliver products via many couriers and bicycle messengers. "But in a country like the United States," he says, "we have such a sophisticated last-mile delivery system that it makes more sense for Amazon to use that system to reach its customers in a rapid and accurate way." When I ask whether he would consider, say, buying UPS, with its 90,000 trucks—or even more radically, purchasing the foundering USPS, with its 213,000 vehicles running daily through America's cities and towns—Bezos scoffs. But he won't precisely say no.

Rivals aren't waiting for an answer. EBay has launched eBay Now, a $5 service that uses its own branded couriers in New York, San Francisco, and San Jose, to fetch products from local retail stores like Best Buy and Toys "R" Us and deliver them to customers within an hour. Google, fully aware that Amazon's market share in product search is substantial (now 30% to Google's 13%), has launched a pilot service called Google Shopping Express, which partners with courier companies. Walmart—which has booted all Kindles from its stores—started testing same-day delivery in select cities during the last holiday season, shipping items directly from its stores. (Joel Anderson, chief executive of Walmart.com, even suggested paying in-store shoppers to deliver online orders to other customers the same day. Come for a handsaw, leave with a job!)

These are the sort of ideas that retailers—both e-commerce and physical, large and small—will have to consider as Amazon expands. Guys like Jeff Jordan, partner at well-known venture firm Andreessen Horowitz, will make sure of it. His firm follows and invests in direct-to-consumer businesses. "We won't invest in a company," he says, "unless they can tell us why they won't get steamrolled by Amazon."

Given the astounding growth of Amazon, and the seemingly infinite ways it has defied the critics, Bezos may have proved himself the best CEO in the world at taking the long view. But he doesn't like talking about it. "Did you bring the crystal ball? I left mine at home today," he quips. He does, however, like discussing what the future might bring for his customers. In fact, he likes talking about his customer so much that the word can seem like a conversational tic; he used it 40 times, by my count, in just one interview. "It's impossible to imagine that 10 years from now, I could interview an Amazon customer and they would tell me, 'Yeah, I really love Amazon. I just wish your prices were a little higher,'" he says. "Or, 'I just wish you'd deliver a little more slowly.'" In Bezos's world, the goal of the coming decade is a lot like the goal of the past two: Be cheap. Be fast. That's how you win.

There is, naturally, no guarantee that Bezos will simply win and win and win. The bigger Amazon gets, the greater the number and variety of stakeholders required to make the Amazon machine hum. Many seem to be getting increasingly frustrated. Consider Amazon's third-party sellers—that group making up 40% of the company's product sales. Earlier this year, Amazon issued a series of fee hikes for use of its fulfillment services, ranging from as low as 5 cents per smallish unit to as much as $100 for heavier or awkwardly shaped items (like a whiteboard, say, or roll-away bed). Many sellers took to Amazon's forums to complain, and others threatened to go to eBay, which mostly leaves fulfillment to its sellers. "I think Amazon is a necessary evil," says Louisa Eyler, distributor for Lock Laces, a shoelace product that sells as many as 3,000 units per week on Amazon. After the price hike, Eyler says her total fees for the $7.99 item went from $2.37 to $3.62. She says Amazon now makes more per unit than she does.

Or consider the frustrations of Amazon employees, who are striking at two of its eight German facilities in an effort to wrest higher wages and overtime pay. At the height of the conflict, on June 17, 1,300 workers walked off the job. (It is one of Amazon's largest walk-offs in its biggest foreign market, and could result in shipping delays.) Meanwhile, Amazon workers in the U.S. have filed a lawsuit claiming that they've been subject to excessive security checks—to search for pilfered items—at warehouses. The suit alleges their wait could last as long as 25 minutes, an inconvenience Amazon would never subject its customers to. "It means there's a broken process somewhere," says Annette Gleneicki, an executive at Confirmit, a software company that helps businesses capture customer and employee feedback. "[Bezos] clearly inspires passion in his employees, but that's only sustainable for so long."

The company could be vulnerable on other fronts as well. Target and Walgreens have "geo-fenced" their stores so their mobile apps can guide customers directly to the products they desire. Walmart and Macy's have begun making their stores do double-duty, both as a place to shop and a warehouse from which to ship products. (The strategy seems to be paying off for Macy's, which recently reported a jump in first-quarter profit and is now fulfilling 10% of its online purchases from its stores.) They're proving that retail won't go away—it'll learn and adapt. "Now you have smart brick-and-mortar stores saying, Why isn't our experience more intuitive, as it is on the web?" says Doug Stephens, author of *The Retail Revival: Re-Imagining Business for the New Age of Consumerism.* "We should know a consumer when they walk in, and what they bought before, in the same way as Amazon's recommendation engine."

Bezos won't admit to any deep concern. While Amazon's paper-thin profits continue to perplex observers (the company netted only $82 million in the first quarter of 2013), the three primary weapons in its retail takeover—fulfillment centers, Amazon Prime, and now AmazonFresh—are coming to maturity. If the next year tells us anything about Amazon's future, it should reveal whether Bezos's decision to plow billions back into these operations will give the company an end-to-end service advantage that might be nearly impossible for its competitors to overcome.

The sun seems to be setting on Bezos's big Day One. Before we part ways in Seattle, I ask him what we can expect to see on Day Two. "Day Two will be when the rate of change slows," he replies. "But there's still so much you can do with technology to improve the customer experience. And that's the sense in which I believe it's still Day One, and that it's early in the day. If anything, the rate of change is accelerating."

Of course, Bezos is the accelerator.

Critical Thinking

1. Define business model and describe what Amazon's business model is. Define value proposition and describe what Amazon's value proposition is. Bezos says his plan is to make Amazon the dominant "servicer" of the entire retail experience. Explain why he uses the term "servicer" rather than "seller" or "marketer."

2. "Day One" is a central motivating idea for Jeff Bezos. What is his "Day One" philosophy? How might he apply this philosophy to AmazonFresh?

3. About the time this article went to press, Jeff Bezos announced his purchase of the *Washington Post* for $250 million. Given what you've learned about Bezos' approach to retail, what changes do you think he might make to the business model of the American newspaper?

Create Central

www.mhhe.com/createcentral

Internet References

Era of Digital Marketing [Infographic]

www.cmswire.com/cms/customer-experience/how-millennials-are-influencing-a-new-era-of-digital-marketing-infographic-021695.php?utm_source=MainRSSFeed&utm_medium=Web&utm_campaign=RSS-News

Will Millennials Change How Cars Are Bought and Sold?

http://business.time.com/2012/08/09/will-millennials-change-how-cars-are-bought-and-sold

J.J. McCorvey is an assistant editor for *Fast Company* magazine, where he covers technology and writes Next, Fast Talk, and feature stories.

Article

Prepared by: Daniel Mittleman, *DePaul University*

Can Online Piracy Be Stopped by Laws?

Considering the legal responsibilities of Internet intermediaries in the aftermath of the Stop Online Privacy Act controversy.

PAMELA SAMUELSON

Learning Outcomes

After reading this article, you will be able to:

- Describe the controversy over piracy of digital media.

- Articulate arguments for and against legislation to protect digital media copyright.

While on a scuba diving trip in the Seychelles Islands earlier this year, I found myself worrying about pirates. Real pirates, as in people who attack boats, take hostages, and sometimes kill their prey. This kind of piracy has become unfortunately common in that part of the world.

On board our ship were four former British special forces soldiers who served as security guards. They were armed with semiautomatic weapons and on patrol, 24/7, for the entire trip. The danger was not just hypothetical. The frigate berthed next to us as we boarded had 25 pirates in its brig.

Waking up every morning to the prospect of encountering real pirates added brio to our excursion. It also induced reflections on use of the word "piracy" to describe copyright infringements. Downloading music is really not in the same league as armed attacks on ships.

As we were cruising from Mahe to Aldabra, I expected to be far away from it all. But the ship got a daily fax of the main stories being published in the *New York Times*. Among them were stories about the controversy over the proposed legislation known as the Stop Online Piracy Act (SOPA). SOPA would have given the entertainment industry new legal tools to impede access to foreign "rogue" Web sites that host infringing content and to challenge U.S.-directed Web sites that the industry thought were either indifferent or acquiescent to storage of infringing materials.

For a time, it seemed virtually inevitable that SOPA would become law. Yet because strong opposition emerged from technology companies, computer security experts, civil liberties groups and members of the general public, SOPA has been put on hold. It is unlikely to be enacted in anything like its original form.

This column will explain the key features of SOPA, why the entertainment industry believed SOPA was necessary to combat online piracy, and why SOPA came to be perceived as so flawed that numerous sponsors withdrew their support from the bill.

Blocking Access to "Foreign Rogue Web Sites"

As introduced, SOPA would have empowered the Attorney General (AG) of the U.S. to seek court orders requiring foreign Web sites to cease providing access to infringing copies of U.S. works. Because "rogue" Web sites seemed unlikely to obey a U.S. court order, SOPA further empowered the AG to serve these orders on U.S. Internet intermediaries who would then have been required to take "technically feasible and reasonable measures" to block their users from accessing the foreign Web sites. This included "measures designed to prevent the domain name of the foreign infringing site . . . from resolving to that domain name's Internet protocol address." These measures needed to be undertaken "as expeditiously as possible," but no later than five days after receipt of the orders.

Upon receiving a copy of a rogue-Web site order, search engines would have been required to block access to the sites even if users were searching for items that would otherwise have brought the sites to their attention. Internet service providers would have had to ensure that users who typed certain URLs (for example, http://thepiratebay.se) into their browsers could not reach those sites. Payment providers (such as Visa or Mastercard) would have had to suspend services for completing transactions. Internet advertising services would have had to discontinue serving ads and providing or receiving funds for advertising at these sites.

Those who failed to comply with the DNS blocking obligations could expect the AG to sue them. The AG was also empowered to sue those who provided a service designed to circumvent this DNS blocking (for example, a plug-in or directory that mapped blocked URLs with numerical DNS representations).

Frustrated by the weak enforcement of intellectual property rights (IPRs) abroad, the U.S. entertainment industry urged Congress to adopt SOPA as the best way to impede online infringements. Foreign rogue Web sites might still be out there, but if U.S.-based Internet intermediaries blocked access to the sites, users would not be able to access infringing materials through U.S. intermediaries.

Because ISPs in the U.S. and abroad have no duty to monitor what users do on their sites, it is easy for sites to become hosts of large volumes of infringing materials. Some operators seemingly turn a blind eye to infringement, some encourage posting of infringing content, while other sites may just be misused by infringers. By cutting off sources of transactional and advertising revenues, the hope was to discourage these sites from continuing to operate.

Challenging U.S.-Directed Web Sites

SOPA would also have given holders of U.S. intellectual property rights (IPRs) power to challenge "U.S.-directed sites dedicated to the theft of U.S. property." At first blush, it might seem that reasonable persons should support a law crafted to target such sites. But "dedicated to the theft of U.S. property" was defined in a troublingly ambiguous and overbroad way. It included operators of sites that were taking "deliberate actions to avoid confirming a high probability of the use of [that] site to carry out acts" in violation of copyright or anti-circumvention rules. Also included was any site that was "primarily designed or operated for the purpose of, ha[d] only a limited use other than, or [wa]s marketed by its operator or another acting in concert with that operator in, offering goods or services in a manner that engages in, enables, or facilitates" violations of copyright or anti-circumvention laws.

SOPA would have enabled firms who believed themselves to be harmed by one of these sites to send letters to payment providers and/or to Internet advertising services to demand that they cease providing services to sites alleged to be "dedicated to the theft of U.S. property" shortly after receiving such letters.

Payment providers and Internet advertising services were then tasked with notifying the challenged sites about the "dedicated-to-theft" allegations against them. Challenged sites could contest these allegations by sending counter-notices to the payment providers and Internet advertising services. But without a counter-notice, payment providers and Internet advertising services had to cease further dealings with the challenged Web sites.

Content owners could also sue dedicated-to-theft sites directly to enjoin them from undertaking further actions that evidenced their dedication to theft. SOPA also authorized content owners to sue payment providers or advertising services who failed to comply with demands that they cease dealing with challenged Web sites.

SOPA's Flaws

The main problems with SOPA insofar as it would have employed DNS blocking to impede access to foreign rogue Web sites were, first, that it would undermine the security and

stability of the Internet as a platform for communication and commerce and second, that it would be ineffective.

SOPA is fundamentally inconsistent with DNSSEC (DNS Security Extensions), a protocol developed to avoid abusive redirections of Internet traffic, whether by criminals, autocratic governments, or other wrongdoers. Computer security experts spent more than a decade developing DNSSEC, which is now being implemented all over the world, including by U.S. government agencies.

As the USACM Public Policy Committee observed in a letter sent to members of Congress, DNSSEC Web site operators cannot reliably block offending sites "and so may be faced with the choice of abandoning DNSSEC or being in violation of issued court orders."

This letter explained why DNS blocking would be ineffective. "[I]t is effectively impossible to bar access to alternate DNS servers around the globe because there are millions of them on the Internet." Use of those servers "allows for bypassing of DNS blocking." Circumvention of DNS blocking is, moreover, "technically simple and universally available." Browser add-ons to avoid DNS blocking have already been developed and would be available on servers outside the U.S., even if illegal in the U.S.

The main problems with the dedicated-to-theft provisions of SOPA were, first, that it was too imprecise and second, that it represented a dramatic change in the rules of the road affecting Internet intermediaries.

What does it mean, for instance, for an Internet intermediary to take "deliberate actions to avoid confirming a high probability" of infringement on the site? If Viacom tells YouTube it has found infringing clips of "South Park" shows on its site, does YouTube become a site dedicated to the theft of Viacom's property if it does not investigate these claims? If Universal Music Group objects to the resale of MP3 files of its music on eBay, does eBay become a site dedicated to theft of Universal's property because one or more of its users offer the MP3 files for sale there?

Many Internet companies considered the dedicated-to-theft definition to be fundamentally inconsistent with the safe harbors established by the Digital Millennium Copyright Act (DMCA). Under the DMCA, Internet intermediaries are obliged to take down infringing materials after they are notified about specific infringements at specific parts of their Web sites. They have no obligation to monitor their sites for infringement. The safe harbors have been an important factor in the extraordinary growth of the Internet economy.

The safe harbors have been an important factor in the extraordinary growth of the Internet economy.

It may be apt to characterize sites such as Napster, Aimster, and Grokster as having been dedicated to the theft of U.S. intellectual property, but existing copyright law supplied copyright owners with ample tools with which to shut down those sites.

Had the entertainment industry sought more narrowly targeted rules aimed at inducing payment providers and Internet advertising services to stop the flow of funds to sites that were really dedicated to infringement, such a law might have passed. But that was not SOPA.

Conclusion

The collapse of support for SOPA was principally due to concerted efforts by Internet service providers (including Wikipedia, which went "dark" one day to protest SOPA), computer security experts, civil society groups, and millions of Internet users who contacted their Congressional representatives to voice opposition to the bill.

Because SOPA was a flawed piece of legislation, the collapse was a good thing.

Because SOPA was a flawed piece of legislation, the collapse was a good thing. It would, however, be a mistake to think the battle over Internet intermediary liability for infringing acts of users has been won for good.

The entertainment industry is almost certainly going to make further efforts to place greater legal responsibilities on Internet intermediaries. This industry believes intermediaries are the only actors in the Internet ecosystem who can actually affect the level of online infringements that contributes to entertainment industry panics.

An odd thing about the entertainment industry is its deeply skewed views about piracy. In movies such as *Pirates of the Caribbean,* the industry glamorizes brigands who attack ships by depicting them as romantic heroes who have great adventures and engage in swashbuckling fun. Yet, it demonizes fans who download music and movies as

pernicious evildoers who are, in its view, destroying this vital part of the U.S. economy. Something is amiss here, and it is contributing to a profound disconnect in perspectives about how much the law can do to bring about changes in norms about copyright.

Critical Thinking

1. The RIAA likens people who acquire music from "rogue" websites (sites populated with mustic, video, games, or software that host torrents or other file sharing applications) to pirates or criminals. Do you agree?

2. If legislation such as SOPA and PIPA are not the answer to protecting copyright in the digital age, what is the answer? Might different, scaled down, legislation work? Might there be a technological solution? Or might there be a business model solution to this dilemma?

Create Central

www.mhhe.com/createcentral

Internet References

The Future of TV: How Do Networks Plan to Stay Competitive?
www.pbs.org/newshour/bb/media/july-dec13/comcast_09-25.html

Lawrence Lessig: Laws that Choke Creativity [TED Talk]
www.ted.com/talks/larry_lessig_says_the_law_is_strangling_creativity.html

What Happens to Traditional TV When Technology Creates New Ways to Watch?
www.pbs.org/newshour/bb/media/july-dec13/tvfuture_09-12.html

PAMELA SAMUELSON (pam@law.berkeley.edu) is the Richard M. Sherman Distinguished Professor of Law and Information at the University of California, Berkeley.

Unit 6

UNIT

Prepared by: Daniel Mittleman, *DePaul University*

IT, Business, and Economy

Innovation may be defined as radical or breakthrough change that improves products, services, or business processes. It is innovation that drives growth in an economy by sparking new investment, creating new markets, and pruning deadwood companies who failed to innovate from the marketplace. When we think of innovation, we think of breakthrough new product design or establishment of new product categories.

Apple computer has seen both. The iPhone, in 2007, quickly dominated its market by completely re-envisioning mobile phone user experience. And the iPad created a whole new market category essentially zooming an iPhone interface to tablet size, which permitted effective movie or business document viewing.

Information technology has been a major driver of innovation the past half century not only by creating new products and product categories (who would have imagined an iTunes store in 1965?), but also by vastly improving productivity through more effective workflow processes. For example, Amazon has 24/7 distribution centers with highly automated "pick, pack, and ship" processes. Amazon's supply-chain automation is responsible, at least in part, for the company's growth and success.

Innovation, however, has a dark side; more than one, actually.

First, there is the issue of patents. Patents are intended to encourage innovation by protecting the inventor and giving him or her an ample head start to earn back development costs, while at the same time promoting more innovation by requiring the details of each invention be revealed, and limiting the amount of time a patent monopoly right can be maintained. While patents, perhaps, work well in other industries to promote innovation, in computer and communication technologies they have become a morass, slowing innovation and adding significant costs to new startups.

A typical new computing device (such as a tablet or cell phone) may contain hundreds of patents, and a networking technology can contain many more. For example, as of 2008, a 4G wireless network would utilize over 18,300 patents, with over 16,000 new patent applications under review. And this is beyond the 80,000 patents used in its underlying backbone.[1] How can a new network vendor innovate in this environment without violating a patent (or worse, have a threatened competitor perceive their patent was violated and sue to delay development of the product)? How can a network innovator even know whether their product violates one of 114,000 potential patents?

It is not surprising, then, that patent lawsuits have become the norm for almost all large scale IT development efforts. And paying patent licensing fees, rather than fighting patent claims, has become the norm as well. Many large firms, Google, Apple, and Microsoft among them, have purchased companies simply to acquire their patent holdings and protect their own development efforts. Further exacerbating the situation is the presence of patent trolls: small companies who have acquired patents from others and exist solely to sue others for patent violation, which given the number of outstanding patents, the complexity of development efforts, and the cost of fighting a patent lawsuit, are easy pickings.

Second to the issue of patents is the issue of innovation and jobs. Economists have long debated whether innovation creates jobs or costs jobs. Today, most economists would agree that in the long term innovation builds a larger economy and with that growth comes more jobs. However, the new jobs may not be direct replacement for the old jobs. The new jobs may require different education or training. The new jobs may be at a different location. And the new jobs, if at the same skill level, may not pay nearly as well. So, the people who lose jobs because of innovation are not necessarily the same people who get jobs. And that leaves specific individuals out of work and unhappy about the change.

Note

1. L. Gilroy, T. D'Amato, How many patents does it take to build an iPhone?, *Intellectual Property Today,* November 2009 (accessed on October 13, 2012 at http://www.iptoday.com/issues/2009/11/articles/how-many-patents-take-build-iPhone.asp)

Article   Prepared by: Daniel Mittleman, *DePaul University*

The Lost Steve Jobs Tapes

A treasure trove of unearthed interviews, conducted by the writer who knew him best, reveals how Jobs's ultimate success at Apple can be traced directly to his so-called wilderness years.

BRENT SCHLENDER

Learning Outcomes

After reading this article, you will be able to:

- Describe the strengths and weaknesses of Steve Jobs's management style.
- Understand how Apple's iPod/iPhone/iPad technologies were informed more by the movie makers at Pixar than by computer makers at Apple and IBM.

If Steve Jobs's life were staged as an opera, it would be a tragedy in three acts. And the titles would go something like this: Act I—The Founding of Apple Computer and the Invention of the PC Industry; Act II—The Wilderness Years; and Act III—A Triumphant Return and Tragic Demise.

The first act would be a piquant comedy about the brashness of genius and the audacity of youth, abruptly turning ominous when our young hero is cast out of his own kingdom. The closing act would plumb the profound irony of a balding and domesticated high-tech rock star coming back to transform Apple far beyond even his own lofty expectations, only to fall mortally ill and then slowly, excruciatingly wither away, even as his original creation miraculously bulks up into the biggest digital dynamo of them all. Both acts are picaresque tales that end with a surge of deep pathos worthy of Shakespeare.

But that second act—The Wilderness Years—would be altogether different in tone and spirit. In fact, the soul of this act would undermine its title, a convenient phrase journalists and biographers use to describe his 1985 to 1996 hiatus from Apple, as if the only meaningful times in Jobs's life were those spent in Cupertino. In fact, this middle period was the most pivotal of his life. And perhaps the happiest. He finally settled down, married, and had a family. He learned the value of patience and the ability to feign it when he lost it. Most important, his work with the two companies he led during that time, NeXT and Pixar, turned him into the kind of man, and leader, who would spur Apple to unimaginable heights upon his return.

Indeed, what at first glance seems like more wandering for the barefoot hippie who dropped out of Reed College to hitchhike around India, is in truth the equivalent of Steve Jobs attending business school. In other words, he grew. By leaps and bounds. In every aspect of his being. With a little massaging, this middle act could even be the plotline for a Pixar movie. It certainly fits the simple mantra John Lasseter ascribes to all the studio's successes, from *Toy Story* to *Up*: "It's gotta be about how the main character changes for the better."

I had covered Jobs for *Fortune* and *The Wall Street Journal* since 1985, but I didn't come to fully appreciate the importance of these "lost" years until after his death last fall. Rummaging through the storage shed, I discovered some three dozen tapes holding recordings of extended interviews—some lasting as long as three hours—that I'd conducted with him periodically over the past 25 years. (Snippets are scattered throughout this story.) Many I had never replayed—a couple hadn't even been transcribed before now. Some were interrupted by his kids bolting into the kitchen as we talked. During others, he would hit the pause button himself before saying something he feared might come back to bite him. Listening to them again with the benefit of hindsight, the ones that took place during that interregnum jump out as especially enlightening.

The lessons are powerful: Jobs matured as a manager and a boss; learned how to make the most of partnerships; found a way to turn his native stubbornness into a productive perseverance. He became a corporate architect, coming to appreciate the scaffolding of a business just as much as the skeletons of real buildings, which always fascinated him. He mastered the art of negotiation by immersing himself in Hollywood, and learned how to successfully manage creative talent, namely the artists at Pixar. Perhaps most important, he developed an astonishing adaptability that was critical to the hit-after-hit-after-hit climb of Apple's last decade. All this, during a time many remember as his most disappointing.

Eleven years is a big chunk of a lifetime. Especially when one's time on earth is cut short. Moreover, many people—particularly creative types—are often their most prolific during their thirties and early forties. With all the heady success of Apple during Jobs's last 14 years, it's all too easy to dismiss these "lost" years. But in truth, they transformed everything.

As I listened again to those hours and hours of tapes, I realized they were, in fact, his most productive.

Steve Jobs did not wander aimlessly into the wilderness after being ousted from Apple in 1985. No happy camper, he was loaded for bear; burning to wreak revenge upon those who had spuriously shoved him into exile, and obsessed with proving to the world that he was no one-trick pony. Within days, he abruptly sold off all but one share of his Apple stock and, flush with a small fortune of about $70 million, set about creating another computer company, this one called NeXT. The startup ostensibly was a vehicle for revolutionizing higher education with powerful, beautiful computers. In reality, it was a bet that one day he would get the better of Apple.

Over all the years Jobs was away from Apple, I can't recall him saying one good thing about the company's brass. Early on, he whined about how CEO John Sculley had "poisoned" the culture of the place. As the years went by, and Apple's fortunes dimmed, Jobs's attacks became more pointed: "Right now it's like the wicked witch in The Wizard of Oz: 'I'm melting. I'm melting,' " he told me in the mid-1990s. "The jig is up. They can't seem to come out with a great computer to save their lives. They need to spend big on industrial design, reintroduce the hipness factor. But no, they hire [Gil] Amelio [as CEO]. It's as if Nike hired the guy that ran Kinney shoes."

At NeXT, Jobs was damn well going to deliver a great computer. He was going to do it with massive resources, raising well over $100 million from the likes of H. Ross Perot, Japanese printer maker Canon, and Carnegie Mellon University. He was going to do it with an astonishing automated factory in Fremont, California, where every surface and piece of equipment would be painted in specific shades of gray, black, and white. He was going to do it in style, working with a full-time architect to give the corporate headquarters in Redwood City a distinctive, austere aesthetic; NeXT HQ looked much like the interior of one of today's Apple Stores. The centerpiece was a staircase that seemed to float in air.

He was also going to do it with a revolutionary organization, something he dubbed the Open Corporation. "Think of it this way," he explained. "If you look at your own body, your cells are specialized, but every single one of them has the master plan for the whole body. We think our company will be the best possible company if every single person working here understands the whole master plan and can use that as a yardstick to make decisions against. We think a lot of little and medium and big decisions will be made better if all our people know that." It was a bold theory.

If Jobs's time in exile can be seen as an extended trip through business school, the heady start of NeXT represents those early days when a student thinks he knows everything and is in a rush to show that to the world. In fact, Jobs had just about every detail wrong. The Open Corporation was a dismal failure in practice. Its hallmark was that employee salaries were not kept secret; there was even an attempt to impose uniform compensation. It didn't work, of course; all kinds of side deals were cut to satiate key employees.

More concretely, Jobs had the whole business plan wrong. It would be two years before NeXT delivered anything to customers. When the NeXTcube computer finally did arrive, it proved too expensive to ever command a serious market. Ultimately, Jobs was forced to admit that the undeniably beautiful machine he and his engineering team concocted was a flop. He laid off most of the staff and turned the company from hardware to software, first to rewrite NeXT's operating system, called NextSTEP, for Intel-based computers. The company also engineered an ingenious development environment called WebObjects, which eventually became its best-selling program.

Jobs didn't know that WebObjects would later prove instrumental in building the online store for Apple and for iTunes, or that NextSTEP would be his ticket back to Apple. The road for NeXT was always rocky, perhaps appropriate for something that was born out of a desire for revenge. It was a good thing he had something else going on the side.

Of the three companies Jobs helped create, Pixar was the purest corporate and organizational expression of his nature. If NeXT was a travail of spite and malice, Pixar was a labor of love.

The Pixar story began even before Jobs left Apple. In early 1985, Apple fellow Alan Kay called his attention to the computer Graphics Group (GG) skunk works in San Rafael, California, an ill-fitting piece of the filmmaking production puzzle George Lucas had assembled for his Skywalker Ranch studios. It was little more than a team of 25 engineers—including a young "user interface designer" named John Lasseter—who desperately wanted to continue to work together even though Lucas, then embroiled in the costly aftermath of a divorce, was looking to sell.

Jobs's trip to take a look-see left an indelible impression. GG's head geek, Ed Catmull, showed him some short demo films made by Lasseter, who was neither a programmer nor a user interface designer, but a talented animator who had left Disney and been given his faux title by Catmull as a way to convince Lucas to put him on the payroll. The films weren't much to look at, but they were three-dimensional, they were generated by computer rather than hand-drawn, and they displayed the whimsy of a master storyteller.

Fascinated, Jobs tried, unsuccessfully, to persuade Apple's board to buy the group. "These guys were way ahead of us on graphics, way ahead," Jobs remembered. "They were way ahead of anybody. I just knew in my bones that this was going to be very important." After getting bounced from Apple, Jobs went back to Lucas and drove a hard bargain. He paid $5 million for the group's assets and provided another $5 million in working capital for the company, which was christened Pixar. In hindsight, the price was a pittance. But in 1985, nobody would have expected Pixar to one day outstrip NeXT. Certainly not Jobs: He didn't build any fancy digs for his motley crew of animators and engineers, who for years made do with used furniture and dowdy offices.

Once again, what Jobs knew in his bones didn't translate into getting the details right. As with NeXT, Jobs initially intended the company to be a purveyor of high-performance computer hardware, this time for two frightfully niche markets: the special-effects departments of Hollywood studios and medical-imaging specialists. By 1989, however, Pixar had sold only a few hundred of its Pixar Image Computers, faux-granite painted cubes originally stickered at $135,000, that had to be paired with expensive engineering workstations to do anything.

This time, the strategy pivot came from the talent. In 1990, Lasseter and Catmull told Jobs they could make a business of creating computer-animated TV commercials—perhaps one day they could even make, and sell, cartoons! Jobs was smitten with Catmull and Lasseter. They were always teaching him something new. Could they deliver on the ultimate promise of the place, to use computers to create an entirely new kind of animation for the cinema and thus upend the entire business model of animation? Jobs decided to focus on this one disruptive opportunity. It was an instinct he would return to, repeatedly, when he rejoined Apple.

In 1991, he fired much of the Pixar staff, announced the new direction to the survivors, and reorganized so that the studio could pursue one animated project at a time. "I got everybody together," Jobs said, "and I said, 'At our heart, we really are a content company. Let's transition out of everything else. Let's go for it. This is why I bought into Pixar. This is why most of you are here. Let's go for it. It's a higher-risk strategy, but the rewards are gonna be much higher, and it's where our hearts are.'" Then he and CFO Lawrence Levy went to work learning everything they could about the dynamics and economics of the animation business. If they were going to start making cartoons, they were going to do it right.

The shift at Pixar occurred at about the same time as the major turn in Jobs's personal life: the blossoming of his romance with Laurene Powell. In 1991, two years after she met him following an informal lecture at Stanford University's Graduate School of Business, Laurene was his pregnant bride, married by a Buddhist monk at the Ahwahnee Hotel in Yosemite National Park.

Jobs had never seemed like the marrying type and hadn't shown much of a sense of responsibility for Lisa, his first daughter, who was born out of wedlock in 1978. He denied paternity initially, even though he had named an Apple computer after her. Egotistical, narcissistic, and manipulative since childhood, Jobs often behaved like a spoiled brat who was accustomed to getting his way.

His personality didn't change overnight after meeting Laurene, but his selfish ways did begin to moderate, especially after his children, Reed, Erin, and Eve, came into the family in 1991, 1995, and 1998, respectively. As is often the case with new parents, Jobs behaved as if he were the first person in the world to discover and fully appreciate the joys of family life. He literally stayed closer to home, converting a clapboard storefront building catty-corner from the Palo Alto Whole Foods into a satellite office so his commute would be a short bike ride. (He didn't use the office all that much after returning to Apple.)

My bureau was a block up the street, and occasionally I'd see him out for a stroll, usually with someone in tow. He always said he could think better when he walked. During these years, his fame had subsided somewhat, so it wasn't like encountering one of the Beatles at the supermarket. People pretty much left him alone.

I bumped into him on one of those walks when he was alone, and wound up joining him as he shopped for a new bicycle for Laurene's upcoming birthday. This was before you could do your homework on the Internet, but he had done his research, so there wasn't much shopping involved. We were in and out of Palo Alto Bicycles in 10 minutes. "I'd never have Andrea do something like this," he said, referring to his longtime administrative assistant. "I like buying presents for my family myself."

Even after he went back to Apple, there was nothing Jobs liked more than spending time at home. Not that he wasn't a workaholic. We were iChat buddies for several years, so his name would pop up whenever he was working at his computer at home. Almost invariably, he was in front of his Mac until after midnight. We'd occasionally have a video chat, and if it took place early in the evening, I'd often see one of his children in the background looking on.

In hindsight, Jobs's having a real family might have been the best thing to happen to Pixar. He was most effective as a marketer and a business leader when he could think of himself as the primary customer. What would he want from a computer-animated movie, both for himself and for his kids? That was the only market-research question he ever asked. He had always demanded great production values and design for his computer products. He was just as picky about what Pixar produced. Lasseter and Catmull couldn't have asked for a more empathetic benefactor.

Shortly after his decision in 1990 to let Lasseter and Catmull start producing commercials and short films, Jobs pulled a rabbit out of his hat: He negotiated a $26 million marketing distribution deal with Disney that provided enough capital to make a full-length, computer-animated motion picture. Because Disney had been a Pixar customer, licensing its software for managing conventional animators, then-CEO Michael Eisner and his head of animation, Jeffrey Katzenberg, were fully aware that the company's technology was solid and unique, and that Lasseter showed flashes of genius as a new breed of animator.

Jobs was candid about the two Disney execs, telling me that both "make the mistake of not appreciating technology. They just assume that they can throw money at things and fix them. They don't have a clue." Once upon a time, he would have been enraged by the ignorance he perceived. When I asked him what had soured an earlier partnership between IBM and NeXT, he ranted: "The people at the top of IBM knew nothing about computers. Nothing. Nothing. The people at the top of Disney," on the other hand, "know a lot about what a really good film is and what is not."

Even though he believed that Katzenberg and Eisner "had no clue" about how far Pixar could take them—Jobs was convinced that Pixar's technology could revolutionize the business model for animation, which was then primarily a hand-drawn art—he recognized that the partnership had more or less saved the company: "It's the biggest thing I've done for Pixar," he said. So he found a common bond between the companies. "There was a certain amount of fear and trepidation, but what always happened was that making a great movie was the focal point of everybody's concerns. One way to drive fear out of a relationship is to realize that your partner's values are the same as yours, that what you care about is exactly what they care about. In my opinion, that drives fear out and makes for a great partnership, whether it's a corporate partnership or a marriage."

Then he set about designing an organization that could deliver a great movie—and many more. His foray into Hollywood had taught him a great deal. "I started to learn about how films are made. Basically, it's bands of gypsies getting together to make a film. After the film, they disband. The problem with that is we want to build a company, not just make a single movie."

This time, there was no flighty discussion of an "open" corporation. "Incentive structures work," he told me. "So you have to be very careful of what you incent people to do, because various incentive structures create all sorts of consequences that you can't anticipate. Everybody at Pixar is incented to build the company: whether they're working on the film; whether they're working on a potential direct-to-video product; whether they're working on a CD-ROM. Whatever their combination of creative and technical talent may be, we want them incented to make the whole company successful."

There was another compensation detail that reflected how completely Jobs was able to mesh the values of Silicon Valley with Hollywood. Pixar paid its animators just as well as its software geniuses (beginning an escalation in salaries that Katzenberg accelerated later that decade at DreamWorks). "We value them both equally," Jobs said of Pixar's two talent camps. "Some people say we should value one higher than the other, but we value them equally, we pay them equally, they have stock equally. We made that decision very early. Ed Catmull made that decision, actually. We will always do that; that's one of Pixar's core values."

These were the decisions that cemented the company's future success. When Disney surprised Jobs by scheduling Pixar's first movie as its 1995 holiday feature, his team was ready, with a little picture called *Toy Story*. And Jobs, armed with a renegotiated Disney deal for three pictures, was ready too; Pixar went public 10 days after *Toy Story's* stunning debut, raising nearly $100 million.

After that, it was as if the company hit the fast-forward button. And for the rest of his life, Jobs enjoyed Pixar as he enjoyed little else. Now was the time to throw away the used furniture and build a proper studio in Emeryville, California. He relished this so much more than the NeXT headquarters—after all, this time he and his team had earned it. The design blended aspects of a Hollywood lot and an old-fashioned brick factory building, perfect for his star animators and programmers, perfect for working with Tom Hanks, Ellen DeGeneres, Owen Wilson, and all the other stars who enjoyed voicing Pixar characters. The custom-made bricks came in 12 shades, and if the colors weren't distributed evenly enough, Jobs would have the bricklayers pull them down and do it again. He would visit the construction site as often as he could as it came together, often clambering around the buildings at night, when no one but the security guards were around.

He also created something called Pixar University for the staff, where his brilliant engineers and clever artists and smart financial people could take classes in all kinds of subjects, to better appreciate what their coworkers did. There were classes in the visual arts, dance, computer programming, foreign languages, drama, mathematics, creative writing, and even

accounting. "It is," he once told me, "the coolest place to work in the world."

When Jobs returned to Apple in 1997, one of the first things he did was trim the product line, focusing employees on four clear projects. He liked to explain his strategy while drawing on a whiteboard, like a professor of management. For all the joy that Pixar brought Jobs, it was NeXT that got him back to Apple. After failing to develop new software architecture for the Mac and bungling a joint venture with IBM, Apple was on its deathbed in 1996. NeXT had a powerful, modern operating system and one very persuasive storyteller, who managed to convince CEO Amelio that his stepchild could be Apple's salvation. In late 1996, Jobs sold NeXT to Apple for $400 million, which he used to pay back Perot, Canon, and some other early investors. Within six months, Jobs had mounted a putsch and became Apple's "iCEO," with the i standing for what proved to be a deeply false "interim."

The ensuing tale, the saga of the modern Apple, is simply the story of the man who emerged from that 11-year business school and implemented the lessons he had learned along the way. As was true when he started at Pixar and NeXT, Jobs had many of the details wrong when he first returned to the Apple helm. He imagined that the company's business would always be selling computers. He thought that what was then called the "information highway" would be primarily of interest to businesses. He dismissed the idea that computer networks would carry lots of video.

But some of the tougher years at NeXT and Pixar had taught him how to stretch a company's finances, which helped him ride out his first couple of years back, when Apple was still reliant on a weak jumble of offerings. With newfound discipline, he quickly streamlined the company's product lines. And just as he had at Pixar, he aligned the company behind those projects. In a way that had never been done before at a technology company—but that looked a lot like an animation studio bent on delivering one great movie a year—Jobs created the organizational strength to deliver one hit after another, each an extension of Apple's position as the consumer's digital hub, each as strong as its predecessor. If there's anything that parallels Apple's decade-long string of hits—iMac, PowerBook, iPod, iTunes, iPhone, iPad, to list just the blockbusters—it's Pixar's string of winners, including *Toy Story, Monsters, Inc., Finding Nemo, The Incredibles, WALL-E,* and *Up*. These insanely great products could have come only from insanely great companies, and that's what Jobs had learned to build.

Jobs had learned how to treat talent at Pixar; he spoke to me about his colleagues there differently from the way he discussed his NeXT coworkers. When he returned to Apple, he often described his very top management team in the same warm terms, with the occasional notable exception. As he had with animators and programmers at Pixar, he integrated designers and technologists at Apple. He cultivated a team he could count on, including the great designer Jonathan Ive, who is to Apple what Lasseter is to Pixar. "We've done so many hardware products where Jony and I have looked at each other and said, 'We don't know how to make it any better than this, we just don't know how to make it,' " Jobs told me. "But we always do; we realize another way. And then it's not long after the new thing comes out that we look at the older thing and go, 'How can we ever have done that?' "

When I listened to this quote again last month, I was struck by something else in it: the combination of adaptability and intuition that proved so critical to Apple's rise. Jobs may have been impulsive at times, but he was always methodical. This kind of nature suited an autodidact with eclectic tastes, empowering him either to obsess impatiently about a pressing problem that had to be dealt with immediately—much like an engineer—or else to let an idea steep and incubate until he got it right. This is why Jobs was so often right on the big picture, even when he got the details wrong. Open salaries was a dumb detail of the Open Corporation, but its core idea, of a workplace where every single person understands the company's goals, is something that most organizations get wrong and that Apple has gotten so right for well over a decade. If Jobs was initially wrong about Apple getting into phones and handheld devices, he was right on about the big idea of the computer at the center of a whirling digital universe. Hence Apple's ability to deliver a great iTunes store after the iPod, even though it was never planned. Hence the great iPhone, despite Jobs's dismissal of "Swiss Army knife" digital devices.

There was one other big lesson he learned from his Hollywood adventure: People remember stories more than products. "The technology we've been laboring on over the past 20 years becomes part of the sedimentary layer," he told me once. "But when *Snow White* was re-released [on DVD, in 2001], we were one of the 28 million families that went out and bought a copy of it. This was a film that is 60 years old, and my son was watching it and loving it. I don't think anybody's going to be beating on a Macintosh 60 years from now."

Once he realized he really was going to die, Jobs quietly began to think more seriously about the story of his own life and creations. At his memorial service, Laurene remarked that what struck her most upon really getting to know him was his "fully formed aesthetic sense." He knew exactly what he liked, and he analyzed it until he could tell you precisely why. Jobs always felt that architecture could be a truly lasting expression of one's aesthetic, reaching beyond the limits of one's lifetime. It wasn't incidental, then, that his last public appearance was at a Cupertino City Council meeting to unveil the breathtaking four-story, doughnut-shaped "mother ship" that's nearly a half-mile in diameter and that will one day become Apple's headquarters.

Of course, Jobs wanted his own official story to measure up. So he enlisted Walter Isaacson—creator of a virtual Mount Rushmore of best-selling biographies of Benjamin Franklin, Albert Einstein, and Henry Kissinger—to tell his tale. Like those giants, Jobs is a man whose history will be told many a time, with fresh insights and new reporting. In the retelling, it may well be that the lessons from his "lost" years in the "wilderness" are the ones that will prove most inspiring.

Critical Thinking

1. Steve Jobs in known for being detail oriented to the point of obsession. The story of him micro-managing the color and pattern of bricks for the Pixar headquarters building is but one of many examples. In what ways did this obsession make him a better inventor or CEO? In what ways did this obsession hinder him? What might the ideal balance be?

2. Schlender refers to the 11 years between Jobs' two terms as Apple CEO as his "business school" education. What key lessons did Jobs learn that can be transferred to your own school and work life?

3. Contrast Jobs' behaviors and policies at NeXT from his behaviors and policies at Pixar. Which differences represented Jobs' growth as a manager, and which differences were simply differences in culture between the two industries?

4. How did Jobs' time at Pixar impact the development of the iPod and iPhone?

Create Central

www.mhhe.com/createcentral

Internet References

The Man Who Invented Our World
www.slate.com/articles/technology/technology/2011/10/steve_jobs_dead_how_the_apple_founder_changed_the_world_.html

Steve Jobs Biography Examines How Rule-Breaker Tied 'Artistry to Engineering'
www.pbs.org/newshour/bb/science/july-dec11/stevejobs_10-28.html

Steve Jobs: How to Live before You Die
www.ted.com/talks/steve_jobs_how_to_live_before_you_die.html

Steve Jobs in 1985: Apple Has "Common Vision" on Changing the World
www.pbs.org/newshour/rundown/2011/10/steve-jobs-in-1985-apple-employees-have-common-vision-on-changing-the-world.html

Article   Prepared by: Daniel Mittleman, *DePaul University*

How Technology Is Destroying Jobs

DAVID ROTMAN

Learning Outcomes

After reading this article, you will be able to:

- Articulate the arguments both for why technology innovation causes unemployment and why it does not.

- Understand what workplace robots are and how the growth in their use may affect employment today.

Given his calm and reasoned academic demeanor, it is easy to miss just how provocative Erik Brynjolfsson's contention really is. Brynjolfsson, a professor at the MIT Sloan School of Management, and his collaborator and coauthor Andrew McAfee have been arguing for the last year and a half that impressive advances in computer technology—from improved industrial robotics to automated translation services—are largely behind the sluggish employment growth of the last 10 to 15 years. Even more ominous for workers, the MIT academics foresee dismal prospects for many types of jobs as these powerful new technologies are increasingly adopted not only in manufacturing, clerical, and retail work but in professions such as law, financial services, education, and medicine.

That robots, automation, and software can replace people might seem obvious to anyone who's worked in automotive manufacturing or as a travel agent. But Brynjolfsson and McAfee's claim is more troubling and controversial. They believe that rapid technological change has been destroying jobs faster than it is creating them, contributing to the stagnation of median income and the growth of inequality in the United States. And, they suspect, something similar is happening in other technologically advanced countries.

Perhaps the most damning piece of evidence, according to Brynjolfsson, is a chart that only an economist could love. In economics, productivity—the amount of economic value created for a given unit of input, such as an hour of labor—is a crucial indicator of growth and wealth creation. It is a measure of progress. On the chart Brynjolfsson likes to show, separate lines represent productivity and total employment in the United States. For years after World War II, the two lines closely tracked each other, with increases in jobs corresponding to increases in productivity. The pattern is clear: as businesses generated more value from their workers, the country as a whole became richer, which fueled more economic activity and created even more jobs. Then, beginning in 2000, the lines diverge; productivity continues to rise robustly, but employment suddenly wilts. By 2011, a significant gap appears between the two lines, showing economic growth with no parallel increase in job creation. Brynjolfsson and McAfee call it the "great decoupling." And Brynjolfsson says he is confident that technology is behind both the healthy growth in productivity and the weak growth in jobs.

It's a startling assertion because it threatens the faith that many economists place in technological progress. Brynjolfsson and McAfee still believe that technology boosts productivity and makes societies wealthier, but they think that it can also have a dark side: technological progress is eliminating the need for many types of jobs and leaving the typical worker worse off than before. Brynjolfsson can point to a second chart indicating that median income is failing to rise even as the gross domestic product soars. "It's the great paradox of our era," he says. "Productivity is at record levels, innovation has never been faster, and yet at the same time, we have a falling median income and we have fewer jobs. People are falling behind because technology is advancing so fast and our skills and organizations aren't keeping up."

Brynjolfsson and McAfee are not Luddites. Indeed, they are sometimes accused of being too optimistic about the extent and speed of recent digital advances. Brynjolfsson says they began writing *Race Against the Machine,* the 2011 book in which they laid out much of their argument, because they wanted to explain the economic benefits of these new technologies (Brynjolfsson spent much of the 1990s sniffing out evidence that information technology was boosting rates of productivity). But it became clear to them that the same technologies making many jobs safer, easier, and more productive were also reducing the demand for many types of human workers.

Anecdotal evidence that digital technologies threaten jobs is, of course, everywhere. Robots and advanced automation have been common in many types of manufacturing for decades. In the United States and China, the world's manufacturing powerhouses, fewer people work in manufacturing today than in 1997, thanks at least in part to automation. Modern automotive plants, many of which were transformed by industrial robotics in the 1980s, routinely use machines that autonomously weld and paint body parts—tasks that were once handled by humans. Most recently, industrial robots like Rethink Robotics' Baxter more flexible and far cheaper than their predecessors, have been introduced to perform simple jobs for small manufacturers in a variety of sectors. The website of a Silicon Valley startup called Industrial Perception features a video of the robot it has designed for use in warehouses picking up and throwing boxes like a bored elephant. And such sensations as Google's driverless car suggest what automation might be able to accomplish someday soon.

A less dramatic change, but one with a potentially far larger impact on employment, is taking place in clerical work and professional services. Technologies like the Web, artificial intelligence, big data, and improved analytics—all made possible by the ever increasing availability of cheap computing power and storage capacity—are automating many routine tasks. Countless traditional white-collar jobs, such as many in the post office and in customer service, have disappeared. W. Brian Arthur, a visiting researcher at the Xerox Palo Alto Research Center's intelligence systems lab and a former economics professor at Stanford University, calls it the "autonomous economy." It's far more subtle than the idea of robots and automation doing human jobs, he says: it involves "digital processes talking to other digital processes and creating new processes," enabling us to do many things with fewer people and making yet other human jobs obsolete.

It is this onslaught of digital processes, says Arthur, that primarily explains how productivity has grown without a significant increase in human labor. And, he says, "digital versions of human intelligence" are increasingly replacing even those jobs once thought to require people. "It will change every profession in ways we have barely seen yet," he warns.

McAfee, associate director of the MIT Center for Digital Business at the Sloan School of Management, speaks rapidly and with a certain awe as he describes advances such as Google's driverless car. Still, despite his obvious enthusiasm for the technologies, he doesn't see the recently vanished jobs coming back. The pressure on employment and the resulting inequality will only get worse, he suggests, as digital technologies—fueled with "enough computing power, data, and geeks"—continue their exponential advances over the next several decades. "I would like to be wrong," he says, "but when all these science-fiction technologies are deployed, what will we need all the people for?"

New Economy?

But are these new technologies really responsible for a decade of lackluster job growth? Many labor economists say the data are, at best, far from conclusive. Several other plausible explanations, including events related to global trade and the financial crises of the early and late 2000s, could account for the relative slowness of job creation since the turn of the century. "No one really knows," says Richard Freeman, a labor economist at Harvard University. That's because it's very difficult to "extricate" the effects of technology from other macroeconomic effects, he says. But he's skeptical that technology would change a wide range of business sectors fast enough to explain recent job numbers.

Employment trends have polarized the workforce and hollowed out the middle class.

David Autor, an economist at MIT who has extensively studied the connections between jobs and technology, also doubts that technology could account for such an abrupt change in total employment. "There was a great sag in employment beginning in 2000. Something did change," he says. "But no one knows the cause." Moreover, he doubts that productivity has, in fact, risen robustly in the United States in the past decade (economists can disagree about that statistic because there are different ways of measuring and weighing economic inputs and outputs). If he's right, it raises the possibility that poor job growth could be simply a result of a sluggish economy. The sudden slowdown in job creation "is a big puzzle," he says, "but there's not a lot of evidence it's linked to computers."

To be sure, Autor says, computer technologies are changing the types of jobs available, and those changes "are not always for the good." At least since the 1980s, he says, computers have increasingly taken over such tasks as bookkeeping, clerical work, and repetitive production jobs in manufacturing—all of which typically provided middle-class pay. At the same time, higher-paying jobs requiring creativity and problem-solving skills, often aided by computers, have proliferated. So have low-skill jobs: demand has increased for restaurant workers, janitors, home health aides, and others doing service work that is nearly impossible to automate. The result, says Autor, has been a "polarization" of the workforce and a "hollowing out" of the middle class—something that has been happening in numerous industrialized countries for the last several decades. But "that is very different from saying technology is affecting the total number of jobs," he adds. "Jobs can change a lot without there being huge changes in employment rates."

What's more, even if today's digital technologies are holding down job creation, history suggests that it is most likely a temporary, albeit painful, shock; as workers adjust their skills and entrepreneurs create opportunities based on the new technologies, the number of jobs will rebound. That, at least, has always been the pattern. The question, then, is whether today's computing technologies will be different, creating long-term involuntary unemployment.

At least since the Industrial Revolution began in the 1700s, improvements in technology have changed the nature of work and destroyed some types of jobs in the process. In 1900, 41 percent of Americans worked in agriculture; by 2000, it was only 2 percent. Likewise, the proportion of Americans employed in manufacturing has dropped from 30 percent in the post-World War II years to around 10 percent today—partly because of increasing automation, especially during the 1980s.

While such changes can be painful for workers whose skills no longer match the needs of employers, Lawrence Katz, a Harvard economist, says that no historical pattern shows these shifts leading to a net decrease in jobs over an extended period. Katz has done extensive research on how technological advances have affected jobs over the last few centuries—describing, for example, how highly skilled artisans in the mid-19th century were displaced by lower-skilled workers in factories. While it can take decades for workers to acquire the expertise needed for new types of employment, he says, "we never have run out of jobs. There is no long-term trend of eliminating work for people. Over the long term, employment rates are fairly stable. People have always been able to create new jobs. People come up with new things to do."

Still, Katz doesn't dismiss the notion that there is something different about today's digital technologies—something that could affect an even broader range of work. The question, he says, is whether economic history will serve as a useful guide. Will the job disruptions caused by technology be temporary as the workforce adapts, or will we see a science-fiction scenario in which automated processes and robots with superhuman skills take over a broad swath of human tasks? Though Katz expects the historical pattern to hold, it is "genuinely a question," he says. "If technology disrupts enough, who knows what will happen?"

Dr. Watson

To get some insight into Katz's question, it is worth looking at how today's most advanced technologies are being deployed in industry. Though these technologies have undoubtedly taken over some human jobs, finding evidence of workers being displaced by machines on a large scale is not all that easy. One reason it is difficult to pinpoint the net impact on jobs is that automation is often used to make human workers more efficient, not necessarily to replace them. Rising productivity means businesses can do the same work with fewer employees, but it can also enable the businesses to expand production with their existing workers, and even to enter new markets.

Take the bright-orange Kiva robot, a boon to fledgling e-commerce companies. Created and sold by Kiva Systems, a startup that was founded in 2002 and bought by Amazon for $775 million in 2012, the robots are designed to scurry across large warehouses, fetching racks of ordered goods and delivering the products to humans who package the orders. In Kiva's large demonstration warehouse and assembly facility at its headquarters outside Boston, fleets of robots move about with seemingly endless energy: some newly assembled machines perform tests to prove they're ready to be shipped to customers around the world, while others wait to demonstrate to a visitor how they can almost instantly respond to an electronic order and bring the desired product to a worker's station.

A warehouse equipped with Kiva robots can handle up to four times as many orders as a similar unautomated warehouse, where workers might spend as much as 70 percent of their time walking about to retrieve goods. (Coincidentally or not, Amazon bought Kiva soon after a press report revealed that workers at one of the retailer's giant warehouses often walked more than 10 miles a day.)

Despite the labor-saving potential of the robots, Mick Mountz, Kiva's founder and CEO, says he doubts the machines have put many people out of work or will do so in the future.

For one thing, he says, most of Kiva's customers are e-commerce retailers, some of them growing so rapidly they can't hire people fast enough. By making distribution operations cheaper and more efficient, the robotic technology has helped many of these retailers survive and even expand. Before founding Kiva, Mountz worked at Webvan, an online grocery delivery company that was one of the 1990s dot-com era's most infamous flameouts. He likes to show the numbers demonstrating that Webvan was doomed from the start; a $100 order cost the company $120 to ship. Mountz's point is clear: something as mundane as the cost of materials handling can consign a new business to an early death. Automation can solve that problem.

Meanwhile, Kiva itself is hiring. Orange balloons—the same color as the robots—hover over multiple cubicles in its sprawling office, signaling that the occupants arrived within the last month. Most of these new employees are software engineers: while the robots are the company's poster boys, its lesser-known innovations lie in the complex algorithms that guide the robots' movements and determine where in the warehouse products are stored. These algorithms help make the system adaptable. It can learn, for example, that a certain product is seldom ordered, so it should be stored in a remote area.

Though advances like these suggest how some aspects of work could be subject to automation, they also illustrate that humans still excel at certain tasks—for example, packaging various items together. Many of the traditional problems in robotics—such as how to teach a machine to recognize an object as, say, a chair—remain largely intractable and are especially difficult to solve when the robots are free to move about a relatively unstructured environment like a factory or office.

Techniques using vast amounts of computational power have gone a long way toward helping robots understand their surroundings, but John Leonard, a professor of engineering at MIT and a member of its Computer Science and Artificial Intelligence Laboratory (CSAIL), says many familiar difficulties remain. "Part of me sees accelerating progress; the other part of me sees the same old problems," he says. "I see how hard it is to do anything with robots. The big challenge is uncertainty." In other words, people are still far better at dealing with changes in their environment and reacting to unexpected events.

For that reason, Leonard says, it is easier to see how robots could work *with* humans than on their own in many applications. "People and robots working together can happen much more quickly than robots simply replacing humans," he says. "That's not going to happen in my lifetime at a massive scale. The semiautonomous taxi will still have a driver."

One of the friendlier, more flexible robots meant to work with humans is Rethinks Baxter. The creation of Rodney Brooks, the company's founder, Baxter needs minimal training to perform simple tasks like picking up objects and moving them to a box. It's meant for use in relatively small manufacturing facilities where conventional industrial robots would cost too much and pose too much danger to workers. The idea, says Brooks, is to have the robots take care of dull, repetitive jobs that no one wants to do.

It's hard not to instantly like Baxter, in part because it seems so eager to please. The "eyebrows" on its display rise quizzically when it's puzzled; its arms submissively and gently retreat when bumped. Asked about the claim that such advanced industrial robots could eliminate jobs, Brooks answers simply that he doesn't see it that way. Robots, he says, can be to factory workers as electric drills are to construction workers: "It makes them more productive and efficient, but it doesn't take jobs."

The machines created at Kiva and Rethink have been cleverly designed and built to work with people, taking over the tasks that the humans often don't want to do or aren't especially good at. They are specifically designed to enhance these workers' productivity. And it's hard to see how even these increasingly sophisticated robots will replace humans in most manufacturing and industrial jobs anytime soon. But clerical and some professional jobs could be more vulnerable. That's because the marriage of artificial intelligence and big data is beginning to give machines a more humanlike ability to reason and to solve many new types of problems.

Even if the economy is only going through a transition, it is an extremely painful one for many.

In the tony northern suburbs of New York City, IBM Research is pushing super-smart computing into the realms of such professions as medicine, finance, and customer service. IBM's efforts have resulted in Watson, a computer system best known for beating human champions on the game show *Jeopardy!* in 2011. That version of Watson now sits in a corner of a large data center at the research facility in Yorktown Heights, marked with a glowing plaque commemorating its glory days. Meanwhile, researchers there are already testing new generations of Watson in medicine, where the technology could help physicians diagnose diseases like cancer, evaluate patients, and prescribe treatments.

IBM likes to call it cognitive computing. Essentially, Watson uses artificial-intelligence techniques, advanced natural-language processing and analytics, and massive amounts of data drawn from sources specific to a given application (in the case of health care, that means medical journals, textbooks, and information collected from the physicians or hospitals using the system). Thanks to these innovative techniques and huge amounts of computing power, it can quickly come up with "advice"—for example, the most recent and relevant information to guide a doctor's diagnosis and treatment decisions.

Despite the system's remarkable ability to make sense of all that data, it's still early days for Dr. Watson. While it has rudimentary abilities to "learn" from specific patterns and evaluate different possibilities, it is far from having the type of judgment and intuition a physician often needs. But IBM has also announced it will begin selling Watson's services to customer-support call centers, which rarely require human judgment that's quite so sophisticated. IBM says companies will rent an updated version of Watson for use as a "customer service agent" that responds to questions from consumers; it

has already signed on several banks. Automation is nothing new in call centers, of course, but Watson's improved capacity for natural-language processing and its ability to tap into a large amount of data suggest that this system could speak plainly with callers, offering them specific advice on even technical and complex questions. It's easy to see it replacing many human holdouts in its new field.

Digital Losers

The contention that automation and digital technologies are partly responsible for today's lack of jobs has obviously touched a raw nerve for many worried about their own employment. But this is only one consequence of what Brynjolfsson and McAfee see as a broader trend. The rapid acceleration of technological progress, they say, has greatly widened the gap between economic winners and losers—the income inequalities that many economists have worried about for decades. Digital technologies tend to favor "superstars," they point out. For example, someone who creates a computer program to automate tax preparation might earn millions or billions of dollars while eliminating the need for countless accountants.

New technologies are "encroaching into human skills in a way that is completely unprecedented," McAfee says, and many middle-class jobs are right in the bull's-eye; even relatively high-skill work in education, medicine, and law is affected. "The middle seems to be going away," he adds. "The top and bottom are clearly getting farther apart." While technology might be only one factor, says McAfee, it has been an "underappreciated" one, and it is likely to become increasingly significant.

Not everyone agrees with Brynjolfsson and McAfee's conclusions—particularly the contention that the impact of recent technological change could be different from anything seen before. But it's hard to ignore their warning that technology is widening the income gap between the tech-savvy and everyone else. And even if the economy is only going through a transition similar to those it's endured before, it is an extremely painful one for many workers, and that will have to be addressed somehow. Harvard's Katz has shown that the United States prospered in the early 1900s in part because secondary education became accessible to many people at a time when employment in agriculture was drying up. The result, at least through the 1980s, was an increase in educated workers who found jobs in the industrial sectors, boosting incomes and reducing inequality. Katz's lesson: painful long-term consequences for the labor force do not follow inevitably from technological changes.

Brynjolfsson himself says he's not ready to conclude that economic progress and employment have diverged for good. "I don't know whether we can recover, but I hope we can," he says. But that, he suggests, will depend on recognizing the problem and taking steps such as investing more in the training and education of workers.

"We were lucky and steadily rising productivity raised all boats for much of the 20th century," he says. "Many people, especially economists, jumped to the conclusion that was just the way the world worked. I used to say that if we took care of productivity, everything else would take care of itself; it was the single most important economic statistic. But that's no longer true." He adds, "It's one of the dirty secrets of economics: technology progress does grow the economy and create wealth, but there is no economic law that says everyone will benefit." In other words, in the race against the machine, some are likely to win while many others lose.

Critical Thinking

1. Define productivity and explain why when technology innovation makes one employee more productive it does not automatically cost other employees their jobs.
2. Brynjolfsson demonstrates that something new happened around 2001 so that increased productivity no longer led to a growth in the number of jobs. Generate at least three

independent hypotheses as to why there appeared a sudden change in this relationshp at that point in time.

Create Central

www.mhhe.com/createcentral

Internet References

Andrew McAfee: Are Droids Taking Our Jobs?
www.ted.com/talks/andrew_mcafee_are_droids_taking_our_jobs.html
Robots at Work: Toward a Smarter Factory
www.wfs.org/futurist/2013-issues-futurist/may-june-2013-vol-47-no-3/robots-work-toward-smarter-factory
Should We Fear "The End of Work"?
www.pbs.org/newshour/businessdesk/2013/07/should-we-fear-the-end-of-work.html

Article   Prepared by: Daniel Mittleman, *DePaul University*

The Patent Problem

STEVEN LEVY

Learning Outcomes

After reading this article, you will be able to:

- To Articulate problems and issues with the current U.S. patent process.
- Understand the role of the U.S. Patent Office and its role in promoting technology innovation.
- Understand what a patent troll is, and how trolls impact technology innovation.

One afternoon in the early 1980s, Mitchell Medina and Robert Lech were hanging out in the dining room of Medina's Essex Fells, New Jersey, home. The two friends got together about once a week. This time the conversation turned to the topic of invention. Lech, a chiropractor, was in the process of computerizing his office. That required converting his claim forms and doctors' reports into an electronic format, an ordeal that involved painstakingly typing in all of the information by hand. It gave Lech an idea: What if you could scan all those documents digitally and store them on the computer? Lech had been chewing on the concept for a while. Now he was eager to share his thoughts with his friend Medina, in part because Medina knew a lot about patents.

The US patent system goes back to the nation's founding; it is explicitly delineated in the Constitution, which, in the name of "the progress of science and the useful arts," gives Congress the power to grant inventors "the exclusive right to their respective writings and discoveries" for a limited time—generally 20 years—during which period competitors are forbidden from selling similar products. Without those assurances, there would arguably be no incentive to innovate; why invest money and effort on a breakthrough that anyone could then take and sell? Patents created a business environment that led to such landmark technologies as the cotton gin, Morse code, the Yale lock, the Xerox machine, the laser, and the Hula Hoop.

But over the years patents became much more than just protection. They were also assets. Inventors who won patents were free to sell them on the open market, giving the buyer the right to their creations. In theory this was another boon for innovation; even if original patent holders couldn't maximize the potential of their inventions, they could still turn a tidy profit by allowing someone else to build on their ideas. But in practice it meant that even people who never invented anything in their lives—a group of lawyers, for instance—could scoop up a bunch of patents and start suing other inventors for infringing on their intellectual property.

Medina had some expertise in patent litigation. He worked for his grandfather's business, Randolph-Rand, which supplied metal parts to the leather industry. Randolph-Rand had acquired a patent for a magnetic snap from a Korean inventor. Medina felt that Randolph-Rand's competitors—who sold their own versions of a magnetic snap—were infringing on that patent, so he set up an "enforcement program," suing rivals if their products included a snap that he considered to be infringing.

Medina didn't immediately embrace the specifics of Lech's scanning idea. There were limits on what kind of concepts could win a patent; if everyone could stake a claim to whatever idea floated into their head, nobody would be able to create anything without infringing on someone else's intellectual property. And so the US Patent and Trademark Office was forbidden from awarding patents to ideas that were too obvious, insufficiently novel, or just plain impractical. It was up to the Patent Office to decide which inventions fell into those categories, but Medina felt sure that the scanning idea was too obvious to pass muster. As they discussed it over the next few weeks, however, he did come up with a twist on the idea that he thought might be patentable. Instead of just scanning and storing the documents, why not create a software process to automatically extract the information and format it on the computer?

Medina had a pretty good grasp of what could and couldn't win a patent. Traditionally, patents could be awarded only to specific technologies, not broad concepts—and the notion of exporting data from scanned documents into a personal computer, before flatbed scanners had become widely available, seemed to fall firmly in the "conceptual" category. But during the 1970s, the Patent Office didn't have the expertise or bandwidth to limn those kinds of distinctions. In the mechanical age, it was relatively easy to determine when a series of equations crossed the line into patentable invention; you couldn't protect the underlying math, but you could protect the machines built from it. Software presented a new kind of challenge. It never left the realm of algorithms; it represented a process, not a physical object. Meanwhile, the industry was exploding, burying the undermanned Patent Office with a burst of applications.

The Supreme Court would eventually provide guidance by declaring that software processes and business practices could indeed be considered patent-worthy. The overwhelmed Patent Office seemed to take this as an OK to apply a rubber stamp to thousands of requests, some of them questionable. "Many patents are approved because examiners don't have time or resources to search all the relevant references," says Colleen Chien, an assistant professor who specializes in intellectual property at Santa Clara University School of Law. And when an examiner did reject an application, candidates would sometimes simply make cosmetic adjustments and keep reapplying until the Patent Office approved it. Hundreds of thousands of patents began to accumulate, resulting in a vast bureaucratic ammunitions dump that could not help but eventually explode.

Several patents would belong to Medina. It took the better part of a decade—until 1990—to find a patent attorney who understood his concept well enough to prepare a filing, which was submitted to the Patent Office in March 1991. (By that time, scanning was commonplace, making the idea of data extraction less of a conceptual leap.) On November 2, 1993, Lech and Medina—along with Catherine Elias, a friend with a computer science degree who had helped draft some specs for the process—were granted a patent for an "Information Processing Methodology." Though written in typically dense and baffling jargon, the very first sentence stated its nature fairly precisely: "The invention is directed to a system for efficiently processing information originating from hard copy documents."

Although the three had never tried to build a working model before they were granted the patent, they now set out to create a business based on the idea. Elias made a prototype, albeit one that Medina would later admit "didn't work particularly well." He claimed to have visited "every big player" they could think of in the computer industry to see if they would like to license his patent and build a commercial version themselves. He also claimed that he had attempted to raise venture capital to create a company of his own. But no corporation or VC would put money into it. According to Medina, they were particularly annoyed when, during a meeting, an executive from IBM's Lotus division rudely dismissed the idea of paying to use the concept. "He acted as if these kinds of patents were somehow laughable," Lech says.

The two main inventors disagreed about what to do next. Lech still wanted a big company to buy the patent and nurture it into a popular product. He devised a legal strategy inspired by the movie *The Hunt for Red October,* in which a rogue Soviet submarine captain appears to be about to attack the US but is really just trying to defect. Lech thought that the team should sue a large company and in so doing lure it into purchasing the patent. "The idea was to feign a missile attack so they could defect and begin a marriage," Lech says.

But Medina apparently had other plans: giving up on the idea of partnering with another company and instead starting his own business to license and litigate the patent.

Lech wasn't crazy about this approach, but Medina did it anyway. Lech later learned that Medina had essentially cut him out of the decisionmaking process, giving himself controlling interest in the fledgling company. Lech walked away. "It

was a matter probably of pride on my part," he says. (Medina would later claim—and Lech does not deny—that Lech sold him the rights and that while he had given Lech the lead inventor credit as a courtesy for the original idea, he—Medina—was "the captain of the ship.") In any case, Lech says, he has not received "even a penny" from any subsequent license fees and settlements.

And there would be plenty of those. Medina transferred the patents to a newly formed company called Millennium, based in the Cayman Islands. "From that time," Medina would later say in a deposition, "Millennium became a patent-enforcement company."

His former partner Lech puts it differently. Medina, he says, "was more inclined to be what has come to be known as a patent troll."

When visiting great technology companies, you often see certificates marking patents, framed and hung in a grid or a long row spanning a hallway. Other times the achievements are commemorated with Lucite squares in an engineer's office. For many years these trophies were regarded as badges of honor, tokens showing that innovators were advancing not just the fortunes of their employers but the public good as well.

But today those Lucite bricks bring to mind a different question: Who's going to get hit in the head with them?

The past three decades of wanton patent-granting have created a disastrous environment for innovation. Today it's practically impossible to build anything without violating a patent of some kind—and risking a multimillion-dollar lawsuit for your troubles. Once intended to protect lone inventors, patents now form a kind of shadow tech industry, in which billions of dollars are spent on amassing huge portfolios. (A recent *New York Times* article noted that Apple and Google, companies that define themselves by innovation, now invest more in patent acquisition and defense than in research and development.)

Why are companies spending so much money on patents? First, as protection. "Patents are like bullets," law professor Chien says. "They're cheap to acquire but can cause a lot of damage." But if you have your own bullets, would-be assassins are less likely to target you. That's the thinking behind RPX (Rational Patent Exchange), whose clients include Google, Microsoft, and IBM. RPX amasses patents, it says, to keep them out of the hands of lawsuit-happy competitors, and it vows not to sue anyone over them.

That's traditionally been the spirit in which large companies have built their patent stockpiles, as a purely defensive measure. They were dissuaded from suing one another because they knew their target likely had patents that covered similar territory and they could be countersued quickly—the legal equivalent of mutually assured destruction. "Typically there's a cross-license that keeps companies from having to assert literally 10,000 or 20,000 patents against each other," Google general counsel Kent Walker says.

But that pact has been broken. What operated for years as an uneasy détente has descended into a Strangelovian shooting war.

The world saw this firsthand in last summer's epic court battle between Apple and Samsung, the geek equivalent of the O. J. Simpson trial. Ostensibly a fight over whether the Korean electronics giant infringed specific Apple smartphone patents, the lawsuit was more appropriately seen as corporate warfare waged not in the marketplace but through the courts—a consequence of Steve Jobs's vow to "go thermonuclear" on Google's Android operating system, which powers Samsung phones. To be fair, the jury seemed to be swayed by evidence that Samsung had consciously copied Apple's device, helping itself to the hard work performed in Cupertino. But the battle was fought over the patents themselves, some of which seemed obvious or overly broad: the "rubber band" function that bounces the names at the end of a contact list, the ability to tap and pinch to zoom on a phone, even the phone's shape. In Apple's previous patent case against Motorola, judge Richard Posner had dismissed the suit with a pox-on-both-your-houses air of disgust. ("As in any jungle, the animals will use all the means at their disposal," he later elaborated to a reporter, "all the teeth and claws that are permitted by their ecosystem.") This time the pox was on only one house: On August 24, Apple was awarded $1 billion in damages. Meanwhile, Apple is defending against several infringement claims. In fact, this year's court docket resembles a high tech lineup of clashes reminiscent of the golden days of professional wrestling. Google versus Oracle. Apple versus HTC. Microsoft versus Google.

Unlike wrestling, though, this is no fun. The technology industry is rife with overly broad patents. Already too much energy and money is spent acquiring and enforcing them. Amazon "owns" the process that allows people to buy things with a single click. Apple now claims the exclusive right to sell rounded-edged, rectangular-shaped communication devices on which icons are arranged in a grid with a row of persistent icons at the bottom. And a small company in Tyler, Texas, once demanded more than $600 million from Google because of the design of the borders around its display ads. Recently companies have begun banding together to buy and share costly patent portfolios at the expense of a shared rival. In 2011, for instance, while telecom giant Nortel Networks was going bankrupt, it was valued at less than a billion dollars. But its patents ended up selling at auction for $4.5 billion to a consortium that called itself Rockstar Bidco. The group included Microsoft and Apple, two companies famous for their rivalry. Google, a third competitor, dropped out of the bidding at $3.14 billion. (Apparently, bidding the value of pi wasn't enough to win the day.)

Of course, some patent suits are clearly justified—as Apple CEO Tim Cook said at a conference this year, infringing on a company's patents is like stealing from a great artist. (Then again, he also said that patent litigation is "a pain in the ass" and that if everyone tried to collect on their patents, no one could afford to make a smartphone.) Cook didn't mention that Apple has aggressively sought patents on practically every conceivable feature it builds into its products, as well as on some ideas it may never end up implementing. That's not the equivalent of Picasso protecting his masterpieces. It's more akin to some artist churning out sketches and storing them in his attic—then claiming theft when someone unwittingly paints the same subjects. (In fact, one of the many books written about how to use patents "to capture and defend markets [and] outflank rivals" is called *Rembrandts in the Attic*.)

The consequences of our current patent crisis reverberate far beyond Silicon Valley, straight into our wallets and pocketbooks. When companies are suddenly paying billions of dollars for patents, who do you think ultimately pays the tab?

But money is only part of the impact on consumers. What can't be measured are the products that are never built—because taking on even bogus patents is too much of a hurdle for some innovators. When Google lost its bid for the Nortel patents, it made a number of public statements arguing that the patent system was being abused in a hostile, organized campaign against Android. Some called it sour grapes. But it would be difficult to argue with senior vice president David Drummond's contention. "Patents were meant to encourage innovation," he blogged in a cri de coeur, "but lately they are being used as a weapon to stop it."

In February 2005, Flagstar Bancorp received a summons stating that it was being sued by Eon-Net, a privately held company based in the British Virgin Islands. Eon-Net, like Millennium, was a company that Medina had set up to protect his intellectual property. Already, with the help of a tireless New Jersey attorney named Jean-Marc Zimmerman, Medina had successfully demanded licensing fees from dozens of other companies for infringing on his patented process of extracting data from scanned documents. But in 2004 Medina was granted another patent, one of several follow-ups to the original. This patent took an even more generous view of his initial idea, covering the extraction of not just scanned data but any information that had been entered using a "multimode information processing system," a term that was not in the first patent. Medina later requested a further tweak, changing 30 phrases to the broadest possible description of his invention—"a method of processing information."

As Zimmerman interpreted it, this extended the domain of the patent to the realm of ecommerce. Under this theory, pretty much anybody who filled out an online form was supposedly infringing on Medina's patents.

It was a powerful claim. Medina and Zimmerman used it to sue more than 100 ecommerce companies. Some considered fighting the claims. A CEO of one ecommerce site was so outraged when he was first served by Eon-Net that he tried to mount his own homegrown defense. He didn't have enough money to pay a legal team, so he drafted his own legal interrogatories. (One example: "Describe the method by which you sleep knowing that you are a scum-sucking pig.") He also contacted the coinventor of several online markup languages to see how much it would cost to have him appear as an expert witness on his behalf. The answer: $25,000, exactly what Eon-Net was demanding in licensing fees, a price that made settling the only rational decision. Grudgingly, the CEO gave up. (He requested anonymity from *Wired* because he didn't want to make himself a target for future lawsuits.)

Such was the situation facing Flagstar's chief legal officer, Matthew Roslin. Flagstar was a bank that prided itself on its technological prowess—it claimed to be one of the first to use the web to expedite mortgage applications. Now it was being sued for just that innovation. "The case was laughable," Roslin says.

Still, logic dictated that he should settle. Eon-Net was asking for less than $100,000—a pittance compared with how much a lawsuit would cost. But the summons rubbed Roslin the wrong way. Flagstar was not a software company—where such suits abounded—and he felt disinclined to submit to what seemed like bullying. He felt that taking a stand would discourage future trolls from filing suit against Flagstar. And the bank—at the time a successful national mortgage lender with billions in assets—could afford the battle.

Flagstar hoped to mitigate costs by sharing its defense with some of the several companies Eon-Net had sued at the same time, in nearly identical suits. But almost all of those firms preferred to pay a settlement and make the problem go away. Only two ecommerce sites agreed to join with Flagstar: drugstore.com and CoolAnimalStuff.com.

The companies successfully petitioned to move the lawsuit from New Jersey to Washington state. Nathan Garnett, drugstore.com's associate general counsel, believed that the inconvenience of fighting a case across the country would discourage Eon-Net. But Eon-Net did not drop out as he had hoped. Soon CoolAnimalStuff.com decided to settle. Its CEO, Richard Leeds, felt the lawsuit was bogus but now calls the settlement amount "a steal" compared with what he would have had to pay for litigation.

Drugstore.com was also doing the unpleasant math. "We felt if we could settle for a reasonable amount of money, we'd do it," Garnett says. "It's absolutely offensive to pay off someone like that, but you have to put your feelings aside." In April 2006, drugstore.com paid Eon-Net, and Flagstar was alone.

In preparing its defense, Flagstar seized on the lack of rigor in Eon-Net's filing. The law required plaintiffs to specify precisely which of a defendant's products infringed on their patents. Flagstar argued that Eon-Net hadn't done that, charging simply that the bank was infringing without going into much detail. "One of our major allegations was that they had no idea what they were suing us about," says Kristina Maritczak, associate general counsel at Flagstar (who has since left the company). "They didn't do due diligence or research on any of the products that we had used."

Even as the case progressed, Eon-Net continued its broad approach to litigation. By Flagstar's count, since its own case began, Eon-Net had filed at least 25 more lawsuits. Barnes & Noble. Burlington Coat Factory. D'Agostino supermarkets. Delta Air Lines. Foot Locker. Gristedes foods. Hammacher Schlemmer. J. Crew. JetBlue. Jos. A. Bank Clothiers. J&R electronics. Liz Claiborne. Somethingsexyplanet.com. Sony Corporation of America. Walgreens. The Wine Messenger.

Over the next few months, district court judge Marsha Pechman came to a conclusion. In August she issued a summary judgment throwing out Eon-Net's case. Two months later she took the rare extra step of sanctioning Eon-Net for filing a frivolous suit, finding that it had made claims that were "wholly without merit . . . in hopes of a quick settlement." "Indicia of extortion are present in the case," she wrote. She directed Eon-Net to pay Flagstar's legal fees. And she ordered Eon-Net to send a copy of her judgment to every other defendant that it was suing. "Eon-Net has chosen filing over investigation

and nuisance settlements to avoid the merits," she wrote. "Eon-Net's conduct violates the rules and other defendants should be made aware."

Eon-Net appealed to the Federal Circuit court.

And to the horror of Flagstar, the appeals court backed Eon-Net.

Pechman, the justices opined, had been too hasty. As a matter of fact, Eon-Net's culpability shouldn't have been reached via summary judgment. Eon-Net should have its day in court. "It was enraging," Maritczak says. "Here was this completely frivolous case, and the federal circuit is telling me that my company has to spend another $500,000 to prove that it's a frivolous case—when a federal judge had just ruled that it was a frivolous case!"

Medina, clearly ecstatic, posted end-zone-dancing comments to a few patent-related blogs. "I have been in the patent enforcement business for 25 years," he wrote on one. "I have never seen a worse judgment than Pechman's: wrong on the facts, wrong on the law, and wrong on procedure."

The flaws of the patent system are most vividly exposed by the rise of trolls. The term, inspired by the stunted opportunists of myth, came from an Intel vice president who had been sued for calling a lawyer a "patent extortionist" and needed another expression. It refers to a company that doesn't make products but exists solely on the revenue of its patents. In the parlance of today's patent ecosystem, trolls are known as nonpracticing entities, or NPEs. Trolling may be frowned upon, but it can present an irresistible business model. It costs a few thousand dollars to secure a patent, which can easily bring millions through litigation. That helps explain why trolling has exploded since the turn of the century. In 2011 NPEs brought 5,842 suits, with a direct cost of $29 billion in legal and settlement fees—more than four times the haul in 2005. (And these sums do not include indirect costs to defendants—like the time and energy spent on a court case that could have gone toward building and selling new products and services.) Apparently many of those claims are baseless—a congressional study found that when defendants fought the trolls, they won 92 percent of the time. But there's no way to know, because the overwhelming majority of patent cases never make it to trial, ending instead in a quick settlement. It is usually more expensive to *win* a case against a troll than to just settle. In other words, the legal system favors the troll. That has helped make trolling a multibillion-dollar industry, albeit one that doesn't benefit consumers in any way.

Perhaps the most famous patent-troll case came in 2006, when an NPE charged that Research in Motion's BlackBerry infringed on patents covering wireless email. RIM had asked the Patent Office to reexamine the patents, but before it could reach a decision, the judge had to decide whether to grant an injunction, which could have shut down RIM's entire business. Fearing the worst, RIM settled for $612.5 million. In a final insult, not long after the case was settled, the Patent Office ruled that many of the disputed patents were indeed invalid.

That labyrinthine process, combined with the intricacies of the court system, have made trolls more powerful than ever. NPEs have nothing to lose. Because they don't create anything,

Patent Wars, a Brief History

Here's a look at some of the major battles in the fight over intellectual property. —*Victoria Tang*

1997

Communications software company Hilgraeve alleges that McAfee's VirusScan infringes a patent on software that performs "in transit detection of computer viruses." The district court sides with McAfee, but an appeals court reverses the summary judgment. A few years later, Symantec acquires the patent and uses it against Computer Associates International (now CA Technologies).

1999

Amazon obtains a preliminary court injunction to stop Barnes & Noble from using a single-click order button, thanks to its patent that covers the system that stores billing and shipping information. In 2002 the two reach a settlement for an undisclosed dollar amount.

2004

Eastman Kodak brings suit against Sony for allegedly encroaching on 10 patents concerning digital cameras and camcorders. Three weeks later, Sony returns the favor with a lawsuit against Kodak that cites 10 different patents. In 2007 the two companies reach a cross-licensing agreement to protect their patent portfolios.

2009

Nokia claims the iPhone violates several of its patents for wireless communication, including one for "bidirectional transmission of packet data." Under the terms of a 2011 settlement, Apple pays a onetime sum and ongoing royalties to Nokia.

2010

Oracle, which gained ownership of several Java-related patents when it purchased Sun Microsystems in 2009, sues Google for unauthorized use of the development technology in Android. A jury rejects the claim.

2011

A series of Apple-Samsung lawsuits commence, as the two smartphone giants square off in courts around the world. In August 2012 a US jury orders Samsung to shell out $1 billion for features that infringe on six of Apple's patents.

2012

Facebook refuses to pay licensing fees to Yahoo for allowing users to customize their pages. Yahoo files suit against the social network for "free riding" on its patents. Facebook manages to avoid a payout, as the two companies agree to cross-licensing.

they can't infringe on anyone else's patents, no matter how overblown. That means they can't be countersued. This isn't mutually assured destruction; it's asymmetric warfare.

The system has its ardent defenders, prime among them Nathan Myhrvold, the former Microsoft CTO who now runs a company called Intellectual Ventures. It conducts periodic invention sessions—Bill Gates often participates—and every year files an average of 500 patents resulting from those discussions. Some of the patents eventually become products, but others may never move beyond the patent stage. Intellectual Ventures also makes money by snapping up patents from individual inventors, which it then licenses or litigates.

Myhrvold has been held up as the poster boy for patent abuse, but he says that by paying inventors for their ideas he is spurring innovation. (He claims to have shelled out more than $300 million to individuals.) He also sees a societal value in a liquid market for patents, which he says can help fund future inventions.

But what's galling is that often, in the wider marketplace, patents aren't valued because of the innovations they might foster. Instead, they are assessed on their potential to exact tolls on existing companies that have veered unintentionally into territory covered by the often bloated claims of the patent holders. Still, Myhrvold believes that despite some overly broad patents, the system is working. "Of course there are bogus patents—just like there are bogus companies listed on Nasdaq," he says. "If you make the proposition that there's lots of bogus patents, then there should be an objective test by which we can measure them. I've looked. There isn't any."

Myhrvold is right that there's no quick, infallible test to distinguish between valid infringement claims and mere trolling. But the current system—requiring a complicated legal process to toss out even the fishiest claim—makes it easy to file lawsuit after lawsuit, always settling before the underlying patent is exposed to the most rudimentary scrutiny.

After the appeals court sided with Eon-Net in overturning Pechman's ruling, Flagstar had good reason to drop the case. On the eve of the mortgage loan crisis, the fortunes of the family-run bank were slipping and clearly about to get much worse. (Indeed, today the bank is controlled by an equity firm, and its share price has dropped more than 99 percent from its high in 2004.) But this had become a moral issue. "The fortunes of the company turned, but I still viewed it as money well spent," says Roslin, Flagstar's former chief legal officer.

Medina, meanwhile, seemed to have thrived. While his lawyer was busy sending infringement notices to dozens of companies, collecting millions of dollars in licensing fees or settlements, Medina was spending much of his time in Kenya. A secular Jew who turned to Christianity in 1973, he had established a ministry there. (He says he has six academic degrees, including a doctorate in theology from Vision International University.) He also got involved in politics ("I am, in effect, the James Carville of Kenya," he told his high school's alumni magazine) and founded an NGO promoting computer literacy, apparently with the proceeds of his litigation and licensing. He and his wife, a Filipino doctor he met in New York City, began to work with a Kenyan professor to develop medicines derived from local flora for the treatment of AIDS. He also started to make videos, including a 64-part series of the life of Jesus that he posted on YouTube. Only rarely did he speak publicly about his lawsuits.

But on June 23, 2008, Medina found himself answering questions under oath. As part of the continuing Eon-Net case, Flagstar had the right to depose him. Accompanied by his wife and lawyer, Medina appeared at the offices of a neutral New Jersey law firm to submit to seven hours of questioning that struck some of the viewers as one of the more unusual depositions they'd ever witnessed. "It was like an acid trip," Roslin says.

Medina set the tone early. When Flagstar attorney Melissa Baily asked him whether he had prepared for the deposition, he answered, "Not really." (Baily, who had joined the Flagstar case as an associate, had worked on it for so long that by this point she had made partner.) She asked whether he had prepared even a tiny bit. "I thought a little bit about it," he said. And what, Baily asked, did he think about? "How much of an inconvenience and a bother this is," Medina said. Not all of Medina's comments were so flip. He proved capable of detailed technical descriptions at times. But when Baily tried to press him about the origins of his idea—and tease out just how a patent about scanning documents had transmogrified into a claim that encompassed almost all commercial activity on the web—he spoke in lofty terms. "It was sort of Athena coming fully clothed from the mind of Zeus, except she wasn't really clothed," Medina said. "It took us a while to clothe her, but it was there from the beginning." When Baily asked why he was unable to provide papers or notes from the invention process indicating that he had the slightest premonition about the Internet or electronic commerce, he told her he had long ago tossed out his notes and files. "I don't save anything so I don't have to look," he said. "There is nobody else to ask and no place else to look." In any case, he admitted that while his team had built an admittedly crude prototype of his original scanning idea, he hadn't done so for the web-based claims he was pursuing in this case. No need to. "We believe broadly that websites implementing ecommerce more than likely infringe our patents."

Did he *really* think that practically every instance of ecommerce infringed on his idea? "That is a belief I hold," he said. And he didn't think he needed to bother even analyzing an ecommerce website to conclude that it infringed his patent? "That is 99 and 44/100 percent true," he said. He and his lawyer simply browsed the Internet, looking for "people doing electronic commerce, which there is a near infinitude," he said. It was all due, he implied, to the almost otherworldly brilliance of his vision many years ago. "This invention was sort of a prophetic flash as to what the future of computing would look like," he said. "And we were fortunate enough that the logic of that inspiration came to dominate the market."

At one point Medina expressed his irritation and impatience at the indignity of having to explain why Flagstar should do what almost every other defendant had already done: pay him thousands of dollars in settlement fees. "I tell you I am so sick of this stuff by now," he told Baily. "Especially this haggling over the stupidities and trivialities which is the name of the game in litigation." Instead he suggested that Baily simply put him in touch with a principal at Flagstar with decisionmaking authority so he could quickly persuade them to pay up. "Why are we playing ring around the rosy with this lawsuit," he asked, "when Flagstar is a money-losing bank that spent a multiple of our license fees on this litigation which (A) it is not going to win and (B) is quixotic at best?"

But that decision would be left to the judge, who would have to determine whether Medina's patent did in fact apply to Flagstar's website. On October 27, 2008, Eon-Net's attorney, Jean-Marc Zimmerman, approached the bench at a Seattle district court to make the case to judge Ricardo Martinez. (Although this was a continuation of the initial lawsuit, Pechman had recused herself after her summary judgment was bounced by the appeals court.) But before Zimmerman could launch his argument, Martinez posed a question that gave some indication of how he felt about Eon-Net's claims. "Before we get started, I'm just kind of curious," Martinez said. "From your perspective, can you tell me what this invention is?"

"Sure," said Zimmerman.

"I mean, what are we talking about? Are we talking about a software system? Are we talking about a hardware system? Are we talking about the method of configuring the computer? *What are we talking about?*"

It was not the first time this question had come up. At an earlier hearing with Pechman, Zimmerman explained his thinking. "There's no product per se," he had told her. "It's a system method. It's a system patent. The claims are system claims comprised of steps, and if those steps are performed, there's an infringement."

"That leads me to a question," Pechman said. "If you are correct, and you have patented a system—"

"Yes," Zimmerman said.

"Then you own the web," Pechman concluded.

Martinez was not swayed by this reasoning any more than Pechman had been. On March 4, 2009, he ruled that the original patent couldn't be extended to cover every online form. The ruling essentially ended the case. (It also made one wonder whether the millions of dollars that Eon-Net had already collected were based on unjustified claims.) Within a few weeks, both parties stipulated to a judgment of noninfringement.

But things were not over. A couple of months later, just as Pechman had done before him, Martinez further ruled that Eon-Net's case had been baseless and unjustifiable. Its attitude toward litigation was "cavalier." Martinez held Eon-Net responsible for abusing the court and ordered it to pay Flagstar's legal fees.

Eon-Net kept fighting. When Flagstar submitted its expenses, Zimmerman went over them line by line, questioning many of them—and losing every time. Of course, Eon-Net appealed the ruling.

But this time the Federal Circuit Court of Appeals affirmed every bit of the decision. In fact, the ruling read like a brief attacking the tactics of trolls in general, citing the high cost of litigation and the tortuous process that defendants have to bear before a meritless case can be dismissed.

When the Supreme Court refused to consider Zimmerman's subsequent appeal, the case was finally over. It had taken more than seven years, but the troll was denied.

The rise of trolls came as a result of a court system that seemed to favor them every step of the way. The vagueness of the underlying patents, the ridiculous ease with which plaintiffs could file a suit, the high costs defendants faced, and the unthinkable consequences of losing—all created an environment in which trolls were routinely rewarded for filing frivolous suits. But by the late 2000s, courts and the legislature began slowly chipping away at these factors. In 2003 a company called MercExchange successfully sued eBay over the provenance of its Buy It Now button. When eBay appealed, MercExchange took the common step of asking for an injunction against the defendant, which would have barred eBay from using the disputed technology as long as the case remained open. This was intended to prevent firms from profiting unfairly from someone else's invention. But all too often it further pressured companies to settle quickly so they could go back to business. Courts could be quick to grant such injunctions, but when the issue came before the Supreme Court in 2006, the justices determined that more care should be taken with that drastic step. This precedent made it harder for challengers to threaten a defendant's entire business.

The federal legislature is also waking up to the problem. Last year Congress passed a patent reform bill, the Leahy-Smith America Invents Act. Though patent activists label it timid, the law does provide some speed bumps for trolls. It has been difficult and pricey to get even the most blatantly abusive infringement case thrown out. But now, thanks to a new inter partes review petition process, the Patent Office itself can rule on egregious claims, throwing them out before defendants are forced to go through the pain and expense of a full trial. When the new process was unveiled on September 16, a flood of challengers poured into the Patent Office.

And a new bill before Congress would further dampen troll activity. The Shield (Saving High-Tech Innovators From Egregious Legal Disputes) Act would require an unsuccessful plaintiff in an infringement suit to pay the defendant's legal fees—just as Eon-Net was forced to do in the Flagstar case. "We think this would be a big disincentive," says Oregon representative Peter DeFazio, who predicts that the legislation could pass in the next session.

Some companies, meanwhile, are taking individual moral stands against weaponized patents. Twitter recently introduced the Innovator's Patent Agreement. It grants its employees some control over the patents that bear their names. This means that Twitter can't file an infringement suit unless the original inventor gives permission—even if the company changes hands or sells off the patents. It may cost Twitter a bit in licensing fees, but it has helped the company in other ways; legal counsel Ben Lee says that its recruiters are already reporting that the program makes Twitter more attractive to prospective hires.

But if the system itself is to be put right, the most significant changes must come from the Patent Office, which helped create this whole mess. Director David Kappos is well aware that there are simply too many patents that never should have been

granted. He is toughening the guidelines and retraining examiners on certain types of patents, and he says that the rate of rejection for those claims has begun to rise. ("As much as we'd like? No," he says, "so we're going to do even more education and training.") Kappos is experimenting with crowdsourcing that will enable outside experts to air objections while patents are still under consideration.

Kappos also says that his office has ended one of its more vexing practices. "Merely putting a business process that existed in the physical world on the Internet is not patentable, and we should've never been issuing patents on that," he says.

Still, even Kappos is not ready to argue that we've turned the corner on our patent problems. "What I am prepared to say is that a lot has been done," he says. "There's a lot under way, and there's even more that we're prepared to do. And we are not done."

Mitchell Medina, who has sued more than 100 companies for infringing his patents, sees himself as a victim. "When Jobs and Wozniak or Hewlett and Packard start in a garage, they're heroes and captains of industry," he says. "If you apply for a patent first, you're a troll." Via email from Africa, he continues to attack the Flagstar decision, claiming that Martinez ignored key evidence and ruled incorrectly. (Medina felt it best not to talk by phone, because, as he put it, "I tend to speak my mind, and it would be unwise for me to do so without the self-censorship of writing.")

"We did nothing improper," he writes. "The judges in this case comported themselves like spectators in a Roman coliseum who wanted to see plenty of blood on the floor in the form of litigant's money before they considered the show worthy of their interest."

Medina says that his preference all along was not to file suits but to develop a product or, barring that, to get licensing fees for his patents, which he says "anticipated the development of ecommerce." He says he even set low royalty fees, "because I did not want to unduly damage anybody's business." The main objective for all his activities was his charitable work, most notably "perfecting an herbal-based remedy for HIV/AIDS." (He and his colleagues already have several patents on this.) Paying Flagstar's legal fees—more than $630,000—has hurt this important effort, he says. "I hope the prevaricators and pettifoggers who made the Eon-Net judgment possible are proud of themselves," he writes.

Surprisingly, for someone who seems to have done pretty well overall with the current system, Medina isn't bullish on it. "The patent system is badly broken," he says. "But it wasn't broken by NPEs. The system is now a playground for the big boys, and the independent inventor can't afford to play the game."

Nevertheless, after Eon-Net he began a new company called Glory Licensing. The company, based in Saint Kitts and Nevis, filed at least a dozen more lawsuits against ecommerce companies. In 2011 a company called Content Extraction and Transmission began filing another set of lawsuits. Attorney Jean-Marc Zimmerman charged San Diego County Credit Union, Bank of America, Wells Fargo, and at least eight other companies with infringing patents whose family history tracks back to Medina's dining room table.

Outrage may one day swing the pendulum back from patent madness to something resembling what the Constitution's framers had in mind. Meanwhile, those defendants will probably continue to pay up. And so will we.

Critical Thinking

1. How are problems with the current patent system inhibiting technology innovation today?
2. Why do many companies settle lawsuits with patent trolls even when they know the patent claim is not valid?

Create Central

www.mhhe.com/createcentral

Internet References

Drew Curtis: How I Beat a Patent Troll [TED Talk]
www.ted.com/talks/drew_curtis_how_i_beat_a_patent_troll.html

Finally: This Is How to Fix the 'Patent Fix' We're All In
www.wired.com/opinion/2013/04/this-is-how-to-fix-the-patent-fix-were-in

The Patent Troll Crisis is Really a Software Patent Crisis
www.washingtonpost.com/blogs/the-switch/wp/2013/09/03/the-patent-troll-crisis-is-really-a-software-patent-crisis

Article   Prepared by: Daniel Mittleman, *DePaul University*

The Tricky Business of Innovation: Can You Patent a Magic Trick?

RICK LAX

Learning Outcomes

After reading this article, you will be able to:

- Understand that Intellectual Property law consists of several independent concepts.
- Define the IP concepts of: Patent, Copyright, Trade Secret, and Trade Dress.

I created a magic trick with a balloon. You stretch out the balloon's nozzle, rip it off, and then magically reattach it as the balloon deflates. No secret props, no extra pieces: just one balloon. I spent months developing this trick, perfecting the psychology and the physiology. Then I spent weeks filming and editing the trick with magic distributor Theory11.com. We released "Detach" in February of 2012.

Some company in Russia copied it a couple months later. But they didn't just copy my trick—move for move, beat for beat—they copied the look and feel of the marketing in the trailer, too. [You can see for yourself by comparing those two links.]

In the field of magic, theft is *rampant.* Close-up magic wholesalers steal from close-up magic wholesalers. Parlor manipulators steal from parlor manipulators. Large-scale illusionists steal from large-scale illusionists.

Why do they do it? Because they can.

David Copperfield spends years developing illusions, perfecting patter, and mastering misdirection. And then lots of large-scale illusionists steal his style, his jokes, his presentations. "French law protects artists much better than U.S. law," Copperfield says. "In France, I sued someone who stole my Flying illusion, and I was successful. The lawsuit prevented him from performing it again without compensating me."

Here in America, intellectual property law offers less help to magicians.

Everyone Steals—And It's Not about Innovation

Since moving to Vegas six years ago, I've gotten to know a handful of notable magicians and every single one of them has been ripped off. Bizzaro makes and sells Color Changing Sponge Balls; two different manufacturers market it without his permission internationally. Losander created a big, beautiful $2,000 illusion floating table; you can now buy a crappy knockoff for $500. Jeff McBride spent years developing a manipulation act that incorporates masks with feathers, canes, umbrellas, and streamers; someone in Thailand copied the entire thing. And that company in Russia continued to copy my other tricks: a card trick, a headphones trick.

Unfortunately, none of this copying is about the kind of competition and innovation that one arguably sees in an industry like fashion.

Just last month, Criss Angel attempted an illusion very similar to one done by German illusionist Jan Rouven in 2009. It goes like this: Six swords are hung above a table, upon which the magician lies. Five swords are positioned to fall inches away from the magician's body; one is positioned over the heart. The swords' handles are connected to ropes and given to a spectator, who releases them, one by one, not knowing which rope is connected to the kill sword. After the magician survives the five drops, he gets off the table to demonstrate what would have happened if the spectator had released the kill sword. It plunges down to where the magician's heart just was.

Rouven tells me that his backstage manager caught Angel examining the prop after one of Rouven's shows, and apparently Angel never asked Rouven for permission to perform the trick. What Angel did do—here's where things get interesting—is get "permission" from fantasy/horror director Clive Barker, whose 1995 film *Lord of Illusions* contained a scene in which a magician performed a trick in which swords dropped onto a table upon which the magician lay. Angel's prop looked a lot like the one in Barker's movie (circular table, gold spiral, extra sword), not like Rouven's.

But the similarities between Angel's trick and the *Lord of Illusions* trick ended there. The *Lord of Illusions* trick was an escape demonstration in which the magician was locked to the table and every sword was positioned to fall on him. In the movie, the swords weren't released by ropes held by a spectator (they dropped automatically), and the table rotated in one direction while the hanging swords rotated in the other. None of these things applied to Angel's trick.

So Angel made a prop that *looked* like Barker's but *functioned* like Rouven's.

The irony? The trick malfunctioned (the kill sword didn't drop; the prop was repaired in full view of the live audience), and Angel's website later rewrote who owned the trick by stating, "Criss is the only magician to whom Clive has given his permission and blessing to recreate this illusion, and no one else should be performing it without Mr. Barker's permission."

The Tricks of the Law

It's not like the rampant copying or stealing has led to any new innovations or advanced the field of magic.

If a magician invents a device that allows him to, say, teleport across the stage in the blink of an eye, he can patent the device. But the patents themselves are open to the public. Anyone can see them. When an R. J. Reynolds tobacco newspaper ad revealed Horace Goldin's "Sawing a Lady in Half" illusion and Goldin sued for "unfair competition," the court sided with Reynolds, essentially arguing something like "if you wanted to keep it a secret you shouldn't have patented it."

Patents don't protect secrets; they reveal them. Plus, many magicians' tricks don't use special devices; they use misdirection and sleight-of-hand.

What about trade secret law? (This is different than trademark law, which only lets you protect the name or logo of your trick.) Liability is found against only those who share secrets "improperly." That means you can't score a job as Copperfield's assistant, promise to keep his secrets, and then turn around and start performing his tricks yourself. However, if you figure out one of his illusions while sitting in the audience, trade secret law won't stop you from copying it and performing it.

Prolific magic creator Andre Kole sued the "Masked Magician" and FOX for exposing his "Table of Death" illusion. It didn't go well. The court said the trick was too similar to a trick that had been published in several magic books in the 1800s, and that under trade secret law, the courts must consider the "ease or difficulty with which the information could be properly acquired or duplicated by others." Because if a trick is published in several books, it's easy to acquire the information.

Copyrighting Magic

Although the federal Copyright Act of 1976 protects original "dramatic works" and "choreographic works," you can't currently copyright a magic trick.

You can only copyright the "pantomimes" surrounding the trick. That's what Teller (of Penn & Teller) did with his "Shadows" illusion. When a Dutch magician started selling a knockoff version, Teller sued him for infringement, even though international litigation can get messy. The suit wasn't about revealing the props' secrets; it was about the stolen choreography.

But should it be?

Let's say I invent a Magic Jacket. I show both sides of the jacket, front and back. Looks totally normal. I slip the jacket on and zip it up. I pull its hood over my head. Then I put my arms behind my back. I pause. And then, as if possessed, the zipper unzips, the hood flies back, and the jacket peels itself off my shoulders and drops to the ground. (Applause here.)

It's a trick jacket, obviously. It looks normal, but it's got all sorts of wires and bands and electronics inside. I might spend years testing and perfecting the mechanics, but when I go to the copyright office, the only thing I can protect is the bit about showing both sides of the jacket and the bit about putting my arms behind my back.

Now let's imagine a rival magician steals my trick. Performs it on TV, on YouTube, at a theater next to mine. So I head to court to enforce my copyright. I tell the judge, "He's showing both sides of the jacket and he's putting his arms behind his back! That's my copyrighted choreography!"

My rival can defend himself with the merger doctrine. He'll say that my choreography is the *only* way to do the jacket trick: He has to show both sides of the jacket to show that it's (ostensibly) normal. *Of course* he has to put his hands behind his back, so his audience doesn't think he's unzipping the jacket from the inside. He'll argue that he *can't* perform the uncopyrightable trick without the copyrightable choreography, and that he's therefore not liable for infringement. And his argument will probably hold up.

This is like saying: It should be legal to bring a gun to a bank robbery because you *need* a gun if you're going to rob a bank effectively, so, actually, let's just make the whole robbery legal.

Look at it like this: You can copyright a choreography, and you can copyright a dramatic monolog, and a magic trick is just a combination of the two. It's a series of particular movements—close-up magic is choreography of the hands—with a series of particular words. Just because some tricks incorporate special props (as the Magic Jacket trick would) doesn't mean they should be less protectable.

The special prop alone is not the "work"; the "work" is a combination of the prop and what you do with it. In magic, the two are inseparable. If you've got a Sawing a Woman in Half box, the only thing you can do with it is make it look like you're cutting a girl in two.

So what can magicians do? Is there any hope for magicians protecting their intellectual property?

Maybe. Hope may lie in Trade Dress law, which could prevent one magician from copying the look and feel of another magician's show. (Think back to the Apple/Samsung lawsuit—that's Trade Dress law.)

Or maybe hope lies within the magic community's informal, internal policing. That's what attorney Jacob Loshin argues in his paper "Secrets Revealed: How Magicians Protect Intellectual Property Without Law."

Loshin points out that good magic secrets are hard to come by, and that the penalty for improperly sharing them, while not court sanctioned, is severe.

And lastly, maybe hope for the magic community as a whole lies in the illusions that haven't yet been created—in innovating the art form.

At least, that's what Copperfield thinks: "I believe it's possible to achieve justice in the American court system, but it takes a lot of time, energy, and money. It's not always worth focusing important bandwidth on that when you can apply the same time and energy to creating something new and different."

Critical Thinking

1. Describe why it is difficult to successfully sue when a magic trick is stolen, despite the existence of several forms of intellectual property law. Proffer an argument as to the best ways for a magician to protect his/her IP.

2. Research online how IP law works in the fashion industry and compare its use in fashion to its use in magic. Why is IP law applied differently in different industries?

Create Central

www.mhhe.com/createcentral

Internet References

Design Patents
www.computer.org/csdl/mags/co/2013/03/mco2013030008.html

Johanna Blakley: Lessons from Fashion's Free Culture [TED Talk]
www.ted.com/talks/johanna_blakley_lessons_from_fashion_s_free_culture.html

Unit 7

UNIT

Prepared by: Daniel Mittleman, *DePaul University*

International Perspectives

Americans may be surprised by how much access people outside of the United States have to the Internet. As of 2012, there were just over 245,000,000 Americans with Internet access, but that was just over 10 percent of the 2.4 billion Internet users worldwide. And those 2.4 billion were not situated only in the world's most developed nations; they include a significant community of users from developing nations as well (see Table 1).

Among the top twenty countries with the most Internet users are China, India, Indonesia, Nigeria, Iran, Korea, Vietnam, and Egypt. Korea even has a higher percentage of its population on the Internet than does the United States.

Tom Friedman wrote *The World is Flat*, a seminal book about the global impact of Internet growth, in 2005.[1] In it he describes several outcomes we are experiencing today. One: we are becoming global citizens. Today, we can withdraw money from our bank accounts using ATMs in Central Turkey, check our e-mail from a terminal located in an Internet café in Florence or Katmandu, and make cell or VoIP phone calls to and from nearly anywhere on the planet. Online education and virtual meetings are becoming the norm, rather than the exception.

Two: there is a global marketplace. E-commerce, via the Internet, allows consumers to buy from almost anyplace in the world; and it allows small entrepreneurs to set up a storefront and sell almost anyplace in the world. This means local businesses no longer have a captive market but have to compete in the global marketplace, increasing competition and narrowing their margins. But it also means they don't have to buy from

Table 1: www.internetworldstats.com/top20.htm

	Population	Internet Users	Percent on Internet	Growth since 2000
China	1,343,239,923	538,000,000	40.1%	2,391%
United States	313,847,465	245,203,319	78.1%	257%
India	1,205,073,612	137,000,000	11.4%	2,740%
Japan	127,368,088	101,228,736	79.5%	215%
Brazil	193,946,886	88,494,756	45.6%	1,770%
Russia	142,517,670	67,982,547	47.7%	2,193%
Germany	81,305,856	67,483,860	83.0%	281%
Indonesia	248,645,008	55,000,000	22.1%	2,750%
United Kingdom	63,047,162	52,731,209	83.6%	342%
France	65,630,692	52,228,905	79.6%	614%
Nigeria	170,123,740	48,366,179	28.4%	24,183%
Mexico	114,975,406	42,000,000	36.5%	1,548%
Iran	78,868,711	42,000,000	53.3%	16,800%
Korea	48,860,500	40,329,660	82.5%	212%
Turkey	79,749,461	36,455,000	45.7%	1,823%
Italy	61,261,254	35,800,000	58.4%	271%
Philippines	103,775,002	33,600,000	32.4%	1,680%
Spain	47,042,984	31,606,233	67.2%	587%
Vietnam	91,519,289	31,034,900	33.9%	15,517%
Egypt	83,688,164	29,809,724	35.6%	6,624%

local suppliers; rather they can negotiate the best price from the same global marketplace.

This leads to three: the growth of a skilled labor market around the world that can easily be outsourced to the United States. And this impacts the U.S. labor market. It used to be that if you were in the United Stats and had technical skills, there were jobs for you. Now, if you are a web designer, a computer programmer, a bookkeeper, or a technical support representative, there is someone in India, Indonesia, Viet Nam, or some other country willing and able to do the same work for less pay. You are competing not only with the person sitting next to you in class for a job, but you are competing with that person on the other side of the planet. The global marketplace grows the economy so there are actually more jobs; but there are even more people available competing for those jobs.

Four: the Internet also provides entrepreneurship opportunities. A programmer in the Ukraine can set up shop for the cost of a PC and an Internet connection. Or a non-programmer can start a business on eBay, Amazon, or any other of a number of global online shopping sites. Digital media can easily be created and replicated. And this portends the dark side of entrepreneurship: the vast gray market of pirated digital goods from movies, to music, to games and software. Differing cultural values and economic realities have made it impossible for copyright holders to stop the pirating of digital media. Rampant pirating has led to proposals for fairly draconian new International Trade Agreements aimed at protecting copyright of these goods.

And five: the unskilled labor market has expanded as well. The supply chain for moving raw materials to finished goods is now managed via the Internet, better enabling the efficiencies of sweatshops of unskilled workers in Bangladesh, Cambodia, China, Indonesia, India, and many other countries to make our clothes, toys, electronics, and other goods. While the Internet provide jobs for these people, it also enables their exploitation through sometimes cruel and unsafe working conditions with little oversight or protection.

Six: the technological infrastructure supporting the Internet is newer and more modern in many countries than it is in the United States. The outcome of this is that many countries are far ahead of the United States in adoption of mobile technology. While only about a third of the world's 7.2 billion people are on the Internet, The ITU reports there are over 6.8 billion mobile phone subscriptions as of mid-2013, with the likelihood there will be more active mobile phones in the world than there are people before the end of 2014.[2] And, while each phone subscription is not necessarily to a different person, even in lesser developed countries mobile phone access is almost universal, averaging 89 percent across all developing nations. It stands to reason we are only a few years away from almost all of those phones being Internet connected smart phones.

Seven: in other parts of the world the Internet has abetted revolution. As early as 1989 with Beijing's Tiananmen Square Protests in June and the fall of the Berlin Wall in November, the Internet was used to transfer photos and immediate accounts of the events to safe locations where they could be shared and published. Totalitarian governments were caught completely off-guard by the communication power of the Internet. More recently during the disputed 2009 Iranian presidential election and during the Arab Spring of 2011, social networking software such as Facebook and Twitter emerged as powerful communication vehicles for the protesters. Opposition Iranian presidential candidate Mir Hussein Moussavi's Facebook fan group reached 50,000 members during the election aftermath. At the peak of the protests, Twitter mentions "Iran" spiked from a steady flow of about 20,000 tweets per hour to over 221,000 tweets.[3] Similar increases in social media use were found during the 2011 Arab spring. Tweets about political change in Egypt rose from about 2,300 to 230,000 a day. The top 23 protest and political commentary YouTube videos were viewed over 5 million times.[4]

For all of these reasons, access to, and policies about, management of the Internet remain at the forefront of diplomatic and trade negotiations.

Notes

1. Thomas L. Friedman, *The World is Flat: A Brief History of the Twenty-first Century,* Farrar, Straus, and Giroux: New York. 2005.

2. _____, *The World in 2013: ICT Facts and Figures,* International Telecommunication Union. Geneva, Switzerland. February, 2013.

3. Ben Parr, *Mindblowing#IranElection Stats: 221,744 Tweets Per Hour at Peak, Mashable Social Media,* June 17, 2009 (See http://mashable.com/2009/06/17/iranelection-crisis-numbers/)

4. Philip N. Howard, Aiden Duffy, Deen Freelon, Muzammil Hussain, Will Mari, Marwa Mazaid, *Opening Closed Regimes: What Was the Role of Social Media During the Arab Spring?,* Working Paper, Project on Information Technology & Political Islam, University of Washington, 2011. (Accessed at http://pitpi.org/wp-content/uploads/2013/02/2011_Howard-Duffy-Freelon-Hussain-Mari-Mazaid_pITPI.pdf1 on October 22, 2013). ·

Article   Prepared by: Daniel Mittleman, *DePaul University*

Internet Freedom and Human Rights

Maintaining the practice of open communication and continuing the system of multi-stakeholder management of the Internet can help advance the principles expressed in the Universal Declaration of Human Rights.

HILLARY RODHAM CLINTON

Learning Outcomes

After reading this article, you will be able to:

- Articulate the threats to human rights that can occur through cyberspace.

- Understand the role of government as both a threat to and potentially a protector of international Internet freedoms.

- Understand the role of private companies in protecting international Internet freedoms.

In the 63 years since the adoption of the Universal Declaration of Human Rights, the world has been implementing a global commitment around the rights and freedoms of people everywhere, no matter where they live or who they are. And today as people increasingly turn to the Internet to conduct important aspects of their lives, we have to make sure that human rights are as respected online as offline. After all, the right to express one's views, practice one's faith, or peacefully assemble with others to pursue political or social change are all rights to which all human beings are entitled, whether they choose to exercise them in a city square or an Internet chat room. And just as we have worked together since the last century to secure these rights in the material world, we must work together in this century to secure them in cyberspace.

This is an urgent task. It is most urgent, of course, for those around the world whose words are now censored, who are imprisoned because of what they or others have written online, who are blocked from accessing entire categories of Internet content, or who are being tracked by governments seeking to keep them from connecting with one another.

In Syria, a blogger named Anas Maarawi was arrested in July 2011 after demanding that President Asad leave. He's not been charged with anything, but he remains in detention. In both Syria and Iran, many other online activists—actually too many to name—have been detained, imprisoned, beaten, and even killed for expressing their views and organizing their

fellow citizens. And perhaps the most well-known blogger in Russia, Alexei Navalny, was sentenced in December 2011 to 15 days in jail after he took part in protests over the Russian elections.

In China, several dozen companies signed a pledge in October, committing to strengthen their "self-management, self-restraint, and strict self-discipline." Now, if they were talking about fiscal responsibility, we might all agree. But they were talking about offering Web-based services to the Chinese people, which is code for getting in line with the government's tight control over the Internet.

These and many other incidents worldwide remind us of the stakes in this struggle. And the struggle does not belong only to those on the front lines who are suffering. It belongs to all of us: first, because we all have a responsibility to support human rights and fundamental freedoms everywhere. Second, because the benefits of the network grow as the number of users grows. The Internet is not exhaustible or competitive. My use of the Internet doesn't diminish yours. On the contrary, the more people that are online and contributing ideas, the more valuable the entire network becomes to all the other users. In this way, all users, through the billions of individual choices we make about what information to seek or share, fuel innovation, enliven public debates, quench a thirst for knowledge, and connect people in ways that distance and cost made impossible just a generation ago.

But when ideas are blocked, information deleted, conversations stifled, and people constrained in their choices, the Internet is diminished for all of us. What we do today to preserve fundamental freedoms online will have a profound effect on the next generation of users. More than two billion people are now connected to the Internet, but in the next 20 years, that number will more than double. And we are quickly approaching the day when more than a billion people are using the Internet in repressive countries. The pledges we make and the actions we take today can help us determine whether that number grows or shrinks, or whether the meaning of being on the Internet is totally distorted.

Delivering on Internet freedom requires cooperative actions, and we have to foster a global conversation based on shared principles and with the right partners to navigate the practical challenges of maintaining an Internet that is open and free while also interoperable, secure, and reliable. Now, this enterprise isn't a matter of negotiating a single document and calling the job done. It requires an ongoing effort to reckon with the new reality that we live in, in a digital world, and doing so in a way that maximizes its promise.

Because the advent of cyberspace creates new challenges and opportunities in terms of security, the digital economy, and human rights, we have to be constantly evolving in our responses. And though they are distinct, they are practically inseparable, because there isn't an economic Internet, a social Internet, and a political Internet. There is just the Internet, and we're here to protect what makes it great.

I'd like to briefly discuss three specific challenges that defenders of the Internet must confront.

The first challenge is for the private sector to embrace its role in protecting Internet freedom, because whether you like it or not, the choices that private companies make have an impact on how information flows or doesn't flow on the Internet and mobile networks. They also have an impact on what governments can and can't do, and they have an impact on people on the ground.

In recent months, we've seen cases where companies, products, and services were used as tools of oppression. In some instances, this cannot be foreseen, but in others, yes, it can. A few years ago, the headlines were about companies turning over sensitive information about political dissidents. Earlier this year, they were about a company shutting down the social networking accounts of activists in the midst of a political debate. Today's news stories are about companies selling the hardware and software of repression to authoritarian governments. When companies sell surveillance equipment to the security agency of Syria or Iran or, in past times, Qadhafi, there can be no doubt it will be used to violate rights.

There are some who would say that in order to compel good behavior by businesses, responsible governments should simply impose broad sanctions, and that will take care of the problem. Well, it's true that sanctions and export controls are useful tools, and the United States makes vigorous use of them when appropriate; and if they are broken, we investigate and pursue violators. And we're always seeking to work with our partners, such as the European Union, to make them as smart and effective as possible. Just last week, for example, we were glad to see our EU partners impose new sanctions on technology going to Syria.

So sanctions are part of the solution, but they are not the entire solution. Dual-use technologies and third-party sales make it impossible to have a sanctions regime that perfectly prevents bad actors from using technologies in bad ways. Sometimes companies say to us at the State Department, "Just tell us what to do, and we'll do it." But the fact is, you can't wait for instructions. In the 21st century, smart companies have to act before they find themselves in the crosshairs of controversy.

I wish there were, but there isn't, an easy formula for this. Making good decisions about how and whether to do business in various parts of the world, particularly where the laws are applied haphazardly or are opaque, takes critical thinking and deliberation and asking hard questions. So what kind of business should you do in a country where it has a history of violating Internet freedom? Is there something you can do to prevent governments from using your products to spy on their own citizens? Should you include warnings to consumers? How will you handle requests for information from security authorities when those requests come without a warrant? Are you working to prevent post-purchase modifications of your products or resale through middlemen to authoritarian regimes?

These and others are difficult questions, but companies must ask them. And the rest of us stand ready to work with you to find answers and to hold those who ignore or dismiss or deny the importance of this issue accountable. A range of resources emerged in recent years to help companies work through these issues. The UN Guiding Principles on Business and Human Rights, which were adopted in June 2011, and the OECD Guidelines for Multinational Enterprises both advise companies on how to meet responsibilities and carry out due diligence. And the Global Network Initiative is a growing forum where companies can work through challenges with other industry partners, as well as academics, investors, and activists.

And of course, companies can always learn from users. The Silicon Valley Human Rights Conference in October 2011 brought together companies, activists, and experts to discuss real-life problems and identify solutions. And some participants issued what they called the Silicon Valley Standard for stakeholders to aspire to.

Working through these difficult questions by corporate executives and board members should help shape your practices. Part of the job of responsible corporate management in the 21st century is doing human rights due diligence on new markets, instituting internal review procedures, identifying principles by which decisions are to be made in tough situations, because we cannot let the short-term gains that all of us think are legitimate and worth seeking jeopardize the openness of the Internet and the human rights of individuals who use it without it coming back to haunt us all in the future. A free and open Internet is important not just to technology companies but to all companies. Whether it's run with a single mobile phone or an extensive corporate network, it's hard to find any business today that doesn't depend in some way on the Internet and doesn't suffer when networks are constrained.

And also I would add that, in this day, brand and reputation are precious corporate assets. Companies that put them at risk when they are careless about freedom of the Internet can often pay a price.

But even as companies must step up, governments must resist the urge to clamp down, and that is the second challenge we face. If we're not careful, governments could upend the current Internet governance framework in a quest to increase their own control. Some governments use Internet governance issues as a cover for pushing an agenda that would justify restricting human rights online. We must be wary of such agendas and united in our shared conviction that human rights apply online.

Right now, in various international forums, some countries are working to change how the Internet is governed. They want to replace the current multi-stakeholder approach, which includes governments, the private sector, and citizens, and supports the free flow of information, in a single global network. In its place, they aim to impose a system cemented in a global code that expands control over Internet resources, institutions, and content, and centralizes that control in the hands of governments.

In a way, that isn't surprising, because governments have never met a voice or public sphere they didn't want to control at some point or another. They want to control what gets printed in newspapers, who gets into universities, what companies get oil contracts, what churches and NGOs get registered, where citizens can gather, so why not the Internet? But it's actually worse than that. It's not just that they want governments to have all the control by cutting out civil society and the private sector; they also want to empower each individual government to make its own rules for the Internet that not only undermine human rights and the free flow of information but also the interoperability of the network.

In effect, the governments pushing this agenda want to create national barriers in cyberspace. This approach would be disastrous for Internet freedom. More government control will further constrict what people in repressive environments can do online. It would also be disastrous for the Internet as a whole, because it would reduce the dynamism of the Internet for everyone. Fragmenting the global Internet by erecting barriers around national Internets would change the landscape of cyberspace. In this scenario, the Internet would contain people in a series of digital bubbles, rather than connecting them in a global network. Breaking the Internet into pieces would give you echo chambers rather than an innovative global marketplace of ideas.

The United States wants the Internet to remain a space where economic, political, and social exchanges flourish. To do that, we need to protect people who exercise their rights online, and we also need to protect the Internet itself from plans that would undermine its fundamental characteristics.

Now, those who push these plans often do so in the name of security. And let me be clear: The challenge of maintaining security and of combating cyber crime, such as the theft of intellectual property, is real—a point I underscore whenever I discuss these issues. There are predators, terrorists, traffickers on the Internet, malign actors plotting cyber attacks, and they all need to be stopped. We can do that by working together without compromising the global network, its dynamism, or our principles.

There's a lot to be said about cyber security, but here I want to emphasize only the basic point that the United States supports the public-private collaboration that now exists to manage the technical evolution of the Internet in real time. We support the principles of multi-stakeholder Internet governance developed by more than 30 nations in the OECD earlier this year. A multi-stakeholder system brings together the best of governments, the private sector, and civil society. And most importantly, it works. It has kept the Internet up and running for years all over the world. So to use an American phrase, our position is, "If it ain't broke, don't fix it." And there's no good reason to replace an effective system with an oppressive one.

The third and final challenge is that all of us—governments, private sector, civil society—must do more to build a truly global coalition to preserve an open Internet. And that's where all of you here today come in, because Internet freedom cannot be defended by one country or one region alone. Building this global coalition is hard, partly because for people in many countries the potential of the Internet is still unrealized. While it's easy for us in the United States or in the Netherlands to imagine what we would lose if the Internet became less free, it is harder for those who have yet to see the benefit of the Internet in their day to day lives. So we have to work harder to make the case that an open Internet is and will be in everyone's best interests. And we have to keep that in mind as we work to build this global coalition and make the case to leaders of those countries where the next generation of Internet users live. These leaders have an opportunity today to help ensure that the full benefits are available to their people tomorrow, and in so doing, they will help us ensure an open Internet for everyone.

The United States will be making the case for an open Internet in our work worldwide, and we welcome other countries to join us. As our coalition expands, countries such as Ghana, Kenya, Mongolia, Chile, Indonesia, and others are sure to be effective at bringing other potential partners on board who have perspectives that can help us confront and answer difficult questions. And new players from governments, the private sector, and civil society will be participating in managing the Internet in coming decades as billions more people from all different regions go online.

So let's lay the groundwork now for these partnerships that will support an open Internet in the future. The first step will be to build support for a new cross-regional group that will work together in exactly the way that I've just discussed, based on shared principles, providing a platform for governments to engage creatively and energetically with the private sector, civil society, and other governments.

The second step is a practical effort to do more to support cyber activists and bloggers who are threatened by their repressive governments. The Committee to Protect Journalists recently reported that of all the writers, editors, and photojournalists now imprisoned around the world, nearly half are online journalists. The threat is very real. Several of us already provide support, including financial support, to activists and bloggers, and I was pleased that the EU recently announced new funding for that purpose. And I know that other governments, including the Netherlands, are also looking for ways to help out.

By coordinating our efforts, we can make them go further and help more people.

As we engage in this work, we must remain aware that some countries are pulling very hard in the opposite direction. They're trying to erect walls between different activities online, economic exchanges, political discussions, religious expression, social interaction, and so on. They want to keep what they like and what doesn't threaten them and to suppress what they don't. But there are opportunity costs for trying to be open for business but closed for free expression, costs to a nation's education system, political stability, social mobility, and economic potential.

And walls that divide the Internet are easier to erect than to maintain. Our government will continue to work very hard to get around every barrier that repressive governments put up, because governments that have erected barriers will eventually find themselves boxed in, and they will face the dictator's dilemma. They will have to choose between letting the walls fall or paying the price for keeping them standing by resorting to greater repression and to escalating the opportunity cost of missing out on the ideas that have been blocked and the people who have disappeared.

I urge countries everywhere to reject that dark and narrow vision, and to join us in betting that an open Internet will lead to stronger, more prosperous countries. This is not a bet on computers or mobile phones. It's a bet on the human spirit. It's a bet on people. And we're confident that together, with our partners and government, the private sector, and civil society around the world, who have made this same bet, we will preserve the Internet as open and secure for all.

We should honor the Universal Declaration of Human Rights, which reminds us of the timeless principles that should be our North Star. And a look at the world around us and the way it is changing reminds us there is no autopilot steering us forward. We have to work in good faith and engage in honest debate, and we have to join together to solve the challenges and seize the opportunities of this exciting digital age.

Critical Thinking

1. Clinton says, "Because the advent of cyberspace creates new challenges and opportunities in terms of security, the digital economy, and human rights, we have to be constantly evolving in our responses." What does she mean by this? What examples can you provide?

2. View the Web Materials associated with this article and discuss how social media can be both a catalyst for freedom and a tool of repression.

3. View the *Guardian* interviews with Edward Snowden as well as the *Tonight Show* interview with President Obama. From these articulate an opinion as to whether the U.S. government is functioning as a protector of or a threat to international Internet freedoms.

Create Central

www.mhhe.com/createcentral

Internet References

Full Interview: President Obama on "The Tonight Show" with Jay Leno
www.realclearpolitics.com/video/2013/08/07/full_interview_president_obama_on_the_tonight_show_with_jay_leno.html

In Egypt, Social Media Tools Act as Protest Catalyst Despite Government Meddling
www.pbs.org/newshour/bb/world/jan-june11/egyptcommunica_01-31.html

Internet Censorship Is Taking Root in Southeast Asia
http://world.time.com/2013/07/18/internet-censorship-is-taking-root-in-southeast-asia

The NSA Files from The Guardian Newspaper
www.theguardian.com/world/the-nsa-files

The Technology Helping Repressive Regimes Spy
www.npr.org/2011/12/14/143639670/the-technology-helping-repressive-regimes-spy

Top 10 Countries That Censor the Internet the Most!
www.bestvpnservice.com/blog/top-10-countries-that-censor-the-internet

---

HILLARY RODHAM CLINTON is U.S. Secretary of State. This article is adapted from a speech she gave at The Hague on December 8, 2011.

Clinton, Hillary Rodham. Reprinted with permission from *Issues in Science and Technology,* Spring 2012, pp. 45, 47–52. Published in 2012 by the University of Texas at Dallas, Richardson, TX.

Article   Prepared by: Daniel Mittleman, *DePaul University*

A Small World After All?

The Internet has changed many things, but not the insular habits of mind that keep the world from becoming truly connected.

ETHAN ZUCKERMAN

Learning Outcomes

After reading this article, you will be able to:

- Understand the barriers that keep the world from becoming truly connected via the Internet.

- Understand where we currently are in the process of achieving true global connectivity.

- Understand how we discover information and make connections with people online.

When the Cold War ended, the work of America's intelligence analysts suddenly became vastly more difficult. In the past, they had known who the nation's main adversaries were and what bits of information they needed to acquire about them: the number of SS-9 missiles Moscow could deploy, for example, or the number of warheads each missile could carry. The U.S. intelligence community had been in search of secrets—facts that exist but are hidden by one government from another. After the Soviet Union's collapse, as Bruce Berkowitz and Allan Goodman observe in *Best Truth: Intelligence in the Information Age* (2002), it found a new role thrust upon it: the untangling of mysteries.

Computer security expert Susan Landau identifies the 1979 Islamic Revolution in Iran as one of the first indicators that the intelligence community needed to shift its focus from secrets to mysteries. On its surface, Iran was a strong, stable ally of the United States, an "island of stability" in the region, according to President Jimmy Carter. The rapid ouster of the shah and a referendum that turned a monarchy into a theocracy led by a formerly exiled religious scholar left governments around the world shocked and baffled.

The Islamic Revolution was a surprise because it had taken root in mosques and homes, not palaces or barracks. The calls to resist the shah weren't broadcast on state media but transmitted via handmade leaflets and audiocassettes of speeches by Ayatollah Khomeini. In their book analyzing the events of 1979, *Small Media, Big Revolution* (1994), Annabelle Sreberny and Ali Mohammad, who both participated in the Iranian

revolution, emphasize the role of two types of technology: tools that let people obtain access to information from outside Iran, and tools that let people spread and share that information on a local scale. Connections to the outside world (direct-dial long-distance phone lines, cassettes of sermons sent through the mail, broadcasts on the BBC World Service) and tools that amplified those connections (home cassette recorders, photocopying machines) helped build a movement more potent than governments and armies had anticipated.

As we enter an age of increased global connection, we are also entering an age of increasing participation. The billions of people worldwide who access the Internet via computers and mobile phones have access to information far beyond their borders, and the opportunity to contribute their own insights and opinions. It should be no surprise that we are experiencing a concomitant rise in mystery that parallels the increases in connection.

The mysteries brought to the fore in a connected age extend well beyond the realm of political power. Bad subprime loans in the United States lead to the failure of an investment bank; this, in turn, depresses interbank lending, pushing Iceland's heavily leveraged economy into collapse and consequently leaving British consumers infuriated at the disappearance of their deposits from Icelandic banks that had offered high interest rates on savings accounts. An American businessman on a flight to Singapore takes ill, and epidemiologists find themselves tracing the SARS epidemic in cities from Toronto to Manila, eventually discovering a disease that originated with civet cats and was passed to humans because civets are sold as food in southern China. Not all mysteries are tragedies—the path of a musical style from Miami clubs through dance parties in the favelas of Rio to the hit singles of British–Sri Lankan singer M.I.A. is at least as unexpected and convoluted.

Uncovering secrets might require counting missile silos in satellite images or debriefing double agents. To understand our connected world, we need different skills. Landau suggests that "solving mysteries requires deep, often unconventional thinking, and a full picture of the world around the mystery."

The unexpected outbreak of the Arab Spring, a mystery that's still unfolding, suggests that we may not be getting this full picture, or the deep, unconventional thinking we need. Had you asked an expert on the Middle East what changes were likely to take place in 2011, almost none would have predicted the Arab Spring, and none would have chosen Tunisia as the flashpoint for the movement. Zine el Abidine Ben Ali had ruled the North African nation virtually unchallenged since 1987, and had co-opted, jailed, or exiled anyone likely to challenge his authority. When vegetable seller Mohamed Bouazizi set himself on fire, there was no reason to expect his family's protests against government corruption to spread beyond the village of Sidi Bouzid. After all, the combination of military cordons, violence against protesters, a sycophantic domestic press, and a ban on international news media had, in the past, ensured that dissent remained local.

Not this time. Video of protests in Sidi Bouzid, shot on mobile phones and uploaded to Facebook, reached Tunisian dissidents in Europe. They indexed and translated the footage and packaged it for distribution on sympathetic networks such as al-Jazeera. Widely watched in Tunisia, al-Jazeera alerted citizens in Tunis and Sfax to protests taking place in another corner of their country, which in effect served as an invitation to participate. As Ben Ali's regime trembled and fell, images of the protests spread throughout the region, inspiring similar outpourings in more than a dozen countries and the overthrow of two additional regimes.

While the impact of Tunisia's revolution is now appreciated, the protests that led to Ben Ali's ouster were invisible in much of the world. *The New York Times* first mentioned Mohamed Bouazizi and Sidi Bouzid in print on January 15, 2011, the day after Ben Ali fled. The U.S. intelligence apparatus was no more prescient. Senator Dianne Feinstein (D.-Calif.), who chairs the Senate Intelligence Committee, wondered to reporters, "Was someone looking at what was going on the Internet?"

A central paradox of this connected age is that while it's easier than ever to share information and perspectives from different parts of the world, we may be encountering a narrower picture of the world than we did in less connected days. During the Vietnam War, television reporting from the frontlines involved transporting exposed film from Southeast Asia by air, then developing and editing it in the United States before broadcasting it days later. Now, an unfolding crisis such as the Japanese tsunami or Haitian earthquake can be reported in real time via satellite. Despite these lowered barriers, today's American television news features less than half as many international stories as were broadcast in the 1970s.

The pace of print media reporting has accelerated sharply, with newspapers moving to a "digital first" strategy, publishing fresh information online as news breaks. While papers publish many more stories than they did 40 years ago (online and offline), Britain's four major dailies publish on average 45 percent fewer international stories than they did in 1979.

Why worry about what's covered in newspapers and television when it's possible to read firsthand accounts from Syria or Sierra Leone? Research suggests that we rarely read such accounts. My studies of online news consumption show that 95 percent of the news consumed by American Internet users is published in the United States. By this metric, the United States is less parochial than many other nations, which consume even less news published in other countries. This locality effect crosses into social media as well. A recent study of Twitter, a tool used by 400 million people around the world, showed that we're far more likely to follow people who are physically close to us than to follow someone outside our home country's borders, or even a few states or provinces away. Thirty-nine percent of the relationships on Twitter involve someone following the tweets of a person in the same metropolitan area. In the Twitter hotbed of São Paulo, Brazil, more than 78 percent of the relationships are local. So much for the death of distance.

As we start to understand how people actually use the Internet, the cyberutopian hopes of a borderless, postnational planet can look as naive as most past predictions that new technologies would transform societies. In 1912, radio pioneer Guglielmo Marconi declared, "The coming of the wireless era will make war impossible, because it will make war ridiculous." Two years later a ridiculous war began, ultimately killing nine million Europeans.

While it's easy to be dismissive of today's Marconis—the pundits, experts, and enthusiasts who saw a rise in Internet connection leading to a rise in international understanding—that's too simple and too cynical a response. Increased digital connection does not automatically lead to increased understanding. At the same time, there's never been a tool as powerful as the Internet for building new ties (and maintaining existing ones) across distant borders.

The challenge for anyone who wants to decipher the mysteries of a connected age is to understand how the Internet does, and does not, connect us. Only then can we find ways to make online connection more common and more powerful.

There are at least three ways we discover new information online. Each of these methods has shortcomings in terms of giving us a broad, global picture of the world. Search engines, while incredibly powerful, are only as good as the queries we put to them. They are designed for information retrieval, not for discovery. If you had been able to ask Google in 1979 how many SS-9 missiles the Soviets possessed, you might have received a plausible answer, but you wouldn't have been told you should be asking about cassette recorders in Iran instead. Search engines tell us what we want to know, but they can't tell us what we might need to know.

Social media such as Facebook or Twitter might tell you to pay attention to cassette recordings in Iran, but only if your friends include Iranians. Social media are a powerful discovery engine, but what you're discovering is what your friends know. If you're lucky enough to have a diverse, knowledgeable set of friends online, they may lead you in unexpected directions. But birds of a feather flock together, both online and offline, and your friends are more likely to help you discover the unexpected in your hometown than in another land.

The most powerful discovery engines online may be curated publications such as *The New York Times* or *The Guardian*. Editors of these publications are driven by a mission to provide their audiences with the broad picture of the world they need in order to be effective citizens, consumers, and businesspeople. But professional curators have their inevitable biases and blind spots. Much as we know to search for the news we think will affect our lives, editors deploy reporting resources toward parts of the world with strategic and economic significance. When mysteries unfold in corners of the world we're used to ignoring, such as Tunisia, curators are often left struggling to catch up.

The limits of online information sources are a challenge both for us and for the people building the next generation of online tools. If we rigorously examine the media we're encountering online, looking for topics and places we hear little about, we may be able to change our behavior, adding different and dissenting views to our social networks, seeking out new sources of news. But this task would be vastly easier if the architects of Internet tools took up the cause of helping to broaden worldviews. Facebook already notices that you've failed to "friend" a high school classmate and tries to connect you. It could look for strangers in Africa or India who share your interests and broker an introduction. Google tracks every search you undertake so it can more effectively target ads to you. It could also use that information to help you discover compelling content about topics you've never explored, adding a serendipity engine to its formidable search function.

Why aren't engineers racing to build the new tools that will help unravel the mysteries of a connected world? They may be waiting for indicators that we want them and are ready to use them.

In 2004, journalist Rebecca MacKinnon and I founded Global Voices, an international news network designed to amplify and spread ideas and perspectives published online in the developing world. Our 800 correspondents translate and summarize content from the blogs of Russian activists protesting election fraud and Nigerian Facebook users discussing the latest hot Nollywood film. The project has won awards and recognition, but it's had only modest success building an audience. When a news story receives global attention, as Iran's Green Movement protests did in 2009, readership spikes. But our in-depth coverage of the protests in Sidi Bouzid went largely unnoticed until Ben Ali's government fell. We continue to report on coups in Madagascar and culture in Malaysia regardless of the audience these stories generate. But to convince Facebook to broker global connections or encourage *The Huffington Post* to cover global stories, people need to demand a broader view.

As Pankaj Ghemawat of Barcelona's IESE Business School reminds us in *World 3.0* (2011), we're not at the endpoint of globalization, but somewhere near the starting line. The age of connection is just beginning. Many people still view the world as dominated by secrets: How close is Iran to building a nuclear bomb? How can Western companies crack the Chinese market?

Where are undiscovered reserves of oil? It's at least as possible that the questions that will dominate the next century are the ones we don't yet know to ask. Those who will thrive in a connected world are those who learn to see broadly and to solve the mysteries that emerge.

Critical Thinking

1. What are the key barriers that keep the world from becoming truly connected via the Internet?

2. Zuckerman writes, "As we start to understand how people actually use the Internet, the cyber utopian hopes of a borderless, postnational planet can look as naive as most past predictions that new technologies would transform societies." Do you agree? Why or why not?

3. Zuckerman quotes Pankej Ghemaway saying, "we're not at the endpoint of globalization, but somewhere near the starting line." How do you think global connectivity will change as we proceed through this journey?

Create Central

www.mhhe.com/createcentral

Internet References

'The End of Big' Argues That Technology Helps The Little Guy
www.pbs.org/newshour/rundown/2013/04/the-end-of-big-argues-technology-helps-the-little-guy.html

Microfinance Combines Charity and Business Savvy
www.pbs.org/newshour/extra/student_voices/microfinance-combines-charity-and-business-savvy

Social Media and Social Change: How Young People are Tapping into Technology
http://blogs.worldbank.org/youthink/social-media-and-social-change-how-young-people-are-tapping-technology

The Surveillance Market and Its Victims
www.bloomberg.com/data-visualization/wired-for-repression

Tim Berners-Lee: The Year Open Data Went Worldwide [TED Talk]
www.ted.com/talks/tim_berners_lee_the_year_open_data_went_worldwide.html

---

ETHAN ZUCKERMAN is director of the Center for Civic Media at MIT. He and Rebecca MacKinnon are cofounders of the international blogging community Global Voices (globalvoicesonline.org), which showcases news and opinion from citizen media in more than 150 nations. His book *Rewire: Rethinking Globalization in an Age of Connection* will be published by W. W. Norton early next year.

Article — Prepared by: Daniel Mittleman, *DePaul University*

7 Reasons Why Sweatshops Still Persist

JOLEEN ONG

Learning Outcomes

After reading this article, you will be able to:

- Understand the relationship between the growth of the Internet and the prevalance of Third World sweatshops.

- Describe what a supply chain is and where ethical issues emerge within computers and smart phone supply chains.

- List several reasons why sweatshops exist.

Talk to any conscious consumer about sweatshops, and they are likely to ask you—"what company *is* 'sweat free'?"

The answer is not simple. Although some companies do a much better job than others, it's easier to name companies that are *not* sweat-free. Strictly talking about factories that produce for export to global retailers, supply chain management practices can enable sweatshop conditions. Since the term 'sweatshop' describes abusive workplace conditions, consumers should be conscious of how this happens, to ask the right questions and become part of the solution.

There are 7 key supply chain realities, which can help us see why sweatshops persist:

1. Not Just in China

Sweatshops are everywhere. Bad working conditions tend especially to be prevalent in workplaces where there are migrant or 'stateless' workers, as labor law does not usually protect them. Additionally, workers who lack basic education have few choices for work. For example, forced labor in Florida's tomato fields, and child labor in Malaysia's palm oil industry are often stateless and/or migrant workers. The bargaining power of these workers is absent, and their disenfranchised status enables exploitative practices.

2. Most Brands Don't Own Their Factories

Almost every large retailer is vertically disintegrated. Aside from Foxconn, it is rare for the general public and mainstream media to know the name of a supplier factory. Vertically disintegrated business models decrease the liability for companies if something goes wrong at the factory, and increase their flexibility in buying. But a retailer's responsibility for their transactional relations is still going to be questioned by the public and media, as their brand reputation is inextricably linked to their social responsibility. A customer wouldn't return a defective shoe to XYZ factory where it was produced in Indonesia, they would return it to the Nike store where they bought it. But, would customers return a shoe if they found it was produced by exploited workers?

3. Unstable Relationships Create Risky Circumstances

Companies might have policies for issues such as forced and child labor, as well as an ethical code of conduct, but in the end it all comes down to the purchase order. Often, but not always, the supplier has a comparably smaller voice and decision-making power than its retail customers. Many suppliers are faced with short-term contracts and inadequate lead-time to produce goods. If a factory doesn't have the security of a long-term customer relationship, it may need to front its own money, and therefore will be fighting to make every purchase order happen on time, by any means necessary. This triggers excessive overtime, which can trigger an increase in workplace accidents and defective products, as well as illegal subcontracting as we've seen in the case of Zara. For retailers, it is important to ask: *does the supplier actually have the capacity and time to produce what we're asking for in the ethical manner that we seek?*

4. The Purchase Order Determines the Degree of Influence

Supplier factories are independent businesses, and their customers are retailers that buy their goods. A scarf factory in India can be producing for 80 brands, and as a result, be audited by different retailers' code of conduct auditors 2–3 times a month. Foxconn wasn't just producing for Apple, it was also producing for others such as Sony and Intel. It's important to see where the money flows and how often, to determine the degree of influence exerted to follow the retailer's code of conduct. For retailers, before suppliers are expected to broadly respect human rights, it's important to do a reality check—*what percentage of the supplier's business are you? Do you have a long-term contract with them?*

5. Audits Alone Don't Create Change

Alone, audits of codes of conduct or voluntary standards are seldom able to change workplace conditions, nor provide a guarantee. Auditors take a snapshot of the factory at a given time and place. Supplier factories will do what is *expected* and *inspected*. Ultimately, it is what is done with the information found in the workplace, whether by an auditor or anyone else, that effects change. On May 20, 2011, an explosion caused by a buildup of aluminum dust killed three workers at Foxconn in Chengdu. Just two days earlier, SACOM publicly documented this as a health and safety violation in a report, after witnessing workers enter Foxconn with aluminum dust coated in their skin and hair. No action was taken in time.

6. Ethically-Made Products Are Not Always More Expensive

Price elasticity varies by product, sector, consumer base, and in the case of Apple—cult following. On the eve of the iPhone 5's release, news reports described the crowds of people that waited outside the Apple store. Consumers were selling their spot in line, and previously there was a report that one consumer sold his kidney to buy an iPad and iPhone. If a price premium were definitively established to ensure an ethical product, would consumers purchase it? Of course this depends on the circumstances, but according to a Harvard case study on ethically labeled towels, coffee and shirts, the answer is—yes, they would.

7. Misaligned Incentives and Unintegrated Retail Departments

In the past decade, many companies have established 'Corporate Social Responsibility' (CSR) departments, where some focus on managing human rights in their supply chains.

Chances are, these departments are silos. If they are not closely cooperating with the other departments that communicate with suppliers, conflicting messages that produce misaligned incentives may occur. For example, the questions suppliers receive might differ substantially:

- Purchasing Department: "Can you produce this by next week?"
- Design Department: "Can you change this now?"
- CSR Department: "Can you cut overtime to legal limits?"

It is important that all departments are integrated with similar goals, objectives and incentives about the code of conduct at the design stage. Otherwise, the supplier might only listen to the department that issues the purchase order.

These are seven key realities about sweatshops I've encountered in my daily work at Social Accountability International (SAI). Can you think of any others?

Critical Thinking

1. In what ways are the use of Third World sweatshops an Information Technology problem? In what ways did the advent of the Internet exacerbate the problem of sweatshops?
2. Why is it difficult for brands to simply decree that sweatshop labor will not be used to create their products?

Create Central

www.mhhe.com/createcentral

Internet References

Apple Supplier Foxconn Pledges Better Working Conditions, but Will it Deliver?
www.pbs.org/newshour/bb/world/jan-june12/apple_03-30.html

Will Technology End Sweatshops?
www.monroenews.com/news/2013/jun/02/
will-technology-end-sweatshops/?news

Workers' Rights 'Flouted' at Apple iPhone Factory in China
www.theguardian.com/technology/2013/sep/05/
workers-rights-flouted-apple-iphone-plant

The World's Least Wired Countries, in 1 Map
www.washingtonpost.com/blogs/the-switch/wp/2013/08/21/
the-worlds-least-wired-countries-in-1-map

Unit 8

UNIT

Prepared by: Daniel Mittleman, *DePaul University*

National Security

Prior to 2013, American cyber war and cyber espionage capabilities were touted as important cogs within our military's arsenal. Stuxnet, for example, leaked into the news in 2010 as a mysterious, very focused attack upon the Iranian nuclear program that must have come from the Americans or Israelis, though neither government owned up to sponsoring it. Stuxnet, while fascinating, has become old news. Much more interesting was Flame, an even more sinister follow up attack upon the Iranian nuclear program, so named by the Russian computer security firm that uncovered and publicized its existence. Flame leads one to wonder: is this what the future of warfare is going to be like?

Things changed in 2013, the year national security and personal privacy found themselves in direct conflict in the United States. The news was dominated by Edward Snowden's exposure of National Security Agency (NSA) information that documents how the United States government has been systematically collecting data on Americans for over two generations—even before the existence of the Internet, and has increased and automated that surveillance since September 2001. Some Americans view Snowden as a national hero: a whistleblower who uncovered longstanding unconstitutional activities. Others, including the government national security and homeland security communities, view Snowden as a traitor and seditionist. However one views the propriety of Snowden's whistleblowing, it is enlightening to read about the processes the United States government has used to infiltrate our telecommunications and computing systems to capture and store vast quantities of data. As of this writing, the story has not yet played out in full. *The Guardian,* publishers of most of Snowden's material, suggests there are more leaks to come. And neither Congress nor the Supreme Court has weighed in on the legality of recent revelations.

Other issues emerging this year include the growing domestic use of drone aircraft by Customs and Border Protection and other federal and local agencies. It appears over 500 domestic drone flights have taken place between 2010 and 2012.[1] There exists little or no policy regulating the use of domestic drones nor addressing constitutional issues that might arise from their use. As drone use by multiple law enforcement agencies grows, courts and Congress will no doubt take a stand on their legality.

And the technologies available to drones are improving to the point of being scary good. Argus, for example, is a 1.8 gigapixel camera that can be mounted on a plane (or drone) and track individuals in real time from more than three miles high.[2] The United States government has not said whether Argus has been deployed over the United States. And, given that Argus' specifications have been declassified, it is not a stretch to imagine something more powerful is already, or soon to be, deployed.

Omnipresent surveillance of U.S. public space has produced benefits. The 2013 Boston Marathon bombers, for example, were quickly identified by crowdsourcing surveillance video that captured them at the race. The presence of recording equipment must be presumed today be friend and foe alike, likely modifying behaviors in the public arena.

Notes

1. See: www.eff.org/deeplinks/2013/09/500-cbp-drone-flights-other-agencies. More recent data has not been released by the government.

2. See: http://video.pbs.org/video/2325492143

Article

Prepared by: Daniel Mittleman, *DePaul University*

Deception Is Futile When Big Brother's Lie Detector Turns Its Eyes on You

ADAM HIGGINBOTHAM

Learning Outcomes

After reading this article, you will be able to:

- Understand the role of technology in lie detection; articulate several approaches to using technology to support lie detection and the relative success of each.

- Understand the role of politics in determining which technologies are funded for research and development.

- Articulate both advantages and disadvantages of having avatars conduct initial border screenings.

Alan Bersin, commissioner of Customs and Border Protection, arrives at the gloomy US border post in Nogales, Arizona, early one winter morning wearing an expression of mildly pained concentration.

He got up before dawn and now looks as if he'd rather be anywhere else. In the immigration lanes downstairs, a procession of pickups and SUVs nudge dejectedly in from Mexico, taillights blinking through a relentless drizzle. Bersin arrived late, and he seems in no mood to assess the state of the art in automated psychophysiological evaluation technology. Yet there it is, pushed up against the wall of a cramped back office at the DeConcini Port of Entry: a gray metal box about the size and shape of an ATM, with two softly glowing video monitors, one on top of the other.

Bersin, a self-assured bureaucrat and a Rhodes Scholar who studied at Oxford with Bill Clinton, approaches the device. The lower monitor displays an icon of an oversize red button; the upper screen shows the head and shoulders of a smoothly rendered, computer-generated young man blinking and occasionally suffering a slight electronic shudder. He appears to be in his twenties and has an improbably luxuriant head of blue-black hair combed back in a sumptuous pompadour. This is the Embodied Avatar, the personification of the latest software developed to help secure the nation's frontiers by delivering what its creator calls "a noninvasive credibility assessment"— sifting dishonest travelers from honest ones. Which is to say, this late-model Max Headroom is a lie detector.

Bersin taps the red button to start the test, and in an agreeable Midwestern voice, the avatar asks Bersin a series of questions.

"Are you a citizen of the United States of America?"

"Yes," Bersin says.

"Have you visited any foreign countries in the past five years?"

"Yes."

"Do you live at the address you listed on your application?"

"Yes."

When the interview is over, Bersin turns to the other people in the room—his entourage, a delegation from the Canadian border agency, and the engineers who are anxiously overseeing this most critical test yet of their invention.

One technician explains to Bersin how the kiosk has instantly analyzed his responses, displayed on a rubber-jacketed iPad and broken down into categories of risk: green, yellow, and red. Bersin's mask of barely suppressed boredom does not crack.

But then the technician points out that one of his answers is flagged in red: The machine is suspicious about his address. Bersin acknowledges that, yes, what he usually describes as his home is not actually where he lives, and that he was thinking about something else when he was answering—it's just that he has a work residence in Washington, DC, but of course his family home remains back in San Diego and—

Bersin's counterpart from Canada, a former intelligence officer, interrupts, cracking an interrogator's indulgent smile: "Do you have a lawyer?"

Afterward, Jay Nunamaker, the sardonic computer engineer overseeing the Embodied Avatar project, allows himself a low chuckle. "I don't think it could have gone better," he says. Within a few hours, the young man with the improbable hair is interviewing members of the public. The first field tests of the US government's state-of-the-art computer-controlled lie-detection device have begun.

Since September 11, 2001, federal agencies have spent millions of dollars on research designed to detect deceptive behavior in travelers passing through US airports and border crossings in the hope of catching terrorists. Security personnel have been trained—and technology has been devised—to identify, as an air transport trade association representative once put it, "bad people and not just bad objects." Yet for all this investment and the decades of research that preceded it, researchers continue to struggle with a profound scientific question: How can you tell if someone is lying?

That problem is so complex that no one, including the engineers and psychologists developing machines to do it, can be certain if any technology will work. "It fits with our notion of justice, somehow, that liars can't really get away with it," says Maria Hartwig, a social psychologist at John Jay College of Criminal Justice who cowrote a recent report on deceit detection at airports and border crossings. The problem is, as Hartwig explains it, that all the science says people are really good at lying, and it's incredibly hard to tell when we're doing it.

In fact, most of us lie constantly—ranging from outright cons to minor fibs told to make life run more smoothly. "Some of the best research I've seen says we lie as much as 10 times every 24 hours," says Phil Houston, a soft-spoken former CIA interrogator who is now CEO of QVerity, a company selling lie-detecting techniques in the business world. "There's some research on college students that says it may be double and triple that. We lie a ton." And yet, statistically, people can tell whether someone is telling the truth only around 54 percent of the time, barely better than a coin toss.

The Interrogation Bot

Just three sensors tell the Embodied Avatar kiosk everything it needs to know about whether someone is telling the truth. An infrared camera records eye movement and pupil dilation at up to 250 frames per second—the stress of lying tends to cause the pupils to dilate. A high-definition video camera captures fidgets such as shrugging, nodding, and scratching, which tend to increase during a deceptive statement. And a microphone collects vocal data, because lies often come with minute changes in pitch. Future versions of the machine might go even further—a weight-sensing platform could measure leg and foot shifts or toe scrunches, and a 3-D camera could track the movements of a person's entire body.—*Sara Breselor*

For thousands of years, attempts to detect deceit have relied on the notion that liars' bodies betray them. But even after a century of scientific research, this fundamental assumption has never been definitively proven. "We know very little about deception from either a psychological or physiological view at the basic level," says Charles Honts, a former Department of Defense polygrapher and now a Boise State University psychologist specializing in the study of deception. "If you look at the lie-detection literature, there's nothing that ties it together, because there's no basic theory there. It's all over the place."

Despite their fixation on the problem of deceit, government agencies aren't interested in funding anything so abstract as basic research. "They want to buy hardware," Honts says. But without an understanding of the mechanics of lying, it seems that any attempt to build a lie-detecting device is doomed to fail. "It's like trying to build an atomic bomb without knowing the theory of the atom," Honts says.

Take the polygraph. It functions today on the same principles as when it was conceived in 1921: providing a continuous recording of vital signs, including blood pressure, heart rate, and perspiration. But the validity of the polygraph approach has been questioned almost since its inception. It records the signs of arousal, and while these may be indications that a subject is lying—dissembling can be stressful—they might also be signs of anger, fear, even sexual excitement. "It's not deception, per se," says Judee Burgoon, Nunamaker's research partner at the University of Arizona. "But that little caveat gets lost in the shuffle."

The US Army founded a polygraph school in 1951, and the government later introduced the machine as an employee-screening tool. Indeed, according to some experts, the polygraph can detect deception more than 90 percent of the time—albeit under very strictly defined criteria. "If you've got a single issue, and the person knows whether or not they've shot John Doe," Honts says, "the polygraph is pretty good." Experienced polygraph examiners like Phil Houston, legendary within the CIA for his successful interrogations, are careful to point out that the device relies on the skill of the examiner to produce accurate results—the right kind of questions, the experience to know when to press harder and when the mere presence of the device can intimidate a suspect into telling the truth. Without that, a polygraph machine is no more of a lie-detector than a rubber truncheon or a pair of pliers.

As a result, although some state courts allow them, polygraph examinations have rarely been admitted as evidence in federal court; they've been dogged by high false-positive rates, and notorious spies, including CIA mole Aldrich Ames, have beaten the tests. In 2003 the National Academy of Sciences reported that the evidence of polygraph accuracy was "scanty and scientifically weak" and that, while the device might be used effectively in criminal investigations, as a screening tool it was practically useless. By then, other devices and techniques that had been touted as reliable lie detectors—voice stress analysis, pupillometry, brain scanning—had also either been dismissed as junk science or not fully tested.

But spooks and cops remain desperate for technology that could boost their rate of success even a couple of points above chance. That's why, in 2006, project managers from the Army's polygraph school—by then renamed the Defense Academy for Credibility Assessment—approached Nunamaker and Burgoon. The government wanted them to build a new machine, a device that could sniff out liars without touching them and that wouldn't need a trained human examiner: a polygraph for the 21st century.

A former college wrestler from Pittsburgh, Nunamaker is a leathery 75-year-old who trained as a mechanical engineer, and his methodical approach to problem-solving has carried him through four decades of developing software. He became interested in deception in the '90s, while building teleconferencing and collaboration software for corporate-scale behemoths including IBM and the US Army and Air Force. His clients suspected that many of their employees' contributions were often deliberately misleading, warped by self-interest and interdepartmental rivalry. Nunamaker discovered that he could pick out liars by looking for a statistical prevalence of evasive language and "hedging words," and he became fascinated with the ways deceitful employees betray themselves.

Burgoon, 64, a brisk and polished psychologist with cropped silver hair, had already done a decade of military-funded deception-detection work when she began collaborating with Nunamaker 12 years ago—both were at the University of Arizona working, it turned out, on similar projects. Burgoon specialized in examining deceit as part of interpersonal communication, a laborious, time-consuming, and—compared with the twitching needles and brain scanning at the other end of the field—unglamorous area of research. Nunamaker suggested they collaborate; her psychology background complemented his engineering expertise.

Instead of simply measuring signs of physiological arousal, Burgoon analyzed liars' body movement—expressions and gestures—and linguistic cues. Like Nunamaker, she had established that liars tend to hedge, equivocate, or fail to deny things directly. One recent study, using publicly available recordings of 911 calls from Florida and Ohio, found that using vague language about things like location and details of the crime often correlated with the caller being the perpetrator. Other research has shown that dishonest stories tend to be better structured than honest ones, although in the end the true story may seem more coherent. True narratives feature richer sensory detail, more direct speech, and more spontaneous corrections. "Deceivers are not going to say, 'Well, I can't remember that, I forgot that,'" Burgoon says. "They'll make something up."

For years, Burgoon collected linguistic data the hard way, transcribing interviews and marking them up by hand. Analyzing body movement was even more painstaking. Trained coders watched video of experimental subjects for hundreds of hours and logged each cue they saw—one blink, a slight smile—manually, using a pen and paper. One research project involved 300 videotaped interviews; the coding took three years. Analyzing the audio was even harder. Burgoon worked with specialists who attempted to hear the changes in vocal pitch in individual phonemes, the units of sound that make up words. Expanding to whole conversations proved almost impossible. "They were used to dealing with a phoneme, not with an entire utterance, much less an entire interview," Burgoon says.

When they first began working together in 2000, Nunamaker found it hard to believe that nobody had tried using machines to simplify this data collection. "It drove me crazy," he says. So Burgoon and Nunamaker started tracking body movement with software that superimposed computer-generated blobs over the video of interviewees; now computer vision tools can find a human being in an image and track more than 80 different landmarks on the face alone. Using transcripts of interviews with indicted Air Force personnel—whose lies were pretty well documented—they worked on artificial-intelligence tools to analyze language, counting hedging words and tracking pronoun use. (This evolved into a suite of software Burgoon dubbed the Agent99 Analyzer—she liked the idea of naming it after the female sidekick from *Get Smart,* famously more competent than her male boss.)

Eventually, Nunamaker and Burgoon came to believe that no single technology could solve the problems of lie detection. "There is no silver bullet answer—which is what everybody wants," Nunamaker says. "It's going to be this basket of cues and figuring out whether you've got the right cues in the

basket." But they also knew that computers could detect the signs they'd identified. The researchers decided to combine as many sensors as possible in a single lie-detecting toolbox. By monitoring potentially hundreds of different psychophysiological, linguistic, and verbal cues, their hypothetical machine would spot tells in even the most polished liar. "A human can only control three or four at a time—so cues leak out no matter how hard you try," Nunamaker says.

One of the first government agencies interested in Nunamaker and Burgoon's work was the Department of Homeland Security. DHS paid for early data collection at the border station at Nogales, a project in which the researchers filmed travelers during screening interviews and then compared their linguistic and physical cues to the way customs officers rated them after screening. But the Science and Technology Directorate at DHS believed that even a working lie detector wouldn't be good enough to fight terrorism. They didn't just want to know when someone was lying—they wanted to look for signs that the person intended to do bad things, or "malintent." So before Nunamaker and Burgoon finished their fieldwork in Nogales, they say, DHS asked them to abandon it and instead study the relationship between emotions, physical cues, and malintent—specifically incorporating the microexpression theories of Paul Ekman.

Ekman is a divisive figure. Now 78, his work on lie detection has made him a rock star among behavioral psychologists, with a best-selling book, a profitable consulting business, and a network TV drama—*Lie to Me*—inspired by his research. In 1969 he theorized that facial muscles that expressed seven human emotions also created "microexpressions" that could reveal concealment, despite the fact that these microexpressions last just 0.04 second. Ekman claims that with his training, it's possible to spot microexpressions and successfully detect deception 70 percent of the time, increasing this to almost 100 percent if other body movements are taken into account.

In 2006 Ekman and his team spent 30 days training TSA officers to read microexpressions as part of a program called SPOT—Screening Passengers by Observational Techniques. These officers deployed to 161 airports across the US. According to the TSA, from January 2006 through March 2012, SPOT officers referred more than 331,280 travelers for secondary screening, but the merest fraction were arrested—just 2,270. In that time, at least 16 people involved in terrorism cases passed unchallenged through airport checkpoints manned by SPOT personnel—some of them more than once. Nobody outside the TSA knows what SPOT officers are looking for, since the details remain classified. The agency admits to being uncertain that it has yet detained a single terrorist. Charles Honts, who was trained by Ekman, says that all his attempts to replicate Ekman's experiments have failed, and in 2009 the researchers studying airports and border crossings found no evidence that microexpressions reliably betray concealed emotion or can be used to detect deceit. The next year the Government Accountability Office reported that the TSA's scheme had never been scientifically tested. (Ekman disputes these criticisms. Of the 9/11 hijackers, for example, he says, "If the behavior that people reported them showing did occur, it would certainly have been picked up by SPOT.")

Nunamaker and Burgoon didn't want to abandon their fieldwork, and they didn't want to focus on microexpressions. "There's not a lot of science to back up Ekman's claims," Nunamaker says. "Applying them to deception detection is a reach." The project manager pulled their funding—because, Nunamaker says, he wouldn't switch the focus of his work. DHS moved ahead with Ekman's research. The new behavioral forecasting program—Future Attribute Screening Technology—is so secret that even Burgoon has no idea what it does.

After falling out with DHS, Nunamaker and Burgoon pressed on. They won new funding from the Pentagon and other agencies. Customs and Border Protection, for example, wanted to help overburdened customs officers screen immigration lines at borders, so the two decided to combine their lie-detecting toolbox with an idea other deception researchers were already playing with: a computer-generated interrogator.

An avatar interrogator has many advantages over its human counterparts. It's consistent, tireless, and susceptible to neither persuasion nor bribery. Douglas Derrick, a researcher at the University of Nebraska who studies human-computer interaction and has worked on the Embodied Avatar since 2007, even suspects that people fear the power they feel it embodies. "They view it as the personification of the system," Derrick says. "They believe they're talking to the computer." One early version was a menacing shaven-headed character nicknamed Scary Guy. On the other hand, Nunamaker says, Las Vegas casinos, which fund their own deception research to catch cheats, have had more success giving casino-goers screen-based directions and advice with avatars that resemble cartoons. Derrick even tried using a camera and morphing software so that an avatar would increasingly resemble the person in front of it, reflecting research that suggests you're more likely to trust someone who looks like you. The one thing they all had in common was skirting the edges of the uncanny valley, where characters look just human enough to be disturbing. "I think we're close with this one," Derrick says of the thick-haired young man used in Nogales. "It's realistic, but we're not in the valley."

The team dug into commercially available lie-detection technology, but most proved unusable. A thermal-imaging camera was enormous and required a cooling fan so noisy that it drowned out the other equipment. The laser Doppler vibrometer, which could monitor blood pressure from 10 feet away, could be circumvented by anyone wearing a turtleneck or even a beard. And the lie/truth analyzer, built into vocal dynamics software provided by the Israeli company Nemesysco, was hopeless under experimental conditions.

Despite those failings, Nunamaker and Burgoon thought that some of the gadgets had potential. Arizona grad student Aaron Elkins found that the Nemesysco software really was finding a correlation between vocal stress and deception, so he wrote his own algorithms to do the same thing—to measure cues like hesitation, changes in tempo and intonation, and spoken errors. It worked; Elkins' approach can identify deceitful speech 75 percent of the time in an experimental setting, and speech dynamics now provide key data points used by the technology being tested in Nogales.

Now, using just three sensors, they can collect as many as 50 different psychophysiological and vocal deception cues. A microphone gathers vocal information. An HD video camera captures body movement—for example, the sudden freezing of a liar attempting to control physical tells. And an infrared camera monitors pupil dilation and gaze pattern. Some of the team's most successful experiments have shown that eye flicker correlates to deception: Examining images of falsified documents, for example, subjects often cannot help looking repeatedly at the details they've doctored.

Separately, these streams of data can provide a good picture of when test subjects might be lying—in the lab, information from the eyes alone correctly flagged liars 60 percent of the time. But when the avatar kiosk combines the data from eye and voice analysis, its accuracy spikes. In an experiment in Poland last year using 37 EU border guards, some of whom were asked to present false documents, the kiosk identified every one of the liars. Taking into account two false positives, the machine scored 94 percent. Human agents asked to perform the same task failed to stop a single impostor.

Yet the success of such experiments has depended on the context of the interrogation. In October 2011, as Nunamaker's team began readying a version of the device for the field tests in Nogales, he admitted that he still wasn't certain how it would perform in the outside world: "We really don't know, until we test it at the border with real people who don't have a vested interest in the system working."

Two months later in Nogales, a uniformed customs officer introduces the avatar kiosk to the public for the first time. In line are a mother and daughter from Tucson, a well-dressed couple from over the border in Mexico, and a portly retiree in a baseball cap there to renew his trusted-traveler card. Each is here as part of a fast-track border crossing program and is first screened by a cheerful immigration specialist trained in interviewing and behavioral analysis techniques. Then they meet the young man with the luxuriant hair. The avatar is set up to deliver the standard final set of questions asked of anyone trying to join a trusted-traveler program. Giving their yes-or-no answers to a five-minute robotic catechism, they seem curious or bemused or visibly anxious. One girl, eager to meet the machine after she heard there was a lie detector in the building, behaves as if she's trying her luck on a carnival midway, giddy and excited. On his way out, the old man remarks, "For guys, you might want to make it look like Salma Hayek."

The Nogales field test, intended to reveal the kind of limitations only everyday use can show, has led to further revisions of the kiosk. It's now bilingual, speaking both English and Spanish, and new lab versions have a camera that can collect eye data regardless of the height of the person it's interrogating. Eventually, if the machine flags a traveler as potentially deceptive, that person will be questioned further by a human customs officer. If the traveler triggers no alert, the machine will tell them they're free to go.

When the avatar catches him out, even commissioner Bersin—soon afterward promoted to assistant secretary of international affairs and chief diplomatic officer at DHS—seems to see its potential. He tells a group of customs officers at the DeConcini crossing station that he hopes the kiosk will soon check more and more people coming across the border. "We start off in this more controlled setting, but eventually the pay-off is getting it into the lanes," he says.

Customs and Border Protection initially expressed interest in installing five kiosks in each of nine different customs stations, where they would conduct preliminary screening for the Nexus and Sentri programs. Budget issues have now postponed those plans, but last year the research team spent a month showing the machine to several DHS agencies in Washington, DC, including Immigration and Customs Enforcement, TSA, and the Secret Service. Nunamaker, Burgoon, and their colleagues now have funding to research countermeasures and identify the ways people might successfully beat the machine. Meanwhile, the TSA's FAST program, built around Paul Ekman's ideas, has been beset by controversy and technical difficulties. TSA officials now say the agency has no plan to deploy it.

Back in December, the last interviewee of the day at the DeConcini crossing station in Nogales is a stocky Mexican engineer wearing an Otis Elevator ID card around his neck. "So this is the future, huh?" he says at the end of his five-minute interrogation, his face unreadable. "Nice."

It is not yet 5 pm, but it's been a long day of cross-examinations. The customs officer pulls her uniform jacket on over her gun and equipment belt and heads into the rain for home. In the corner of the office, the tech from the university clicks on a wireless mouse a few times. The screen on the Embodied Avatar kiosk flickers, and the device goes to sleep where it stands.

Critical Thinking

1. The researchers in the article say that DHS asked them to study the relationship among emotions, physical cues, and malintent presumably so DHS can predict bad acts before

they occur. Do you think this is something we (as a society) should be developing? If we have a tool that can predict malintent and be right most of the time, what should the government do when they find indications of such malintent?

2. The article mentions that Las Vegas casinos use technology to catch cheats. Should private casinos be permitted to evaluate potential cheats with deception detection equipment similar to these avatars? Should retail stores be permitted to evaluate potential shoplifters this way? Should the IRS be permitted to use this during audits? Should a traffic cop be permitted when asking you how much you've had to drink? What general principles should guide acceptable use of deception detection tools?

3. Research in deception detection runs parallel to development of facial recognition technologies. [See the web link to "Privacy is Dead"]. What implications can you imagine—either good or bad—if these two technologies are combined for use at a single checkpoint?

Create Central
www.mhhe.com/createcentral

Internet References
Are Faces the New Fingerprints?
www.pbs.org/newshour/bb/science/jan-june13/facial_05-29.html
Can Software That Predicts Crime Pass Constitutional Muster?
www.npr.org/2013/07/26/205835674/
can-software-that-predicts-crime-pass-constitutional-muster
Met's Minority Report: They Use Computer Algorithms to Predict Where Crime Will Happen
www.dailymail.co.uk/news/article-2437206/Police-tackle-burglars-muggers-using-Minority-Report-style-technology-tackle-future-crime.html
PRIVACY IS DEAD: Here Are 5 Places Where You Can Be Identified with Facial Recognition Technology
www.businessinsider.com/privacy-is-dead-here-are-5-places-where-you-can-be-identified-with-facial-recognition-technology-2011-9
What Drones Can See.
http://video.pbs.org/video/2325492143

Article Prepared by: Daniel Mittleman, *DePaul University*

Know Your Rights!

Your computer, your phone, and your other digital devices hold vast amounts of personal information about you and your family. This is sensitive data that's worth protecting from prying eyes—including those of the government.

HANNI FAKHOURY

Learning Outcomes

After reading this article, you will be able to:

- Articulate the basic principles of the U.S. Constitution Fourth Amendment, and the implications for those principles with the advent of digital communication and storage technologies.

- Understand both the rights and the limitations on search and seizure protections you have under the U.S. Constitution.

- Understand appropriate both legal and behaviors to exhibit if law enforcement requests to search or seize your property in the United States.

The Fourth Amendment to the Constitution protects you from unreasonable government searches and seizures, and this protection extends to your computer and portable devices. But how does this work in the real world? What should you do if the police or other law enforcement officers show up at your door and want to search your computer?

EFF has designed this guide to help you understand your rights if officers try to search the data stored on your computer or portable electronic device, or seize it for further examination somewhere else.

Because anything you say can be used against you in a criminal or civil case, before speaking to any law enforcement official, you should consult with an attorney.

Q: Can the police enter my home to search my computer or portable device, like a laptop or cell phone?

A: No, in most instances, unless they have a warrant. But there are two major exceptions: (1) you consent to the search;[1] or (2) the police have probable cause to believe there is incriminating evidence on the computer that is under immediate threat of destruction.[2]

Q: What if the police have a search warrant to enter my home, but not to search my computer? Can they search it then?

A: No, typically, because a search warrant only allows the police to search the area or items described in the warrant.[3]

But if the warrant authorizes the police to search for evidence of a particular crime, and such evidence is likely to be found on your computer, some courts have allowed the police to search the computer without a warrant.[4] Additionally, while the police are searching your home, if they observe something in plain view on the computer that is suspicious or incriminating, they may take it for further examination and can rely on their observations to later get a search warrant.[5] And of course, if you consent, any search of your computer is permissible.

Q: Can my roommate/guest/spouse/partner allow the police access to my computer?

A: Maybe. A third party can consent to a search as long as the officers reasonably believe the third person has control over the thing to be searched.[6] However, the police cannot search if one person with control (for example a spouse) consents, but another individual (the other spouse) with control does not.[7] One court, however, has said that this rule applies only to a residence, and not personal property, such as a hard drive placed into someone else's computer.[8]

Q: What if the police want to search my computer, but I'm not the subject of their investigation?

A: It typically does not matter whether the police are investigating you, or think there is evidence they want to use against someone else located on your computer. If they have a warrant, you consent to the search, or they think there is something incriminating on your computer that may be immediately destroyed, the police can search it. Regardless of whether you're the subject of an investigation, you can always seek the assistance of a lawyer.

Q: Can I see the warrant?

A: Yes. The police must take the warrant with them when executing it and give you a copy of it.[9] They must also knock and announce their entry before entering your home[10] and must serve the warrant during the day in most circumstances.[11]

Q: Can the police take my computer with them and search it somewhere else?

A: Yes. As long as the police have a warrant, they can seize the computer and take it somewhere else to search it more thoroughly. As part of that inspection, the police may make a copy of media or other files stored on your computer.[12]

Q: Do I have to cooperate with them when they are searching?

A: No, you do not have to help the police conduct the search. But you should not physically interfere with them, obstruct the search, or try to destroy evidence, since that can lead to your arrest. This is true even if the police don't have a warrant and you do not consent to the search, but the police insist on searching anyway. In that instance, do not interfere but write down the names and badge numbers of the officers and immediately call a lawyer.

Q: Do I have to answer their questions while they are searching my home without a warrant?

A: No, you do not have to answer any questions. In fact, because anything you say can be used against you and other individuals, it is best to say nothing at all until you have a chance to talk to a lawyer. However, if you do decide to answer questions, be sure to tell the truth. It is a crime to lie to a police officer and you may find yourself in more trouble for lying to law enforcement than for whatever it was they wanted on your computer.[13]

Q: If the police ask for my encryption keys or passwords, do I have to turn them over?

A: No. The police can't force you to divulge anything. However, a judge or a grand jury may be able to. The Fifth Amendment protects you from being forced to give the government self-incriminating testimony. If turning over an encryption key or password triggers this right, not even a court can force you to divulge the information. But whether that right is triggered is a difficult question to answer. If turning over an encryption key or password will reveal to the government information it does not have (such as demonstrating that you have control over files on a computer), there is a strong argument that the Fifth Amendment protects you.[14] If, however, turning over passwords and encryption keys will not incriminate you, then the Fifth Amendment does not protect you. Moreover, even if you have a Fifth Amendment right that protects your encryption keys or passwords, a grand jury or judge may still order you to disclose your data in an unencrypted format under certain circumstances.[15] If you find yourself in a situation where the police are demanding that you turn over encryption keys or passwords, let EFF know.

Q: If my computer is taken and searched, can I get it back?

A: Perhaps. If your computer was illegally seized, then you can file a motion with the court to have the property returned.[16] If the police believe that evidence of a crime has been found on your computer (such as "digital contraband" like pirated music and movies, or digital images of child pornography), the police can keep the computer as evidence. They may also attempt to make you forfeit the computer, but you can challenge that in court.[17]

Q: What about my work computer?

A: It depends. Generally, you have some Fourth Amendment protection in your office or workspace.[18] This means the police need a warrant to search your office and work computer unless one of the exceptions described above applies. But the extent of Fourth Amendment protection depends on the physical details of your work environment, as well as any employer policies. For example, the police will have difficulty justifying a warrantless search of a private office with doors and a lock and a private computer that you have exclusive access to. On the other hand, if you share a computer with other co-workers, you will have a weaker expectation of privacy in that computer, and thus less Fourth Amendment protection.[19] However, be aware that your employer can consent to a police request to search an office or workspace.[20] Moreover, if you work for a public entity or government agency, no warrant is required to search your computer or office as long as the search is for a non-investigative, work-related matter.[21]

Q: I've been arrested. Can the police search my cell phone without a warrant?

A: Maybe. After a person has been arrested, the police generally may search the items on her person and in her pockets, as well as anything within her immediate control.[22] This means that the police can physically take your cell phone and anything else in your pockets. Some courts go one step further and allow the police to search the contents of your cell phone, like text messages, call logs, emails, and other data stored on your phone, without a warrant.[23] Other courts disagree, and require the police to seek a warrant.[24] It depends on the circumstances and where you live.

Q: The police pulled me over while I was driving. Can they search my cell phone?

A: Maybe. If the police believe there is probably evidence of a crime in your car, they may search areas within a driver or passenger's reach where they believe they might find it—like the glove box, center console, and other "containers."[25] Some courts have found cell phones to be "containers" that police may search without a warrant.[26]

Q: Can the police search my computer or portable devices at the border without a warrant?

A: Yes. So far, courts have ruled that almost any search at the border is "reasonable"—so government agents don't need to get a warrant. This means that officials can inspect your computer or electronic equipment, even if they have no reason to suspect there is anything illegal on it.[27] An international airport may be considered the functional equivalent of a border, even if it is many miles from the actual border.[28]

Q: Can the police take my electronic device away from the border or airport for further examination without a warrant?

A: At least one federal court has said yes, they can send it elsewhere for further inspection if necessary.[29] Even though you may be permitted to enter the country, your computer or portable device may not be.

References

1. Schneckloth v. Bustamonte, 412 United States 218, 219 (1973); United States v. Vanvilet, 542 F.3d 259 (1st Cir. 2008).
2. Ker v. California, 374 United States 23 (1963); see also United States v. Vallimont, 378 Fed.Appx. 972 (11th Cir. 2010) (unpublished); United States v. Smith, 2010 WL 1949364 (9th Cir. 2010) (unpublished).
3. See Maryland v. Garrison, 480 United States 79, 84–85 (1987) (citing cases).
4. See e.g., United States v. Mann, 592 F.3d 779 (7th Cir. 2010); see also Brown v. City of Fort Wayne, 752 F.Supp.2d 925 (N.D. Ind. 2010).
5. Horton v. California, 496 United States 128 (1990); see also United States v. Walser, 275 F.3d 981 (10th Cir. 2001); United States v. Carey, 172 F.3d 1268 (10th Cir. 1999).
6. Illinois v. Rodriguez, 497 United States 177 (1990); United States v. Stabile, 633 F.3d 219 (3d Cir. 2011); United States v. Andrus, 483 F.3d 711 (10th Cir. 2007).
7. Georgia v. Randolph, 547 United States 103 (2006).
8. United States v. King, 604 F.3d 125 (3d Cir. 2010) (court approved search and seizure where two housemates shared a desktop computer, and one housemate granted the police access to the entire computer over the other housemate's objections, even though the objecting housemate was the sole owner of a hard drive in the computer).
9. Federal Rule of Criminal Procedure 41(f)(1)(C).
10. Wilson v. Arkansas, 514 United States 927 (1995).
11. Federal Rule of Criminal Procedure 41(e)(2)(A)(ii).
12. See e.g., United States v. Hill, 459 F.3d 966 (9th Cir. 2006); In re Search of 3817 W. West End, First Floor Chicago, Illinois 60621, 321 F.Supp.2d 953 (N.D. Ill. 2004); see also Federal Rule of Criminal Procedure 41(e)(2)(B).
13. Compare 18 United StatesC. § 1001(a) (maximum punishment for first offense of lying to federal officer is 5 or 8 years) with 18 United StatesC. §§ 1030(a)(2) and (c)(2)(A) (maximum punishment for first offense of simply exceeding authorized computer access is generally 1 year).
14. See United States v. Kirschner, 2010 WL 1257355 (E.D. Mich. Mar. 30, 2010) (unpublished) (relying on United States v. Hubbell, 530 United States 27 (2000)).
15. See e.g., United States v. Hatfield, 2010 WL 1423103 (E.D.N.Y. April 7, 2010) (unpublished); In re Boucher, 2009 WL 424718 (D. Vt. Feb. 19, 2009) (unpublished).
16. Federal Rule of Criminal Procedure 41(g).
17. See 18 United StatesC. § 983, Federal Rule of Criminal Procedure 32.2.
18. Mancusi v. DeForte, 392 United States 364 (1968); United States v. Ziegler, 474 F.3d 1184 (9th Cir. 2007).
19. See e.g., Schowengerdt v. United States, 944 F.2d 483 (9th Cir. 1991).
20. See Ziegler, 474 F.3d at 1191 (citing Mancusi).
21. City of Ontario v. Quon, 130 S.Ct. 2619 (2010); O'Connor v. Ortega, 480 United States 709 (1987).
22. Chimel v. California, 395 United States 752 (1969).
23. See e.g., United States v. Murphy, 552 F.3d 405 (4th Cir. 2009); United States v. Wurie, 612 F.Supp.2d 104 (D. Mass. 2009); People v. Diaz, 51 Cal.4th 84, 244 P.3d 501 (2011).
24. See e.g., United States v. Wall, 2008 WL 5381412 (S.D.Fla. Dec. 22, 2008) (unpublished); United States v. Park, 2007 WL 1521573 (N.D. Cal. May 23, 2007) (unpublished); State v. Smith, 124 Ohio St.3d 163, 920 N.E.2d 949 (2009).
25. Arizona v. Gant, 129 S.Ct. 1710 (2009).
26. See e.g., United States v. Finley, 477 F.3d 250 (5th Cir. 2007); Wurie, 612 F.Supp.2d at 109–110; United States v. Cole, 2010 WL 3210963 (N.D.Ga. Aug. 11, 2010) (unpublished); United States v. McCray, 2009 WL 29607 (S.D.Ga. Jan. 5, 2009) (unpublished).
27. United States v. Flores-Montano, 541 United States 149 (2004); United States v. Ickes, 393 F.3d 501 (4th Cir. 2005).
28. Almeida-Sanchez v. United States, 413 United States 266, 273 (1973); United States v. Arnold, 533 F.3d 1003 (9th Cir. 2008); United States v. Romm, 455 F.3d 990 (9th Cir. 2006); United States v. Roberts, 274 F.3d 1007 (5th Cir. 2001).
29. United States v. Cotterman, 637 F.3d 1068 (9th Cir. 2011).

Critical Thinking

1. Of the questions answered at the site, which answer surprised you the most? Of the questions answered at the site, did you disagree with any of the rights currently in force? If so, which ones and why?
2. Research online the historical motivation for creating the Fourth Amendment to the U.S. Constitution. As the framers of the Constitution were naïve to electronic technologies, what rules do you think they would have found appropriate for protecting against unreasonable search and seizure of digital information?
3. Since this article was published in 2011, we have learned the NSA has been collecting vast amounts of electronic information on Americans under provisions of the Patriot Act that render national security considerations sufficient to collect such information. How do you think national security considerations should be balanced against Fourth Amendment protections against unreasonable search and seizure?

Create Central

www.mhhe.com/createcentral

Internet References

Bruce Schneier: The Security Mirage [TED Talk]
www.ted.com/talks/bruce_schneier.html
Era of Online Sharing Offers Benefits of 'Big Data,' Privacy Trade-Offs
www.pbs.org/newshour/bb/science/jan-june13/nsa2_06-12.html
4 Things You Should Know about Metadata, Hackers And Privacy That Edward Snowden Would Never Tell You
www.forbes.com/sites/gregsatell/2013/08/03/4-things-you-should-know-about-metadata-hackers-and-privacy-that-edward-snowden-would-never-tell-you
Hasan Elahi: FBI, Here I Am! [TED Talk]
www.ted.com/talks/hasan_elahi.html
Mikko Hypponen: Three Types of Online Attack [TED Talk]
www.ted.com/talks/mikko_hypponen_three_types_of_online_attack.html

Article   Prepared by: Daniel Mittleman, *DePaul University*

Bride of Stuxnet

Webcraft as spycraft.

Jonathan V. Last

Learning Outcomes

After reading this article, you will be able to:

- Understand the contours of cyber warfare and cyber espionage.
- Articulate a hypothesis of the relationship between what we know of the Stuxnet and Flame viruses and what we more recently have learned from the Snowden/NSA leaks.

Last April, the Iranian Oil Ministry and the National Iranian Oil Company noticed a problem with some of their computers: A small number of machines were spontaneously erasing themselves. Spooked by the recent Stuxnet attack, which had wrecked centrifuges in their nuclear labs, the Iranians suspected a piece of computer malware was to blame. They went to the United Nations' International Telecommunications Union and asked for help. After an initial investigation, it was determined that the Iranians had been hit with a new piece of malicious software; it was temporarily labeled Wiper. Or Viper. After translating the moniker into different languages, no one is quite sure what the original nickname was.

The experts from Turtle Bay quickly realized they were out of their depth with Wiper/Viper and contracted a Russian computer security firm, Kaspersky Lab, to help. As the techs at Kaspersky investigated, they began to find bits and pieces of a much bigger program. What they eventually uncovered forced them to put aside Wiper/Viper and send out an all-hands call to the tech community: a cyber-weapon that made Stuxnet look primitive. They called it Flame.

Stuxnet was like a guided missile with a targeted payload. It was created to spread rapidly, but always to be seeking a particular set of computers—machines made by Siemens and used to control centrifuge operations at a uranium enrichment plant. Once Stuxnet reached its destination, it had very precise instructions: It altered the speed of the centrifuges in such a manner as to slowly degrade the equipment and destroy the uranium they contained—all while sending false readings back to the operating console so that neither the computer nor the human supervisors would notice the damage being done.

If Stuxnet was like a missile, then Flame is more like a surveillance satellite.

Once a computer is infected by Flame, the program begins a process of taking over the entire machine. Flame records every keystroke by the user, creating a perfect log of all activity. It takes pictures of the screen every 60 seconds—and every 15 seconds when instant message or email programs are in use. It records all administrative action on the computer—taking note of network passwords, for instance. And it rummages through the computer's hard drive copying documents and files.

But that's not all. Flame also takes control of the machine's Bluetooth capability and turns it into a hub for a small wireless network, bonding with other Bluetooth-enabled devices in the vicinity, such as cell phones. It then uses the Bluetooth connection to case whatever information is on the remote device—say, an address book, calendar, or email list. Most spectacularly, Flame is able to turn on the computer's built-in microphone and record the user, or anyone else who happens to be chatting in the vicinity.

Flame then compiles all of this information—the passwords, the documents, the keystroke logs, the screenshots, and the audio recordings—encrypts it, and secretly uploads it to a command-and-control server (C&C), where someone is waiting to analyze it.

The first thing the white hats noticed about Flame was its size. Most malware is designed to be tiny—the smaller the package of code, the harder it is for your computer's constantly updating security protocols to intercept it. It took half a megabyte of code to build Stuxnet, which was a remarkably large footprint by the standards of malware. When completely deployed, Flame takes up 20 megabytes. Which is positively gargantuan.

But Flame is deployed in stages. When it works its way onto a new machine, Flame comes in an initial package of six megabytes. After the worm takes control of the box, it inventories the machine and the surrounding networks, and then begins communicating with a remote C&C server. On the other end of the line, a team takes in the data being sent by Flame, makes a determination of the new host's value, and then returns instructions to the waiting worm. Depending on what the C&C team see, they might instruct Flame to install any of 14 additional modules—mini add-on programs which, for instance, would give Flame the ability to take over the computer's microphone, or Bluetooth functionality. One module, named "browse32," is a kill module. When activated by the C&C, browse32 systematically moves through the computer, deleting every trace of Flame's existence. Its wipe is so thorough that once it's been triggered, no one—not even computer security techs—can tell if Flame was ever there in the first place.

No one is sure how long Flame has been operational. There is evidence of its existence in the wild dating to March 2010, but Flame may be older than that. (Stuxnet was discovered in June 2010 and is believed to have been released 12 months before then.) It's difficult to date Flame because its makers went to some trouble to disguise its age. Computer code typically has meta-data describing its "compilation date"—that is, the time and date it was assembled in final form. Flame's 20 modules all have compilation dates set in 1994 and 1995. Which is impossible, because they're written in a language that was released just a few years ago.

Neither are analysts certain exactly how Flame spreads. It has the ability to move from one computer to another by piggybacking onto a USB flash drive (just like Stuxnet). Alternately, it can migrate across a local network by exploiting a shared printer (again, like Stuxnet). But Flame is also able to spread across a network without a printer if it finds itself on a computer that has administrative privileges. When that happens, the worm is smart enough to create backdoor accounts for all the other computers on the network and copy itself into those machines.

As for the question of security—how does Flame talk its way past the computer's antivirus protections? No one knows. The techs at Kaspersky Lab watched Flame attack a PC running the fully updated Windows 7 security suite. The worm took over the computer effortlessly. This suggests that the worm's designers have access to one or more vulnerabilities in the operating system that even the people who designed the OS don't know about. (Stuxnet utilized four of these so-called zero-day exploits.)

Engineers are only two weeks into the teardown, but they already believe that Flame and Stuxnet were created by different development teams. The code and workings are dissimilar. And besides, the timelines on the two projects are too close. It is estimated that coding Stuxnet required 10,000 man-hours. For a team of 30 to 50 programmers, that's a year or two of work. The same squad simply would not have had the time to build both Stuxnet and the much larger Flame.

That said, Kaspersky Lab notes that the worms do share two interesting similarities: They use the same rootkit-based exploit to hijack USB drives and the same print-spooler vulnerability to spread over a network's shared printer. There are three possible explanations for this: (1) The teams that developed Flame and Stuxnet discovered these identical mechanisms independently; (2) the team which developed Flame learned about

them from analyzing an early version of Stuxnet; (3) the teams that developed the two worms were working in parallel, for the same organization(s), and thus were able to share information about these mechanisms.

Yet the most interesting aspect of Flame is the strategic ways it differs from Stuxnet. As a weapon, Stuxnet was a tool conceived in urgency. Every piece of malware has to balance virulence with stealth. The more aggressively a worm propagates, the more likely it is to be caught. Stuxnet was designed to spread at a fairly robust rate. Its creators wanted it to get on lots of different computers and they were willing to risk quicker discovery on the chance that the worm would find its way to the very specific system it was meant for and deliver its payload. In the end, Stuxnet's engineers made a good trade. Because it eventually spread to 100,000 computers, Stuxnet was caught reasonably quickly. Yet this aggressive approach got it to its target—Iran's Natanz refinery—where it wrecked at least a year's worth of work.

Flame, on the other hand, is a study in stealth and patience. Unlike Stuxnet, with its single-minded search for a specific computer system, Flame seems to have wandered in many directions: onto computers used by governments, universities, and private companies. It moved slowly, and the overall number of infected systems seems to be quite low. Current estimates put it at 1,000 computers, nearly all of them located in Iran, the Palestinian territories, Sudan, Syria, and Lebanon. Flame kept the number of infections low because it never moved from one computer to another without explicit instructions from its C&C. According to Kaspersky Lab, the method went something like this:

> [T]hey infect several dozen [machines], then conduct analysis of the data of the victim, [and] uninstall Flame from the systems that aren't interesting, leaving the most important ones in place. After which they start a new series of infections.

It was a detailed, deliberate process of identifying and exploiting targets that must have required significant manpower and intelligence capability on the C&C side. In other words, the design and deployment of Flame was only half of the job. Another team, with a different skill set, was needed to run the operation once it was in the field.

But once Flame was running, it was like something out of science fiction. Flame could watch a target even when he was completely alone. It could listen to every word he said on the telephone, or through Skype, or to a colleague walking past his desk. It could rifle through his computer files and find any document. Or peek into a cell phone sitting in someone's pocket in the next room. It never had to worry about getting caught in the act. And on a moment's notice, it could erase any sign that it was ever there. It kept up constant communication with its handlers, even when they were thousands of miles away, and it always followed orders.

Whoever engineered Flame didn't just build the most spectacular computer worm ever made. They created the perfect spy.

Critical Thinking

1. How would the American public react if it found out spies from another country infiltrated the networks used by the U.S. military or nuclear scientists? Beyond the initial reaction, what would an appropriate U.S. government response be to such an infiltration?

2. As these software techniques become better known among hackers, inevitably a commercial system will be infiltrated in a similar manner either by outside thieves looking to profit, or by a competitor looking for intelligence. How does such a commercial attack compare to military-style attacks of this sort by government?

3. Build an ethical argument for infiltrating the computer networks of an enemy we are not at war with. Build an ethical argument against such an infiltration.

Create Central

www.mhhe.com/createcentral

Internet References

Guy-Philippe Goldstein: How Cyberattacks Threaten Real-World Peace [in French with sub-titles]
www.ted.com/talks/guy_philippe_goldstein_how_cyberattacks_threaten_real_world_peace.html

Is U.S. Less Secure after Chinese Hack Weapons Designs?
www.pbs.org/newshour/bb/asia/jan-june13/china_05-28.html

New Tools for War and Peace: Technology Game Changers
www.wfs.org/futurist/2013-issues-futurist/july-august-2013-vol-47-no-4/new-tools-for-war-and-peace-technology-ga

Ralph Langner: Cracking Stuxnet, a 21st-Century Cyber Weapon [TED Talk]
www.ted.com/talks/ralph_langner_cracking_stuxnet_a_21st_century_cyberweapon.html

Welcome to the Malware-Industrial Complex
www.technologyreview.com/news/507971/welcome-to-the-malware-industrial-complex

---

JONATHAN V. LAST is a senior writer at *The Weekly Standard.*

Unit 9

UNIT

Prepared by: Daniel Mittleman, *DePaul University*

Projecting the Future

As Yogi Berra once famously said, "It's tough to make predictions, especially about the future." And indeed it is. For example, Thomas Watson Jr., then the Chairman of IBM, predicted in 1953 that IBM would be able to market "maybe five computers."[1] (That is not a typo; although to his credit, at the time each 701 computer was the size of a backyard shed, required more air conditioning than a commercial freezer, and rented for $12,000 to $20,000 a month.) Twenty-four years later, Ken Olson, President of Digital Equipment Corporation (DEC) then one of the largest computer companies in the world, looked at the newly released Apple II computer by an unknown start up in California and surmised, "There is no reason anyone would want a computer in their home." Today, of course, Apple is, by measure of total stock, the largest company in the world, valued at almost a half-trillion dollars. Apple's iPhone5s is, by measure of instructions per second, more than 300,000 times faster than the early IBM 701.[2] DEC ceased to exist as an independent company in 1998, subsumed by Compaq Computers, which was later subsumed by Hewlett-Packard in 2002.[3]

Clearly, predicting the future is risky business.

We tend to view the future through the lens of the present day, thinking the future will simply be an improved variation of what is now. In the short term this sometimes works, but the history of technology shows that every so often a new technology completely reshapes not only that technological domain, but economic, social, and political structures impacted by it. This certainly was true with Gutenberg's printing press, which in the mid-fifteenth century changed not only the field of printing, but became a catalyst for the Protestant movement against the Church, increased levels of literacy, and, therefore, the end of the middle ages. Watt's steam engine, in 1781, led to revolutions in transportation (both railroad and shipping) as well as factory work, making it a principle catalyst of the industrial revolution. Not to mention the sweeping effects of the commercialization of the automobile at the beginning of the twentieth century.

Since the commercialization of the computer in the early to mid-1950s, we have experienced a punctuated leap in technological capability roughly once a decade. Computers in the first decade of commercialization were large, expensive, and difficult to program. Only the largest, most data intensive organizations considered acquiring them. Each computer was hand crafted, sometimes modified for individual customers.

The integrated circuit was invented in 1958 and found its way into mass produced computers by the mid-1960s. This reduced the size and price of computers, making them affordable for many more businesses—and large organizations often bought several. This generation of computers led to computerization of government records, computerized billing by utility companies and department stores, and—because information now had to fit into limited fields of data records—standardization among almost everything business and government did.[4] At about the same time, the U.S. Department of Defense commissioned the development of a self-healing network technology with no central hub that would be impossible for the enemy to defeat with a single well-placed strike. This network was named ARPANET and is the precursor to today's Internet.[5] ARPANET, which went live in 1969, enabled email, electronic file transfers, remote computer login, and discussion boards. Though access to these networking features was largely limited to government workers and academics, within those communities they were widely used by the late 1970s.

The microprocessor was invented in 1971 and it led to later inventions at both ends of the spectrum. At the high end, Cray Computers shipped the world's first supercomputer in 1976 enabling sophisticated computational intensive simulation and modeling applications. And the low end, the microprocessor enabled personal computers beginning with the Altair 8800 in 1975. Other computers quickly followed, including the original Apple II in 1977. IBM released its PC in 1981 and brought this form factor into the mainstream. PC-sized computing, along with parallel developments in Ethernet networking technology enabled computing on almost every office desktop, shared file space within a company, and email. It also enabled people to have computers in their homes.

In 1993, Marc Andreessen built Mosaic, the first graphical browser, and ushered in the era of the World Wide Web (WWW), which is primarily a file sharing application that runs on top of the basic Internet protocols. And in 1995, the WWW went commercial with the founding of Yahoo, eBay, and Amazon, initiating the era of e-commerce. By the middle of the following decade, an amalgam of technical developments improved synchronous interactivity on the web. These developments enabled social media and social networking, what we now call Web2.0.

At about the same time, improvements in wireless connectivity (both WiFi and cellular) made rich mobile computing possible. The introduction of the iPhone in 2007 solidified the user interface and led to mass adoption.

Every one of the computing epochs recounted above contributed to significant shifts in economic, social, and political institutions and behaviors. There is no reason to believe this timeline has run its course. And that is why we are interested in predictions. Were the future easy to predict, we all would have bought IBM stock in 1952, Microsoft stock in 1986, and Apple in 1997 (when Steve Jobs returned). But the future is so hard to predict that CEOs of major computer companies got it wrong in embarrassing ways.

So, is there a framework or process we might apply to evaluate ideas for the future? The articles in this unit propose methods for evaluation, suggesting phenomena and drivers that might explain technology adoption.

Further, as you read these articles, look for repeating common themes. For example, we know there is buzz in 2014 about driverless cars, about wearable computing (in the form of smart watches and Google Glass), and about augmented reality. The commonality among these technologies is smart software working as an agent to provide timely useful information for the user. Some such technology is already present, such as iPhone's Siri. In fact, it has long been suspected that artificially intelligent agents, working on their user's behalf, would be the hallmark of Web3.0. It just may be that Web3.0 has arrived, but has not yet fully announced itself.

Notes

1. This quote is often attributed to his father, Thomas Watson Sr., as saying he predicted a world market of maybe five computers. But there is no evidence Watson Sr. ever said such a thing. Watson Jr. did say something to this effect as IBM began marketing their first commercial computer, the 701, in 1953. While he predicted they would sell five of them, they actually sold 18 during their first sales pitch.

2. It comes in three times as many colors, too.

3. The only thing that would make this ironic would be if Apple now owned what is left of DEC.

4. For those of you interested in the societal impact of this standardization, read Les Earnest, *Can Computers Cope with Human Races,* Communications of the ACM, February 1989, v32, n2, 174–182.

5. The Internet is simply the interconnection of many networks that run on TCP/IP, a descendent of the ARPANET protocol.

Article

Prepared by: Daniel Mittleman, *DePaul University*

How to Spot the Future

Thomas Goetz

Learning Outcomes

After reading this article, you will be able to:

- Apply a model for evaluating potential future technologies.

- Understand that technology evolution can be viewed through a lens of themes or patterns.

Thirty years ago, when John Naisbitt was writing *Megatrends,* his prescient vision of America's future, he used a simple yet powerful tool to spot new ideas that were bubbling in the zeitgeist: the newspaper. He didn't just read it, though. He took out a ruler and measured it. The more column inches a particular topic earned over time, the more likely it represented an emerging trend. "The collective news hole," Naisbitt wrote, "becomes a mechanical representation of society sorting out its priorities"—and he used that mechanism to predict the information society, globalism, decentralization, and the rise of networks.

As clever as Naisbitt's method was, it would never work today. There's an infinite amount of ink and pixels spilled on most any topic. These days, spotting the future requires a different set of tools. That's why at *Wired,* where we constantly endeavor to pinpoint the inventions and trends that will define the future, we have developed our own set of rules. They allow us to size up ideas and separate the truly world-changing from the merely interesting. After 20 years of watching how technology creates a bold and better tomorrow, we have seen some common themes emerge, patterns that have fostered the most profound innovations of our age.

This may sound like a paradox. Surely technology always promises something radically new, wholly unexpected, and unlike anything anybody has seen before. But in fact even when a product or service breaks new ground, it's usually following a familiar trajectory. After all, the factors governing thermodynamics, economics, and human interaction don't change that much. And they provide an intellectual platform that has allowed technology to succeed on a massive scale, to organize, to accelerate, to connect.

So how do we spot the future—and how might you? The seven rules that follow are not a bad place to start. They are the principles that underlie many of our contemporary innovations. Odds are that any story in our pages, any idea we deem potentially transformative, any trend we think has legs, draws on one or more of these core principles. They have played a major part in creating the world we see today. And they'll be the forces behind the world we'll be living in tomorrow.

Look for Cross-Pollinators

It's no secret that the best ideas—the ones with the most impact and longevity—are transferable; an innovation in one industry can be exported to transform another. But even more resonant are those ideas that are cross-disciplinary not just in their application but in their origin.

This notion goes way back. When the mathematician John von Neumann applied mathematics to human strategy, he created game theory—and when he crossed physics and engineering, he helped hatch both the Manhattan Project and computer science. His contemporary Buckminster Fuller drew freely from engineering, economics, and biology to tackle problems in transportation, architecture, and urban design.

Sometimes the cross-pollination is potent enough to create entirely new disciplines. This is what happened when Daniel Kahneman and Amos Tversky started to fuse psychology and economics in the 1970s. They were trying to understand why people didn't behave rationally, despite the assumption by economists that they would do so. It was a question that economists had failed to answer for decades, but by cross-breeding economics with their own training as psychologists, Kahneman and Tversky were able to shed light on what motivates people. The field they created—behavioral economics—is still growing today, informing everything from US economic policy to the produce displays at Whole Foods.

More recently, the commonalities between biology and digital technology—code is code, after all—have inspired a new generation to reach across specialties and create a range of new cross-bred disciplines: bioinformatics, computational genomics, synthetic biology, systems biology. All these fields view biology as a technology that can be manipulated and industrialized. As Rob Carlson, founder of Biodesic and a pioneer in this arena, puts it, "The technology we use to manipulate biological systems is now experiencing the same rapid improvement that has produced today's computers, cars, and airplanes." These similarities and common toolsets can accelerate the pace of innovation.

The same goes for old industries, as well. The vitality we see in today's car industry resulted from the recognition that auto manufacturing isn't a singular industry siloed in Detroit. In the past decade, car companies have gone from occasionally dispatching ambassadors to Silicon Valley to opening lab space there—and eagerly incorporating ideas from information technology and robotics into their products. When Ford CEO Alan Mulally talks about cars as the "all-time mobile application," he's not speaking figuratively—he's trying to reframe the identity of his company and the industry. That's testimony to a wave of cross-pollination that will blur the line between personal electronics and automobiles.

The point here is that by drawing on threads from several areas, interdisciplinary pioneers can weave together a stronger, more robust notion that exceeds the bounds of any one field. (One caveat: Real cross-pollination is literal, not metaphorical. Be wary of flimflam futurists who spin analogies and draw equivalences without actually identifying common structures and complementary systems.)

Surf the Exponentials

Some trends are so constant, they verge on cliché. Just mentioning Moore's law can cause eyes to roll, but that overfamiliarity doesn't make Gordon Moore's 1965 insight—that chips will steadily, exponentially get smaller, cheaper, faster—any less remarkable. Not only has it been the engine of the information age, it has also given us good reason to believe in our capacity to invent our future, not just submit to it. After all, Moore's law doesn't know which silicon innovation will take us to the next level. It just says that if the previous 50 years are any indication, something will come along. And so far, it always has.

Moore's law has been joined by—and has itself propelled—exponential progress in other technologies: in networks, sensors, and data storage (the first iPod, in 2001, offered 5 gigabytes for $399, while today's "classic" model offers 160 gigs for $249, a 51-fold improvement). Each of these cyclically improving technologies creates the opportunity to "surf exponentials," in the words of synthetic biologist Drew Endy—to catch the wave of smaller, cheaper, and faster and to channel that steady improvement into business plans and research agendas.

This was the great insight that inspired YouTube, when cofounder Jawed Karim realized (while reading *Wired*, it so happens) that broadband was becoming so cheap and ubiquitous that it was on the verge of disrupting how people watched videos. And it's what Dropbox did with digital storage. As the cost of disc space was dropping at an exponential rate, Dropbox provided a service capitalizing on that phenomenon, offering to store people's data in the cloud, gratis. In 2007 the two free gigabytes the company offered were really worth something. These days 2 gigs is a pittance, but it remains enough of a lure that people are still signing up in droves—some fraction of whom then upgrade to the paid service and more storage.

And it's what allowed Fitbit to outdo Nike+. As accelerometers dropped in cost and size, Fitbit could use them to measure not just jogging, but any activity where movement matters, from walking to sleep. For all its marketing muscle, Nike didn't recognize that accelerometers were the dynamo of a personal health revolution. The new FuelBand shows that the company has now caught on, but Fitbit recognized the bigger trend first.

Exponentials, it turns out, are everywhere. Just choose one, look where it leads, and take a ride.

Favor the Liberators

Liberation comes in two flavors. First are those who recognize an artificial scarcity and move to eliminate it by creating access to goods. See the MP3 revolutionaries who untethered music from the CD, or the BitTorrent anti-tyrannists who created real video-on-demand.

Sometimes, of course, the revolution takes longer than expected. Back in 1993, George Gilder pointed out in these pages that the cost of bandwidth was plummeting so fast as to be imminently free. Gilder's vision has been proven correct, paving the way for Netflix and Hulu. And yet telcos are today—still!—trying to throttle bandwidth. But this is just biding time on the scaffold. In the words of investor Fred Wilson, "scarcity is a shitty business model."

The second flavor of liberation takes a more subtle approach to turning scarcity into plenty. These liberators use the advent of powerful software to put fallow infrastructure to work. Think of how Netflix piggybacked on a national distribution infrastructure by having the US Postal Service carry its red envelopes. Or how the founders of Airbnb recognized our homes as a massive stock of underutilized beds, ready to be put into the lodging market. Or how Uber turns idling drivers into on-call icons on a Google map, blipping their way to you in mere minutes. Reid Hoffman, the philosopher-investor, describes these companies as bringing liquidity to locked-up assets. He means this in the financial sense of "liquidity," the ability to turn capital into currency, but it also works in a more evocative sense. These companies turn static into flow, bringing motion where there was obstruction.

What's it like to live in the future? Ask an Uber driver—these guys are electrons pulsing through a real-life network, and they're delighted by it. So should we all be.

Give Points for Audacity

When "big hairy audacious goal" entered the lexicon in 1994 (courtesy of *Built to Last,* the management tome by James Collins and Jerry Porras), it applied to ambitious executives eager to set high targets for annual revenue growth and increased market share. Yawn. But the term—shortened to BHAG—also coincided with the birth of the web, when innovators began to posit a whole new sort of audacity: to make every book, in every language, available in less than a minute; to organize all the world's information; or to make financial transactions frictionless and transparent.

Audacity is easily written off as naïveté, as overshooting your resources or talents. And that's a danger. Plenty of would-be Napoleons have called for revolutions that never found an army. But you can't make the future without imagining what it might look like.

Too much of the technology world is trying to build clever solutions to picayune problems. Better parking apps or restaurant finders might appeal to venture capitalists looking for a niche, but they are not ideas that seed revolutions. Instead, take a lesson from Tesla Motors, which had the pluck to spend $42 million of its precious capital to buy a factory roughly the size of the Pentagon, stock it with state-of-the-art robots, and begin making wholly viable electric cars. Or look to Square, which has pronounced the cash register a counter-cluttering vestige of the 19th century and created an alternative that will not only make buying things easier but will deliver retailers from their sclerotic relationship with credit card companies.

These times especially call for more than mere incrementalism. Let's demand that our leaders get in over their heads, that they remain a little bit naive about what they're getting into. As venture capitalist Peter Thiel told wired two years ago, "Am I right and early, or am I just wrong? You always have to wonder." This kind of willingness to take a chance and be early is what keeps the world moving.

Bank on Openness

In 1997 *Wired's* founding executive editor, Kevin Kelly, wrote a story called "New Rules for the New Economy" (it was in many ways the inspiration for this very piece). His focus was on networks, the "thickening web" that was forging connections of catalytic power. Many of his radical rules have become commonalities today, but two of them are just coming into their own: Connected individuals with shared interests and goals, he argued, create "virtuous circles" that can produce remarkable returns for any company that serves their needs. And organizations that "let go at the top"—forsaking proprietary claims and avoiding hierarchy—will be agile, flexible, and poised to leap from opportunity to opportunity, sacrificing short-term payoffs for long-term prosperity. Since Kelly wrote his piece, these forces have flourished. Back then open source software was a programming kibbutz, good for creating a hippy-dippy operating system but nothing that could rival the work of Oracle or Microsoft. Today open source is the default choice for corporations from IBM to Google. Even Microsoft is on board, evangelizing Hadoop and Python and opening the Xbox Kinect controller so it can be a platform for artists and roboticists. Supported by coder clubhouses like SourceForge and GitHub, collaborative circles can emerge with stunning spontaneity, responding elastically to any programming need.

More tellingly, in many organizations openness itself has become a philosophical necessity, the catalyst that turns one employee's lark into a billion-dollar business. Companies from Lego to Twitter have created a product and then called on its users to chart its course, allowing virtuous circles to multiply and flourish. Time after time, the open option has prevailed, as Zipcar has gained on Hertz and users have upvoted Reddit over Digg.

The best example may be nearly invisible, even to a dedicated user of the Internet: blogging platforms. Less than a decade ago there were a multitude of services competing for the emerging legion of bloggers: Movable Type, TypePad, Blogger, WordPress. Today, only the last two remain relevant, and of these, the small, scrappy WordPress is the champ. WordPress prevailed for several reasons. For one, it was free and fantastically easy to install, allowing an aspiring blogger (or blogging company) to get off the ground in hours. Users who wanted a more robust design or additional features could turn to a community of fellow users who had created tools to meet their own needs. And that community didn't just use WordPress—many made money on it by selling their designs and plug-ins. Their investment of time and resources emboldened others, and soon the WordPress community was stronger than any top-down business model forged inside the walls of their competition.

Sure, there are Apples and Facebooks that thrive under the old rules of walled gardens and monocultures. But even they try to tap into openness (albeit on their own terms) by luring developers to the App Store and the Open Graph. And for all the closed-world success of these companies, the world at large is moving the other way: toward transparency, collaboration, and bottom-up innovation. True openness requires trust, and that's not available as a plug-in. When transparency is just a marketing slogan, people can see right through it.

Demand Deep Design

Too often in technology, design is applied like a veneer after the hard work is done. That approach ignores how essential design is in our lives. Our lives are beset by clutter, not just of physical goods but of ideas and options and instructions—and design, at its best, lets us prioritize. Think of a supremely honed technology: the book. It elegantly organizes information, delivering it in a compact form, easily scanned asynchronously or in one sitting. The ebook is a worthy attempt to reverse-engineer these qualities—a process that has taken decades and chewed up millions in capital. But still, despite the ingenuity and functionality of the Kindle and the Nook, they don't entirely capture the charms of the original technology. Good design is hard.

Indeed, good design is much, much harder than it looks. When Target redesigned its prescription pill bottle in 2005, the improvement was instantly recognizable—an easy-to-read label that plainly explains what the pill is and when to take it. It was a why-didn't-I-think-of-it innovation that begged to be replicated elsewhere. But judging by the profusion of products and labels that continue to baffle consumers, it has been largely ignored. Same with Apple: The company's design imperative is forever cited as intrinsic to its success, but Apple still stands curiously alone as a company where engineers integrate design into the bones of its products.

Thankfully, we are on the verge of a golden age of design, where the necessary tools and skills—once such limited resources—are becoming automated and available to all of us. This timing is critical. "Too much information" has become the chorus of complaint from all quarters, and the cure is not more design but deeper design, design that filters complexity into accessible units of comprehension and utility. Forget Apple's overpraised hardware aesthetic; its greatest contribution to industrial design was to recognize that nobody reads user's manuals. So it pretty much eliminated them. You can build as many stunning features into a product as you like; without a design that makes them easy to use, they may as well be Easter eggs.

No company has managed this better than Facebook, which outstripped MySpace because it offered constraint over chaos and rigor over randomness. Facebook has tweaked its interface half a dozen times over the years, but it has never lost the essential functionality that users expect. Indeed, its redesigns have been consistently purposeful. Each time, the company's goal has been to nudge users to share a little more information, to connect a little more deeply. And so every change has offered tools for users to better manage their information, making it easier to share, organize, and access the detritus of our lives. Privacy concerns aside, Facebook has helped people bring design into their lives as never before, letting us curate our friends, categorize our family photos, and bring (at least the appearance of) continuity to our personal histories. Services like Pinterest only make this more explicit. They promise to let us organize our interests and inspirations into a clear, elegant form. They turn us into designers and our daily experience into a lifelong project of curation. This is deep design commoditized—the expertise of IDEO without the pricey consulting contract. And done right, it is irresistible.

Spend Time with Time Wasters

The classic business plan imposes efficiency on an inefficient market. Where there is waste, there is opportunity. Dispatch the engineers, route around the problem, and boom—opportunity seized.

That's a great way to make money, but it's not necessarily a way to find the future. A better signal, perhaps, is to look at where people—individuals—are being consciously, deliberately, enthusiastically inefficient. In other words, where are they spending their precious time doing something that they don't have to do? Where are they fiddling with tools, coining new lingo, swapping new techniques? That's where culture is created. The classic example, of course, is the Homebrew Computer Club—the group of Silicon Valley hobbyists who traded circuits and advice in the 1970s, long before the actual utility of personal computers was evident. Out of this hacker collective grew the first portable PC and, most famously, Apple itself.

This same phenomenon—people playing—has spurred various industries, from videogames (thank you, game modders) to the social web (thank you, oversharers). Today, inspired dissipation is everywhere. The maker movement is merging bits with atoms, combining new tools (3-D printing) with old ones (soldering irons). The DIY bio crowd is using off-the-shelf techniques and bargain-basement lab equipment, along with a

dose of PhD know-how, to put biology into garage lab experiments. And the Quantified Self movement is no longer just Bay Area self-tracking geeks. It has exploded into a worldwide phenomenon, as millions of people turn their daily lives into measurable experiments.

The phenomenon of hackathons, meanwhile, converts free time into a development platform. Hackathons harness the natural enthusiasm of code junkies, aim it at a target, and create a partylike competition atmosphere to make innovation fun. (And increasingly hackathons are drawing folks other than coders.) No doubt there will be more such eruptions of excitement, as the tools become easier, cheaper, and more available.

These rules don't create the future, and they don't guarantee success for those who use them. But they do give us a glimpse around the corner, a way to recognize that in this idea or that person, there might be something big.

Critical Thinking

1. What are Wired magazine's seven rules for spotting the future? Do you agree that all seven rules make sense? Would you revise any of them?

2. Research online about Moore's Law. How does Moore's Law impact evaluation of the future of IT markets and consumer behavior? How does Moore's Law fit with the seven rules described in this article?

3. What one rule can you think of outside of these seven rules (and Naisbitt's news hole rule) for predicting the future of IT?

Create Central

www.mhhe.com/createcentral

Internet References

The Future Is Now: What We Imagined for 2013 — 10 Years Ago
 www.wired.com/gadgetlab/2013/01/2013-the-way-we-were

How Do You Predict the Future? [NPR Interview from TED Radio Hour]; also includes 1984 video of Negroponte making five predictions of the future in 1984.
 www.npr.org/2013/09/13/215827198/how-do-you-predict-the-future

Mobile Fourth Wave: The Evolution of the Next Trillion Dollars
 http://allthingsd.com/20130826/mobile-fourth-wave-the-evolution-of-the-next-trillion-dollars/?refcat=voices

The Origin of Moore's Law and What it May (Not) Teach Us about Biological Technologies
 www.synthesis.cc/2009/04/the-origin-of-moores-law-and-what-it-may-not-teach-us-about-biological-technologies.html

THOMAS GOETZ (thomas@wired.com) is the executive editor of *Wired*.

Article Prepared by: Daniel Mittleman, *DePaul University*

From Smart House to Networked Home

Two foresight specialists describe how tomorrow's integrated, networked, and aware home systems may change your family life.

CHRIS CARBONE AND KRISTIN NAUTH

Learning Outcomes

After reading this article, you will be able to:

- Recognize that new technologies follow an adoption curve from niche to mainstream.
- Recognize that it is the interaction of technological advances and societal drivers that determine which technologies go mainstream.
- Recognize that advances being made across several broad technical areas are what eventually lead to new commercial products.

In the last decade, a range of digital technologies and services have hit the market and moved quickly from niche use to the mainstream. Consider that just seven years after being founded, Facebook is used by more than 50% of the online population in the United States and India, and much higher percentages in global markets from Chile to South Africa to Indonesia. And flat-panel TVs, e-readers, smartphones, and even augmented-reality apps—all largely missing from the consumer landscape just a few years ago—continue to be eagerly adopted even in the face of economic uncertainty.

As we look toward the next decade, it's clear that we are in for even more dramatic changes in the roles that technology will play in daily life. But what technologies are poised to move from niche toward the mainstream in the next 10 years? And how will these technologies change everyday activities?

To bring this into sharper focus, Innovaro Inc.'s futures consulting group identified 10 key themes that it feels will help define the tech experience in the coming decade. These 10 "technology trajectories" will give people a powerful new "toolkit"—new devices, services, and capabilities—that will forever alter the way that we go about everyday activities, from dating and shopping to learning and working.

This glimpse of Innovaro's 10 Technology Trajectories presents several forecasts for how these new capabilities could reshape family and home life in the next decade. And although these themes were identified with the United States and other

advanced economies in mind, the Technology Trajectories have global potential to reshape life in emerging economies as they're adopted and explored there as well.

10 Technology Trajectories

1. **Adaptive Environments.** Advances in materials will make the home and work environment "smart." Everyday objects, surfaces, and coatings will gain the ability to adapt to changing conditions or people's needs (e.g., becoming self-cleaning, self-insulating, or protective). The built environment will no longer be simply structural and passive; it will become adaptive, functional, and smart.

2. **Cloud Intelligence.** The cloud will evolve from being a static repository of data into an active resource that people rely on throughout their daily lives. With new capabilities for accessing online expert systems and applications, we'll tap into information, analysis, and contextual advice in more integrated ways. Virtual agents will migrate from being an automated form of phone-based customer service to a personalized form of support and assistance that provides information and—more importantly—performs useful tasks. For example, such agents might design a weekly menu based on a family's health profile, fitness goals, and eating preferences, and automatically order ingredients.

3. **Collaboration Economy.** The power of collective intelligence will enable us to accomplish cognitive tasks not easily handled by virtual agents and machines in the cloud. We'll get advice and recommendations and solve problems by tapping into the social graph, and this cognitive outsourcing will be applied to both business issues and personal and lifestyle questions (e.g., "Which diet will work best for me?").

4. **Contextual Reality.** People will navigate through their daily activities thanks to multiple layers of real-time and location-specific information. This contextual overlay for everyday life will give us a new way to see

our surroundings and provide new forms of decision support. We will move from a world where information and connections are hidden to one where real-time, contextual information generates ambient awareness.

5. **Cutting the Cable.** Personal devices will be largely untethered from wired power and data connections. Access to the Internet will be ubiquitous, and the tech infrastructure—from electronics to sensors to cars—will be powered by a more diverse set of technologies, including micro-generation, wireless power transmission, and advanced power storage. We will move beyond plugging in, and even beyond the "plug and play" model, to a world where data, power, and inter-networking are ubiquitous.

6. **Information Fusion.** It will become possible for people to generate useful insights about their own habits and behaviors by fusing personal data (e.g., social media profiles, tweets, location data, purchasing histories, health sensor data). But these insights will only be as good as a user's ability to understand and act on them. Personal data will become comprehensible through visualization and other services.

7. **Interface Anywhere, Any Way.** Intuitive interfaces will become the dominant form of interaction with personal electronics and computing devices. We'll be freed from the rigidity of conventional input devices (e.g., keyboard, mouse, screen, remotes) and able to interact with the digital world anywhere—and any way—using a combination of gesture, touch, verbal commands, and targeted use of traditional interfaces.

8. **Manufacturing 3.0.** Manufacturing will be reconceived—from a far-flung, global activity to more of a human-scale and re-localized endeavor. As consumers continue to call for both personalization and attention to environmental pressures, demand will grow for a more local manufacturing infrastructure where product schematics in certain categories are digitized and distributed to commercial tabbing services (or in-home 3-D printers) for final fabrication.

9. **Personal Analytics.** Data analytics will increasingly become a consumer tool as much as a business tool. This will open up analytics to a wide variety of personal and lifestyle applications. We'll collect, store, interpret, and apply the vast amounts of data being created by and about ourselves during our everyday activities.

10. **Socially Networked Stuff.** Many of our possessions will interact with each other and with the broader digital infrastructure. This will create a world of socially networked stuff, where things can actively sense, communicate, and share data. Rather than owning a fragmented set of possessions and devices, passively sitting next to each other, we'll manage a dynamic ecosystem of belongings that interact and work in concert for our benefit.

Societal Drivers Influence Technological Advancements

So, how will the new capabilities described in the 10 Technology Trajectories change home and family life? What will our homes look and feel like? How will they support our activities and lifestyles?

Technology is not the only driver at play here, and the Technology Trajectories are not emerging in a vacuum. There are numerous social, generational, and values drivers at play as well. Of the many drivers that our team at Innovaro considered while generating these forecasts, we especially noted the impact of digital natives on adoption of technology in the home, shifting demographics, and economic considerations.

- **The maturing of the digital natives.** Digital natives—people who have grown up never knowing a world without the Internet, smartphones, Facebook, etc.—have far different attitudes toward technology than do older generations. There are now two distinct generations of digital natives in the United States: millennials (born 1979–1998) and Gen Z (born 1999 and after). The technology behaviors of these groups will affect adoption of technologies that impact family and home life in coming years, as more millennials become parents and as members of Gen Z hit their tween (10–12) and teen years.

- **Shifting demography.** Delayed marriage and parenthood is shrinking family size. At the same time, the strong connection between millennials and their baby-boomer parents has led to a rise in multigenerational households in the United States, a trend that has been further intensified by the Great Recession. The changes in the form and function of the home will happen within the larger context of these continued demographic shifts.

- **Digital DIY.** Digital natives grew up in a world where building, modifying, and hacking consumer technology is taken for granted (think *MAKE* magazine and sites like In-structables and even YouTube). The participatory and DIY proclivities of younger generations could drive a move to more customizable home technology and help weave advanced technologies deeply into home life.

- **New family dynamics.** Social media and mobile devices are altering family relationships. Studies have found high ratios of Americans saying Internet use has reduced time spent with family members. Conversely, technologies can increase family connectedness over distance (e.g., by enabling nearly continuous parental oversight via Face-book or weekly Skype conversations with far-flung relatives).

- **Constrained family finances.** It's likely that families' heightened focus on value will persist for years to come. Some people will invest only in home technologies that either directly save money or offer exceptionally compelling new functionality or experience, such as immersive entertainment systems. A two-tier market could emerge in which well-off families adopt smart-home technology while less-well-off households stick to twentieth-century-style home systems.

In the decade ahead, a confluence of these sorts of social factors with the Technology Trajectories will begin to change the very nature and function of homes, give family members new roles, and further alter family dynamics.

Homes Will Become Aware and Adaptive

Homes and home systems could become far more aware, adaptive, and responsive to their residents. New interfaces, for instance, will make home technology more ubiquitous, as flexible displays finally reach commercialization. Nearly any home surface could become a touchscreen, providing finger-tip control of home electronics, as well as access to "cloud intelligence." Interfaces will also be more intuitive, with voice control, eye-tracking, and even emotion analysis that monitors facial expressions to help determine what the user wants.

For example, a house or apartment might monitor you walking through the door at the end of the day and look for clues on how to best serve your needs. It might remotely sense body temperature or interpret body language; compare these with past arrivals, known schedule for the day, etc.; and "know" if you were likely returning from a workout at the gym or a 15-hour workday.

With this information, the system might adjust lights, music, and temperature in the house or display different information based on cues that it picked up from you. It might automatically pull up exercise tracking stats and healthy recipes after a work-out, or carry-out food options when it senses that you might have just worked overtime. While this future may sound far-off, vending kiosks in Japan are already using sensors to detect age, gender, and emotional state in order to offer shoppers a more targeted selection of products.

New materials and power technologies may also change the way homes look and feel. LED wall coatings will change colors or designs to match the season or holiday—or show a movie or ballgame during dinner. A wave of the hand might turn any part of a kitchen counter into an induction cook top. Counters could also be self-sterilizing, using ultraviolet light, and have built-in touch-screen controls. And advances in short-range wireless electricity transmission may eliminate plugs and cords entirely for our electronic devices.

Digital Natives Will Drive Home-Tech Adoption

More millennials are buying homes and starting families, and Gen Z is moving into its tween and teen years. These groups will spur adoption of next-generation home technology. It's well known that teens rely on their constant connectedness to friends via texting and social media to process their feelings:

As MIT researcher Sherry Turkle noted in her book *Alone Together,* "They need to be connected in order to feel like themselves."

This intense need for a connected lifestyle will shape the kinds of home products that kids—and their parents—buy, and younger family members will become the de facto DIY mavens for their households: staying current on new technologies, knowing how to customize them, and guiding family purchases. Digital natives of 2020 could be the family experts at customizing household technology—just as in the 2000s they were the social networking experts, with parents often asking their kids to help them set up Facebook pages.

Digital natives may also drive greater personalization of the home. They have grown up with the ability to personalize the look of their Wii character, cobble together personal media feeds, and express themselves visually on sites like Pinterest. Based on the control they've grown accustomed to in the digital world, they may expect to customize and modify their families' home systems to a greater degree than previous generations. This could be especially true of entertainment systems, but could also apply to adaptive walls or other smart infrastructures in the home.

Much of the demand for virtual products (i.e., digital possessions that exist locally on their devices or in the cloud) will be from digital natives as well. It will be increasingly possible to render the artifacts of our digital lives in the real world, and millennials could be big adopters of 3-D printing. People may print household and hobby items they design or modify themselves. Imagine, for example, a crafter taking a 3-D scan of a sea shell, modifying the shape and texture using design software, and then 3-D printing her digital creation as a piece of art or jewelry. Already, a prototype 3-D printer called Origo is being developed for the tween market. Children who grow up with toys like Origo will be proficient in the technology—and as young adults in 2020, they may expect to be able to fabricate things at home to personalize and customize their home environment.

Technological Advances Will Change Society and the Home

The Technology Trajectories outlined above will alter the home and its physical artifacts, as well as the families that adopt them. These family and home environment alterations may have repercussions well beyond the household into daily life and society at large.

- **Living in "glass houses."** Levels of transparency in the home will rise. Home systems and processes that have been opaque to homeowners, such as energy consumption or the off-gassing of paint, will become transparent. For people who are interested in the "quantified self" movement, smart homes will make it easier to measure and track one's own behavior. For example, your home could help record and analyze your activities to uncover insights about your behavior over time (e.g., that you tend to argue with your spouse more on days that you don't exercise, or that you sleep poorly when you eat dinner after 8 p.m).

- **House layouts will change.** Houses will change to accommodate the new technologies and the behaviors they enable. As the need for wired power and data access falls away—and new interfaces emerge—more-flexible home designs may come into vogue. Rather than dedicated media rooms or home offices, spaces may be more flexible and adaptive; residents may be able to work or play in any room that suits their preferences.
- **Homes could become even more central to daily life.** Homes will be more personalized, responsive, and attuned to residents' preferences. As this becomes the case, people may find that the experiences that they have in their homes will be superior to what they can have in public spaces for certain activities. For example, productivity levels working at home in a space personalized for one's physical, mood/emotional, and practical needs will likely exceed what can be achieved with a rented desk at the local telecommuting space. Homes could become the preferred location for core activities such as work, education, and entertainment. People could become more dependent on their homes and home systems.
- **Creating new divisions.** With so much more control available over home devices and systems, issues of who controls what will go far beyond tugs-of-war over the remote. Being granted access to or control over certain home systems—such as refrigerator-mediated food ordering or immersive multimedia systems—could become a new rite of passage for younger family members, just as getting your own set of house keys has been in the past.
- **Family impacts could have pros and cons.** With all of these new capabilities at hand, home life could be more engaging, convenient, and fun. On the flip side, learning curves could be steep, especially for generations who are not digital natives. To sidestep this problem, some families may simply outsource management of these next-generation home systems—creating a new business opportunity. Others, feeling stressed out by tech complexity and the prospect of another monthly bill, may choose to opt out.
- **A new digital divide?** Cost will be an issue, and not all families will be able to afford emerging home technologies. Whereas the digital divide used to be about access to PCs and broadband Internet, in the future it could be about access to adaptive and aware living spaces.

A final outcome of these changes is that the market for advanced home technology will grow much larger, more complex, and more competitive than today. Rather than having a few key technology nodes in the home (e.g., PC, tablet, Internet-enabled TV, and smartphones), all key home systems might well become networked devices—from water and electric meters to electrochro-mic windows.

This will open up myriad opportunities for new home products and the potential for exciting collaborations across previously unrelated industries—from consumer electronics and computing to home furnishing, decor, and home improvement. As the Technology Trajectories are realized, tomorrow's families could be far more connected with each other and with their communities than ever before. And when you call home, your home will answer.

Critical Thinking

1. The authors name ten technology trajectories. For each trajectory name one area of significant impact—other than Smart Home related advances—where we have already seen products hit the market. And for each trajectory suggest at least one area of significant impact—other than Smart Home related advances—that we are likely to experience in the coming decade.
2. For each of the twenty product areas you've suggested in question one, discuss which of the five drivers are impacting growth and acceptance of this new technology, and discuss how those drivers are impacting it.

Create Central

www.mhhe.com/createcentral

Internet References

Apple's Next Innovation
www.technologyreview.com/featuredstory/511091/apples-next-innovation-tv
Cars Are Fast Becoming Smartphones on Wheels
www.technologyreview.com/news/516851/cars-are-fast-becoming-smartphones-on-wheels
Is Home Automation the Next UX Frontier?
http://mashable.com/2013/02/27/home-automation-ux-design
Smart Devices That Make Life Easier May Also Be Easy To Hack, Says FTC
www.pbs.org/newshour/bb/science/july-dec13/internet_09-05.html

Chris Carbone is a director with Innovaro's foresight group, where he oversees the Global Lifestyles and Technology Foresight projects and contributes to the firm's custom futures research projects.

Kristin Nauth is a founding partner of Foresight Alliance and has 15 years of experience as a foresight professional, including six with Innovaro.

Article   Prepared by: Daniel Mittleman, *DePaul University*

Augmented Reality Is Finally Getting Real

As smartphones explode in popularity, augmented reality is starting to move from novelty to utility.

Rachel Metz

Learning Outcomes

After reading this article, you will be able to:

• Articulate what augmented reality is, and how it is differentiated from virtual reality.

• Be aware of several practical applications of augmented reality that already exist in the marketplace.

In the summer of 2009, Yelp quietly added a feature to its iPhone app that blurred the line between the real and the virtual. If you held your handset up and looked at the world through its screen, you'd see little floating tags containing the names, user ratings, and other details of businesses around you.

The feature, called Monocle, was an experiment with augmented reality—one of many that appeared around this time, as companies tossed around various ways to mesh digital content with the real world, hoping to catch consumers' eyes.

Several years later, augmented reality is still mostly used by early tech adopters, but it's starting to graze the mainstream, helped by the massive popularity of smartphones and tablets, and their constantly improving processors and sensors, along with the growth of high-speed wireless data networks. Apps featuring augmented reality are available for everything from gaming to driving to furniture arrangement. Slowly but surely, augmented reality is becoming less of a novelty and more of a utility.

While the term is only just becoming common parlance among consumers, augmented reality's history stretches back years: it has long been an area of academic research. Boeing used it with head-mounted displays in the 1990s to aid in aircraft wiring.

Early augmented-reality smartphone apps used a device's GPS and digital compass to determine your location and direction. More recently, app makers have begun incorporating computer vision and increasingly powerful processors to provide greater accuracy.

Jon Fisher, CEO and cofounder of San Francisco-based CrowdOptic, is one entrepreneur trying to take augmented reality mainstream. His startup's software can recognize the direction in which a crowd of people have their phones pointed while taking photos or videos at events, and invite the group to communicate, share content, or get more information about the object of their attention, via an app.

The software uses a smartphone's GPS, accelerometer, and compass to determine a user's position and line of site; but also to triangulate with other phones using the same software to determine specifically what everyone in a cluster is looking at. The company's technology has been used in a number of apps, including one for a recent NASCAR race in which fans, who couldn't see the entire 2.5-mile track, could point their phones at distant turns and get photos and videos generated by others who were closer to the action.

Another company, iOnRoad, offers an augmented-reality collision-warning app for drivers using smartphones that run Google's Android software (an iPhone version is in the works).

IOnRoad CEO Alon Atsmon says the app uses the phone's camera stream along with image processing software to identify relevant objects like the lane in which you're driving and the position of the car in front of you. GPS on your phone determines your speed. The app measures the distance between you and the car in front of you, and divides this by your speed to get a time gap. If the gap is perceived as too small, iOnRoad will warn you that you're not keeping enough distance. Among other things, the app can determine what lane you're driving in, and give you a warning if you start to drift, he says.

So far, nearly 500,000 people have downloaded the Android app since it was released late last year. Most of those chose a free version over a premium one that costs $4.99.

Moves by major companies—Google in particular—have helped make augmented reality seem less far-fetched. This spring, Google confirmed it is working on glasses that can show maps, messages, and other data to the wearer. In June, Google started allowing developers to preorder, for $1,500, a prototype called Project Glass that will be available in early 2013. While not strictly focused on augmented reality, Project Glass draws attention to the idea of a digital layer on top of the physical world.

"Definitely, the attention is good," says Pattie Maes, a professor at MIT's Media Lab who has done extensive research on augmented reality. "It will motivate all the other consumer electronics companies and cell-phone companies to look at this a lot more seriously."

For augmented reality to really become popular, however, a widespread number of apps will have to adopt it. Creative Strategies analyst Ben Bajarin believes the breakthrough could be apps for museums or zoos—while standing cage-side, you might hold up your smartphone to learn more about a bear or a giraffe, for example.

In fact, several zoos and museums already have experimented with the technology. At Toronto's Royal Ontario Museum, for example, visitors can use iPads at a dinosaur exhibit to see how the beasts would have looked in real life. And augmented reality is about to get its biggest mass-market push yet: Swedish furniture maker Ikea's 2013 catalog, 211 million copies of which were shipped out Wednesday, includes additional content that readers can see with an Android or iOS app.

The move could be a good one, Bajarin says, assuming it works well. "You don't want people to try it and hate it, and go, 'Eh, I'm not going to use that again,'" he says.

Critical Thinking

1. How will augmented reality impact the experience of retail shopping (such as at the grocery store or in the shopping mall)? How will augmented reality impact using Yelp to select a restaurant?

2. Metz mentions the use of augmented reality at a NASCAR race. How might it be used to enhance the experience of watching a football, basketball, or baseball game? Should athletes be permitted to use augmented reality while playing a sport?

Create Central

www.mhhe.com/createcentral

Internet References

From Battlefield to Operating Room: Augmented Reality Gets Practical

www.pbs.org/newshour/rundown/2012/09/from-the-operating-room-to-the-battlefield-using-augmented-reality-to-see-more-clearly.html

The Future of Augmented Reality

www.youtube.com/watch?feature=player_embedded&v=tnRJaHZH9lo

A Look Ahead at 2014 – Augmented Reality

www.agilenceinc.com/a-look-ahead-at-2014-augmented-reality

7 Ways Augmented Reality Will Improve Your Life

http://mashable.com/2012/12/19/augmented-reality-city

10 Industries Being Reinvented with Augmented Reality

http://augmentedworldexpo.com/awe2013/awe2013_news/10-business-verticals-being-reinvented-with-augmented-reality

Article Prepared by: Daniel Mittleman, *DePaul University*

I Used Google Glass: The Future, but with Monthly Updates

Up close and personal with Google's visionary new computer.

Joshua Topolsky

Learning Outcomes

After reading this article, you will be able to:

- Understand what Google Glass is, and what it does. Articulate both pros and cons to this new technology platform.

- Surface specific privacy or security risks resulting from the use of Glass. Articulate how these risk might be mitigated by technology or policy.

- Understand how the introduction of a new product category has a rippling impact far beyond its direct use. Articulate both positive and negative anticipated ripples from Glass.

The frosted-glass doors on the 11th floor of Google's NYC headquarters part and a woman steps forward to greet me. This is an otherwise normal specimen of humanity. Normal height, slender build; her eyes are bright, inquisitive. She leans in to shake my hand and at that moment I become acutely aware of the device she's wearing in the place you would expect eyeglasses: a thin strip of aluminum and plastic with a strange, prismatic lens just below her brow. Google Glass.

What was a total oddity a year ago, and little more than an experiment just 18 months ago is now starting to look like a real product. One that could be in the hands (or on the heads, rather) of consumers by the end of this year. A completely new kind of computing device; wearable, designed to reduce distraction, created to allow you to capture and communicate in a way that is supposed to feel completely natural to the wearer. It's the anti-smartphone, explicitly fashioned to blow apart our notions of how we interact with technology.

But as I release from that handshake and study the bizarre device resting on my greeter's brow, my mind begins to fixate on a single question: who would want to wear this thing in public?

Finding Glass

The Glass project was started "about three years ago" by an engineer named Babak Parviz as part of Google's X Lab initiative, the lab also responsible for—amongst other things—self-driving cars and neural networks. Unlike those epic, sci-fi R&D projects at Google, Glass is getting real much sooner than anyone expected. The company offered developers an option to buy into an early adopter strategy called the Explorer Program during its I/O conference last year, and just this week it extended that opportunity to people in the US (http://www.google.com/glass/start/how-to-get-one-/faq/) in a Twitter campaign which asks potential users to explain how they would put the new technology to use. Think of it as a really aggressive beta—something Google is known for.

I was about to beta test Glass myself. But first, I had questions.

Seated in a surprisingly bland room—by Google's whimsical office standards—I find myself opposite two of the most important players in the development of Glass, product director Steve Lee and lead industrial designer Isabelle Olsson. Steve and Isabelle make for a convincing pair of spokespeople for the product. He's excitable, bouncy even, with big bright eyes that spark up every time he makes a point about Glass. Isabelle is more reserved, but speaks with incredible fervency about the product. And she has extremely red hair. Before we can even start talking about Glass, Isabelle and I are in a heated conversation about how you define the color navy blue. She's passionate about design—a condition that seems to be rather contagious at Google these days—and it shows.

Though the question of design is at the front of my mind, a picture of why Glass exists at all begins to emerge as we talk, and it's clearly not about making a new fashion accessory. Steve tries to explain it to me.

"Why are we even working on Glass? We all know that people love to be connected. Families message each other all the time, sports fanatics are checking live scores for their favorite teams. If you're a frequent traveler you have to stay up to date on flight status or if your gate changes. Technology allows us to connect in that way. A big problem right now are the distractions that technology causes. If you're a parent—let's say your child's performance, watching them do a soccer game or a musical. Often friends will be holding a camera to capture that moment. Guess what? It's gone. You just missed that amazing game." Isabelle chimes in, "Did you see that Louis C.K. stand up when he was telling parents, 'your kids are better resolution in real life?'" Everyone laughs, but the point is made.

Human beings have developed a new problem since the advent of the iPhone and the following mobile revolution: no one is paying attention to anything they're actually doing. Everyone seems to be looking down at something or through something. Those perfect moments watching your favorite band play or your kid's recital are either being captured via the lens of a device that sits between you and the actual experience, or being interrupted by constant notifications. Pings from the outside world, breaking into what used to be whole, personal moments.

Steve goes on. "We wondered, what if we brought technology closer to your senses? Would that allow you to more quickly get information and connect with other people but do so in a way—with a design—that gets out of your way when you're not interacting with technology? That's sort of what led us to Glass." I can't stop looking at the lens above his right eye. "It's a new wearable technology. It's a very ambitious way to tackle this problem, but that's really sort of the underpinning of why we worked on Glass."

I get it. We're all distracted. No one can pay attention. We're missing all of life's moments. Sure, it's a problem, but it's a new problem, and this isn't the first time we've been distracted by a new technology. Hell, they used to think car radios would send drivers careening off of the highways. We'll figure out how to manage our distraction, right?

Maybe, but obviously the Glass team doesn't want to wait to find out. Isabelle tells me about the moment the concept clicked for her. "One day, I went to work—I live in SF and I have to commute to Mountain View and there are these shuttles—I went to the shuttle stop and I saw a line of not 10 people but 15 people standing in a row like this," she puts her head down and mimics someone poking at a smartphone. "I don't want to do that, you know? I don't want to be that person. That's when it dawned on me that, OK, we have to make this work. It's bold. It's crazy. But we think that we can do something cool with it."

Bold and crazy sounds right, especially after Steve tells me that the company expects to have Glass on the market as a consumer device by the end of *this year.*

Google-level Design

Forget about normal eyeglasses for a moment. Forget about chunky hipster glasses. Forget about John Lennon's circle sunglasses. Forget The Boys of Summer; forget how she looks with her hair slicked back and her Wayfarers on. Pretend that stuff doesn't exist. Just humor me.

The design of Glass is actually really beautiful. Elegant, sophisticated. They look human and a little bit alien all at once.

Futuristic but not out of time—like an artifact from the 1960s, someone trying to imagine what 2013 would be like. This is Apple-level design. No, in some ways it's beyond what Apple has been doing recently. It's daring, inventive, playful, and yet somehow still ultimately simple. The materials feel good in your hand and on your head, solid but surprisingly light. Comfortable. If Google keeps this up, soon we'll be saying things like "this is Google-level design."

Even the packaging seems thoughtful.

The system itself is made up of only a few basic pieces. The main body of Glass is a soft-touch plastic that houses the brains, battery, and counterweight (which sits behind your ear). There's a thin metal strip that creates the arc of the glasses, with a set of rather typical pad arms and nose pads which allow the device to rest on your face.

Google is making the first version of the device in a variety of colors. If you didn't want to get creative, those colors are: gray, orange, black, white, and light blue. I joke around with Steve and Isabelle about what I think the more creative names would be. "Is the gray one Graphite? Hold on, don't tell me. I'm going to guess." I go down the list. "Tomato? Onyx? Powder—no Avalanche, and Seabreeze." Steve and Isabelle laugh. "That's good," Isabelle says.

But seriously. Shale. Tangerine. Charcoal. Cotton. Sky. So close.

That conversation leads into discussion of the importance of color in a product that you wear every day. "It's one of those things, you think like, 'oh, whatever, it is important,' but it's a secondary thing. But we started to realize how people get attached to the device . . . a lot of it is due to the color," Isabelle tells me.

And there is something to it. When I saw the devices in the different colors, and when I tried on Tangerine and Sky, I started to get emotional about which one was more "me." It's not like how you feel about a favorite pair of sunglasses, but it evokes a similar response. They're supposed to feel like yours.

Isabelle came to the project and Google from Yves Behar's design studio. She joined the Glass team when their product was little more than a bizarre pair of white eyeglass frames with comically large circuit boards glued to either side. She shows me—perhaps ironically—a Chanel box with the original prototype inside, its prism lens limply dangling from the right eye, a gray ribbon cable strewn from one side to the other. The breadboard version.

It was Isabelle's job to make Glass into something that you *could* wear, even if maybe you still weren't sure you *wanted* to wear it. She gets that there are still challenges.

The Explorer edition which the company will ship out has an interchangeable sunglass accessory which twists on or off easily, and I must admit makes Glass look slightly more sane. I also learn that the device actually comes apart, separating that center metal rim from the brains and lens attached on the right. The idea is that you could attach another frame fitted for Glass that would completely alter the look of the device while still allowing for the heads-up functionality. Steve and Isabelle won't say if they're working with partners like Ray-Ban or Tom Ford (the company that makes my glasses), but the *New York Times* (http://www.nytimes.com/2013/02/21/technology/google-looks-to-make-its-computer-glasses-stylish.html) just reported that Google is speaking to Warby Parker, and I'm inclined to believe that particular rumor. It's obvious the company realizes the need for this thing to not just look wearable—Google needs people to want to wear it.

So yes, the Glass looks beautiful to me, but I still don't want to wear it.

Topolsky in Mirrorshades

Finally I get a chance to put the device on and find out what using Glass in the real world actually feels like. This is the moment I've been waiting for all day. It's really happening.

When you activate Glass, there's supposed to be a small screen that floats in the upper right-hand of your field of vision, but I don't see the whole thing right away. Instead I'm getting a ghost of the upper portion, and the bottom half seems to melt away at the corner of my eye.

Steve and Isabelle adjust the nose pad and suddenly I see the glowing box. Victory.

It takes a moment to adjust to this spectral screen in your vision, and it's especially odd the first time you see it, it disappears, and you want it to reappear but don't know how to make it happen. Luckily that really only happens once, at least for me.

Here's what you see: the time is displayed, with a small amount of text underneath that reads "ok glass." That's how you get Glass to wake up to your voice commands. Actually, it's a two-step process. First you have to touch the side of the device (which is actually a touchpad), or tilt your head upward slowly, a gesture which tells Glass to wake up. Once you've done that, you start issuing commands by speaking "ok glass" first, or scroll through the options using your finger along the side of the device. You can scroll items by moving your finger backwards or forward along the strip, you select by tapping, and move "back" by swiping down. Most of the big interaction is done by voice, however.

The device gets data through Wi-Fi on its own, or it can tether via Bluetooth to an Android device or iPhone and use its 3G or 4G data while out and about. There's no cellular radio in Glass, but it does have a GPS chip.

Let me start by saying that using it is actually nearly identical to what the company showed off in its newest demo video. That's not CGI—it's what Glass is actually like to use. It's clean, elegant, and makes relative sense. The screen is not disruptive, you do not feel burdened by it. It is there and then it is gone. It's not shocking. It's not jarring. It's just this new thing in your field of vision. And it's actually pretty cool.

Glass does all sorts of basic stuff after you say "ok glass." Things you'll want to do right away with a camera on your face. "Take a picture" snaps a photo. "Record a video" records ten seconds of video. If you want more you can just tap the side of the device. Saying "ok glass, Google" gets you into search, which plugs heavily into what Google has been doing with Google Now and its Knowledge Graph. Most of the time when you ask Glass questions you get hyper-stylized cards full of information, much like you do in Google Now on Android.

The natural language search works most of the time, but when it doesn't, it can be confusing, leaving you with text results that seem like a dead-end. And Glass doesn't always hear you correctly, or the pace it's expecting you to speak at doesn't line up with reality. I struggled repeatedly with Glass when issuing voice commands that seemed to come too fast for the device to interpret. When I got it right however, Glass usually responded quickly, serving up bits of information and jumping into action as expected.

Some of the issues stemmed from a more common problem: no data. A good data connection is obviously key for the device to function properly, and when taking Glass outside for stroll, losing data or experiencing slow data on a phone put the headset into a near-unusable state.

Steve and Isabelle know the experience isn't perfect. In fact, they tell me that the team plans to issue monthly updates to the device when the Explorer program starts rolling. This is very much a work in progress.

But the most interesting parts of Glass for many people won't be its search functionality, at least not just its basic ability to pull data up. Yes, it can tell you how old Brad Pitt is (49 for those keeping count), but Google is more interested in what it can do for you in the moment. Want the weather? It can do that. Want to get directions? It can do that and display a real-time, turn-by-turn overlay. Want to have a Google Hangout with someone that allows them to see what you're seeing? Yep, it does that.

But the feature everyone is going to go crazy with—and the feature you probably most want to use—is Glass' ability to take photos and video with a "you are there" view. I won't lie, it's amazingly powerful (and more than a little scary) to be able to just start recording video or snapping pictures with a couple of flicks of your finger or simple voice commands.

At one point during my time with Glass, we all went out to navigate to a nearby Starbucks—the camera crew I'd brought with me came along. As soon as we got inside however, the employees at Starbucks asked us to stop filming. Sure, no problem. But I kept the Glass' video recorder going, all the way through my order and getting my coffee. Yes, you can see a light in the prism when the device is recording, but I got the impression that most people had no idea what they were looking at. The cashier seemed to be on the verge of asking me what I was wearing on my face, but the question never came. He certainly never asked me to stop filming.

Once those Explorer editions are out in the world, you can expect a slew of use (and misuse) in this department. Maybe misuse is the wrong word here. Steve tells me that part of the Explorer program is to find out how people want to (and will) use Glass. "It's really important," he says, "what we're trying to do is expand the community that we have for Glass users. Currently it's just our team and a few other Google people testing it. We want to expand that to people outside of Google. We think it's really important, actually, for the development of Glass because it's such a new product and it's not just a piece of software. We want to learn from people how it's going to fit into their lifestyle." He gets the point. "It's a very intimate device. We'd like to better understand how other people are going to use it. We think they'll have a great opportunity to influence and shape the opportunity of Glass by not only giving us feedback on the product, but by helping us develop social norms as well."

I ask if it's their attempt to define "Glass etiquette." Will there be the Glass version of Twitter's RT? "That's what the Explorer program is about," Steve says. But that's not going to answer questions about what's right and wrong to do with a camera that doesn't need to be held up to take a photo, and often won't even be noticed by its owner's subjects. Will people get comfortable with that? Are they supposed to?

The privacy issue is going to be a big hurdle for Google with Glass. Almost as big as the hurdle it has to jump over to convince normal people to wear something as alien and unfashionable as Glass seems right now.

But what's it actually like to have Glass on? To use it when you're walking around? Well, it's kind of awesome.

Think of it this way—if you get a text message or have an incoming call when you're walking down a busy street, there are something like two or three things you have to do before you can deal with that situation. Most of them involve you completely taking your attention off of your task at hand: walking down the street. With Glass, that information just appears to you, in your line of sight, ready for you to take action on. And taking that action is little more than touching the side of Glass or tilting your head up—nothing that would take you away from your main task of not running into people.

It's a simple concept that feels powerful in practice.

The same is true for navigation. When I get out of trains in New York I am constantly jumping right into Google Maps to figure out where I'm headed. Even after more than a decade in the city, I seem to never be able to figure out which way to turn when I exit a subway station. You still have to grapple with asking for directions with Glass, but removing the barrier of being completely distracted by the device in your hand is significant, and actually receiving directions as you walk is even more significant. In the city, Glass make you feel more powerful, better equipped, and definitely less diverted.

I will admit that wearing Glass made me feel self-conscious, and maybe it's just my paranoia acting up (or the fact that I look like a huge weirdo), but I felt people staring at me. Everyone who I made eye contact with while in Glass seemed to be just about to say "hey, what the hell is that?" and it made me uncomfortable.

Steve claims that when those questions do come, people are excited to find out what Glass is. "We've been wearing this for almost a year now out in public, and it's been so interesting and exciting to do that. Before, we were super excited about it and confident in our design, but you never know until you start wearing it out and about. Of course my friends would joke with me 'oh no girls are going to talk to you now, they'll think it's strange.' The exact opposite happened."

I don't think Glass is right for every situation. It's easy to see how it's amazing for parents to capture all of the adorable things their kids are doing, or for skydivers and rock climbers who clearly don't have their hands free and also happen to be having life changing experiences. And yes, it's probably helpful if you're in Thailand and need directions or translation—but this might not be that great at a dinner party, or on a date, or watching a movie. In fact, it could make those situations very awkward, or at the least, change them in ways you might not like.

Sometimes you want to be distracted in the old-fashioned ways. And sometimes, you want people to see you—not a device you're wearing on your face. One that may or may not be recording them right this second.

And that brings me back to the start: who would want to wear this thing in public?

Not If, but When

Honestly, I started to like Glass a lot when I was wearing it. It wasn't uncomfortable and it brought something new into view (both literally and figuratively) that has tremendous value and potential. I don't think my face looks quite right without my glasses on, and I didn't think it looked quite right while wearing Google Glass, but after a while it started to feel less and less not-right. And that's something, right?

The sunglass attachment Google is shipping with the device goes a long way to normalizing the experience. A partnership with someone like Ray-Ban or Warby Parker would go further still. It's actually easy to see now—after using it, after feeling what it's like to be in public with Glass on—how you could get comfortable with the device.

Is it ready for everyone right now? Not really. Does the Glass team still have a huge distance to cover in making the experience work just the way it should every time you use it? Definitely.

But I walked away convinced that this wasn't just one of Google's weird flights of fancy. The more I used Glass the more it made sense to me; the more I wanted it. If the team had told me I could sign up to have my current glasses augmented with Glass technology, I would have put pen to paper (and money in their hands) right then and there. And it's that kind of stuff that will make the difference between this being a niche device for geeks and a product that everyone wants to experience.

After a few hours with Glass, I've decided that the question is no longer 'if,' but 'when?'

Critical Thinking

1. Glass is such a different product category from anything previously on the market it is likely to spur the development of totally new types of software that do things for us we didn't imagine before. What new types of software can you imagine being developed for glass?

2. Watch Google's promotional video for Glass (if no longer available at the link provided, check YouTube for promotional videos). Describe you initial reactions to experiencing Glass through this video. Describe both any excitement or exhilaration as well as any fears or hesitations that came to mind during your viewing. Reflect, now, on whether your initial reactions during the viewing will remain with you long term and influence your opinion of this product category.

3. Several critics of Glass have surfaced a wide array of security concerns as Glass becomes a commonly used product. What three or so security issues do you think are most critical? How do you think each might be addressed either through technology advances or public policy?

Create Central

www.mhhe.com/createcentral

Internet References

Google Augments Reality with Futuristic Glasses [Newshour Extra]
www.pbs.org/newshour/extra/2012/04/
google-augments-reality-with-futuristic-glasses

How It Feels [Google promotional video]
www.google.com/glass/start/how-it-feels

Project Glass is Scary Enough to Deserve some Respect
www.manifestdensity.net/2013/05/02/
project-glass-is-scary-enough-to-deserve-some-respect

Tech and Privacy Advocates Clash over Possibilities for Google Glass
www.pbs.org/newshour/extra/2013/08/
tech-and-privacy-advocates-clash-over-possibilities-for-google-glass